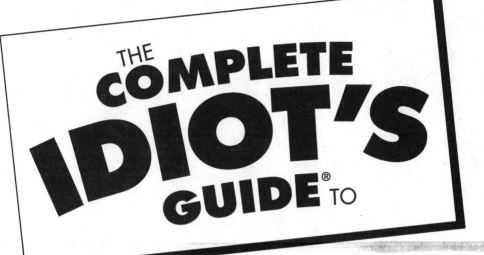

THE COMPLETE IDIOT'S GUIDE® TO

Hockey

D0927476

by Malcolm G. Kelly and Mark Askin

ALPHA

A Pearson Education Company

JAN 0 2 2002

DISCARDED

Originally published as *The Complete Idiot's Guide to the History of Hockey, First Edition*, by Malcolm G. Kelly and Mark Askin, published by Pearson Education Canada, Inc., publishing as Alpha Books, Prentice Hall Canada, Copyright © 2000 by Malcolm G. Kelly and Mark Askin.

The Complete Idiot's Guide to Hockey edition published by Pearson Education, Inc., publishing as Alpha Books, Copyright © 2002 by Malcolm G. Kelly and Mark Askin.

THE COMPLETE IDIOT'S GUIDE TO and Design are registered trademarks of Pearson Education, Inc.

International Standard Book Number: 0-02-864257-0
Library of Congress Catalog Card Number: 2001094727

04 03 02   8 7 6 5 4 3 2 1

Interpretation of the printing code: The rightmost number of the first series of numbers is the year of the book's printing; the rightmost number of the second series of numbers is the number of the book's printing. For example, a printing code of 02-1 shows that the first printing occurred in 2002.

Printed in the United States of America

Note: This publication contains the opinions and ideas of its authors. It is intended to provide helpful and informative material on the subject matter covered. It is sold with the understanding that the authors and publisher are not engaged in rendering professional services in the book. If the reader requires personal assistance or advice, a competent professional should be consulted.

The authors and publisher specifically disclaim any responsibility for any liability, loss, or risk, personal or otherwise, which is incurred as a consequence, directly or indirectly, of the use and application of any of the contents of this book.

Publisher
Marie Butler-Knight

Product Manager
Phil Kitchel

Managing Editor
Jennifer Chisholm

Acquisitions Editor
Mike Sanders

Senior Production Editor
Christy Wagner

Illustrator
Jody Schaeffer

Cover Designers
Mike Freeland
Kevin Spear

Book Designers
Scott Cook and Amy Adams of DesignLab

Layout/Proofreading
Angela Calvert
John Etchison

Contents at a Glance

Contents

Foreword

A visitor arrives from Peru or Pakistan or drops down from outer space. How would I explain hockey to him, or her, or it? To people from Brantford or Parry Sound or Floral, Saskatchewan, from hockey's heartland, what might they know very well but have forgotten, and might be reminded of again?

Step back from this game—

What minds, where, would even conceive of strapping metal blades on their feet to propel themselves across the most frictionless, out-of-control surface they could find? Then make a game of it? Hockey is so bizarre, so odd, so utterly different. Those who play it, the home country that would embrace it, how weird, how incomprehensible must they be?

Now step back into it—

Look past the ice and the metal blades, and what you see is every stick-and-ball game that's ever been played everywhere through all time.

And that's what hockey is. It's the different, and it's the familiar. It's the instinct in every one of us to come together and play. It's a big story, and it's little stories. It's the important and the unimportant. It's the quirky, the stupid, the moving, and the dumb. It's place, names, dates. And it's people. It is understandable. It's also fun.

And that is the spirit of this book.

Ken Dryden

Introduction

Welcome to *The Complete Idiot's Guide to Hockey.*

As you've probably already surmised, you don't have to be an idiot to enjoy this book or to learn something new about the fastest game in the world. We've written it to appeal to a lot of different people:

> ➤ To those who simply like reading about hockey, no matter the subject matter.
> ➤ To those who have a lot of hockey knowledge and want to learn a little more.
> ➤ To those who have very little hockey knowledge and want to begin exploring the world on ice—young people, newcomers to the sport, and those who have a pressing need to pick up a little something—say, those who have a date with a hockey fan and want to make an impression with what you know. And why should your date have to know you've just learned it?

This book is a general, beginning look at the history of hockey, designed to lead readers to some of the best writers on the game in the world. At the back of this volume you'll find an extensive bibliography for further enjoyment and education.

The guide is divided into seven parts, plus appendixes and an index.

Part 1, "A Little History, Repeated," looks at the invention of the game and similar sports that developed into ice hockey, including bandy, shinny, and others. Plus, we'll look at the creation of the Stanley Cup, which eventually would become the symbol of the National Hockey League professional champion, how hockey first made it into the United States and Europe, and early international games and tournaments.

Part 2, "The National Hockey League," tells the story of the NHL, from its creation through the violent early years, the war years, the time of the "Original Six," and up to today, with special focus on the players who made the league great and the problems that have occasionally plagued it.

Part 3, "International Incidents," includes the Miracle on Ice in 1980, the growth of the world championships, and a chapter on the Summit Series—the most important event in hockey history outside of the game's invention. It will also look at international tournaments, the Olympics, and more.

Part 4, "Beyond the Iron Curtain," takes us to the Soviet Union, where ice hockey replaced bandy as the national winter game and became the most important sport across the Russian-led communist world. Included is a look at the men who led the explosion of the Big Red Machine on the world and what happened to the sport when the Iron Curtain fell. We'll also look at hockey's growth in Czechoslovakia and later the Czech Republic and Slovakia.

Part 5, "Scandinavia," follows the game's birth and life in Sweden and Finland—two countries that would not only develop many fine professional players but would also create a rivalry with each other every bit as important to them as Canada or the United States vs. the Soviet Union. And we'll follow Scandinavian players into the NHL.

Part 6, "Other Voices," includes the history of women's hockey from its birth in the nineteenth century to today, how blacks and other minorities first broke into the pro ranks and are changing the face of the game, junior hockey in Canada and around the world, and the college and high school game in the United States.

Part 7, "The Rules," includes a look at the entire National Hockey League rule book, how all the rules work, and how they interact with each other. It also contains stories, trivia, and quotes from the history of the game that relate directly to the rule book or referees.

The appendixes include hints from a hockey television producer on how to watch a game on the big box, plus four lists—the top 10 players, teams, moments, and most influential people in hockey history.

Extras

As with all *Complete Idiot's Guides,* this one includes elements designed to make for a more enjoyable and informative read. Catch them as they skate by:

Aw, I Knew That!

More than 200 skill-testing trivia questions about hockey from the easy to the very difficult. Amaze your friends! Bore your neighbors!!

I Remember ...

Players, coaches, and officials from around the world tell their favorite stories about the game of hockey and their involvement in it.

Quote, Unquote

A look at some of the best remarks about hockey in the media.

Great Games

These are stories that relive some of the most exciting games ever played in hockey.

We hope you come out of this book loving the game as much as we have all of our lives.

Acknowledgments

From MK: First of all, thanks to Mark for the momentary mind loss, during which he agreed to write this book with me. Thanks to Ken Dryden for being kind enough to write the foreword. At Prentice Hall Canada, there is Andrea Crozier (the boss lady), who was supportive the whole way, and at Colborne Communications, copy editor Wendy Yano, who proved once again to be argumentative, intuitive, tough, and unyielding—all the things a good copy editor needs to be. At Pearson Education U.S., Mike Sanders was terrific, and Christy Wagner did a fine job, especially in taking out all the "Ehs" (kidding). Thanks to Dick Irvin, a legend in Canadian broadcasting, for reading the entire manuscript and correcting our mistakes. We stole merrily from dozens of fine authors to write this book, but especially a big thank you goes out to Kevin Allen of *USA Today,* Jack Falla, Brian McFarlane, Igor Kuperman of the Phoenix Coyotes, and Stan Fischler. Thanks to Lawrence Martin for his work on Soviet hockey. Out of all the sources we used, the biggest nod has to go to the editors and writers of *Total Hockey*—simply the best reference book on the sport out there. Personally, as always, all my love goes out to my wife, Barbara, my son, Patrick, and Auggie Doggie, who all had to put up with me. And finally, I'd like to thank Paul Woods for everything he did to get my book career up and running.

From MA: Though it has nothing to do with hockey, it has everything to do with love: Without my wife, Avis, I would never have made much of my life. She taught me patience, respect, how to love, and more valuable life lessons than I could describe in this space. My parents, Yvonne and Harold, encouraged my love of sports and, in particular, hockey. To Bob McCown, I give heartfelt thanks. Bob gave me my start in radio production in 1977. To the folks at Global Television for allowing a young producer to grow on *Sportsline.* To my great pal, Harry Neale, thank you for your friendship, wisdom, and humor. Jim Marshall gets a big thank you—the finest director in the history of Canadian sports television has given 14 years of friendship and comradeship. To Scott Morrison, Chris Cuthbert, Paul Hendrick, and my close friends in the sports industry, thank you. And to Malcolm, I learned a lot throughout the writing of this book, most of it about you and your talent. Finally, to my son Christopher, I hope throughout your life you will be fortunate enough to have had the friends and memories that your dad has had. You already have one best friend for life.

Trademarks

All terms mentioned in this book that are known to be or are suspected of being trademarks or service marks have been appropriately capitalized. Alpha Books and Pearson Education, Inc., cannot attest to the accuracy of this information. Use of a term in this book should not be regarded as affecting the validity of any trademark or service mark.

Part 1
A Little History, Repeated

Hockey has been around in a recognizable form since the beginning of the nineteenth century. But at a time when rowing was the world's most popular spectator sport, baseball was taking a strong foothold in North America, and the idea of a modern Olympiad began forming in the mind of Baron Pierre de Coubertin, hockey was still taking baby steps.

It wasn't until the middle of the 1870s that the game first appeared in Montreal, where it would experience its first real growth. And though the sport would quickly show up in the United States before the end of the century, and even make its debut in modern form in Europe, it was still considered an infant when it came to big-time endeavours. It would take an offering of a small silver cup by a Canadian Governor-General and the rancorous rantings and ravings of early fans and players to push the game into the twentieth century as one that larger numbers of people would finally notice and begin to hold dear to their hearts.

Chapter 1

Whose Game Is This, Anyway?

In This Chapter

➤ Hockey's early ancestors

➤ Bandy's influences

➤ The boys of King's College

➤ Hockey comes to Montreal

➤ First steps south

Hockey is the Canadian game. Invented in Canada. Nurtured in Canada. Perfected by Canadians. Given to the world by the Land of the Maple Leaf and Endless Hockey Games on Television.

Well, yes and no.

Hockey, like many sports, was more developed than created—it was brought together from games with similar elements and molded into its final form over a period of almost two centuries. While it's fair to say that Canadians developed the game we know today, as Americans did with baseball, it's also fair to say that many people from many different countries and cultures see things in both those sports that they recognize from their own experiences and history. In this chapter, we'll look at hockey's early influences, how they were brought together, and the game's baby steps toward respectability.

Not Quite the National Dream

Just who invented the game of ice hockey, and when?

Few discussions have kept hockey historians locked in the throes of happy argument than that launched by those two simple questions.

It's difficult to find answers, however.

There are as many ideas on the subject as there are about how the Civil War began, or about what caused the 100 Years' War in Europe, or about whether Bonnie and Clyde were heroes or criminals.

Writer Teena Spencer, a newcomer in hockey historiography, went looking and wound up as confused as the rest of us. England in Medieval times? Denmark two centuries ago? Scotland around the time of the Battle of Culoden? Ancient Greece?

Bandy fanatic Per Olsson points out that Egyptian hieroglyphics show pictures of youngsters hitting a round object with sticks, but that could more easily be traced as the invention of field hockey than the further reach to the game on ice.

The Dutch seem a fair bet for an early version; the Japanese had one of their own called *Kaichi/Dakyu;* the Aztecs had *Cheucha;* and it goes on and on.

So, where to start? How about with two games—one played across all of Europe and the other that seemed to mostly catch the interest of the Irish.

Bands of Brothers Bothering the Bard

"All right, you kids, get out of the street, I'm trying to write!"

Okay, William Shakespeare might not have yelled that out a window in England, but he does mention the game of "bandy" (which is in itself an early form of field hockey that was eventually played on an ice-covered football pitch) in *Romeo and Juliet.*

Quote, Unquote

Bandy isn't a Russian game, you know. It's a Swedish game."

—Mats Sundin, Toronto Maple Leafs captain, 1999. Originally, it wasn't either.

"The Prince expressly hath forbidden Bandying in the Verona streets," quoth the Bard, which, according to Olsson, refers directly to the game and not hanging about on the street corners with nothing to do.

Bandy and field hockey seemed to develop almost in parallel with each other, switching from grass pitches to iced ones as the seasons changed. And despite the claims of many Russian and Scandinavian enthusiasts, bandy's true modern roots are English.

Having said that, it was the Russians and the Scandinavians who really took to the game and adopted it to their hearts after introduction in the 1890s (more on that in later sections).

There have been bandy world championships since 1957, which have been totally dominated by Sweden and Russia. It's typical for the English—they invented soccer as well, and haven't won a World Cup for over 30 years.

Windsor vs. Kingston: Hockey's First Serious Rivalry

Let's get our opinion on the table right away. Yes, a form of hockey was played in Kingston, Ontario (the birthplace of one Donald S. Cherry), as far back as the 1830s. Yes, that's pretty early. No, the game was not invented there.

Please don't sick your dog on us, Don.

The rules for hockey as we recognize it today were developed and finally written down in Windsor, Nova Scotia, which is home to King's College—in itself the womb for many a rich Bluenoser's boy. King's was opened in 1789, and by 1800, there were already a number of written accounts of the young pups playing "ice hurley," a winter version of an Irish game that features short sticks with rounded ends, a hard ball, a large pitch, and a lot of blood.

It didn't take long for the boys and their teachers, under a not inconsiderable influence from local Mi'kmaq natives (who had their own version of hockey, called shinny), to realize that ice hurley needed some improvements—longer sticks; a smaller ice surface; less gaping goals.

Ingredients for the King's College game must have been going into the pot like ingredients on a television cooking show. A little field hockey. A little cricket. A touch of hurley. A lot of shinny. Some bandy.

All of this took some years of trial and error, until eventually the Halifax Rules were accepted in that Nova Scotia city. As the rules of baseball were first set down on the Elysian Fields of New Jersey and then passed on to the world, so, too, were hockey's first rules sent west, mostly by word of mouth, on the first train available.

Those Halifax Rules

Listen up fellas. We're going to get a little organization out here whether you like it or not. And stop trying to kick the ball into the net—the new rules say you can't!

Writer Garth Vaughan, quoting Colonel B. A. Weston (a famous Dartmouth resident of the time), says the earliest version of the Halifax Rules stated that stones would mark the goal, which was pointed toward the

Quote, Unquote

"Whenever the ball is put through the ricket [goal] a shout 'Game, Ho!' resounds from shore to shore and dies away in a hundred echoes through the hills."

—*Boston Globe*, reporting on "ice ricket" in Dartmouth, Nova Scotia, 1859.

side, not the end; the wooden puck had to stay on the ice at all times; you couldn't carry your stick over your shoulder (this rule remains today); and every time a goal was scored, the players, who numbered seven a side, changed ends.

I Remember ...

One of the most interesting early hockey stories revolves around the British royal family and a game played at Windsor Palace in 1853. According to Ian Gordon, a British journalist writing in 1937, royal family members went to a house party at the country palace after a hard frost and decided to play field hockey on the ice-covered grounds. They chose sides, took a wooden plug from a barrel, put skates on, and had a game with the royal guards. The Prince Consort guarded a goal.

Interestingly, the forward pass was allowed in the Halifax Rules, but when the game finally made its way to Montreal after 1872, it was banned there. Imagine a game with no forward pass! (The argument might be made that the Soviets of the 1960s and 1970s seemed willing to return to that era with the way they cycled the puck forever backward when they couldn't skate it into the offensive zone.)

Quote, Unquote

"I recollect John Cunard [the brother of Sir Samuel of steamship fame] having his front teeth knocked out with a hurley by Pete Delancey of Annapolis."

—Anonymous writer, writing of his life at King's College, 1816–1818.

Who Invented That?

Organizing the rules into an accepted form wasn't the only advancement in the game that came from Nova Scotia.

➤ The Starr Manufacturing Company of Dartmouth created the first self-fastening skates in 1863 and then came up with specific hockey skates (with the rockered, or rounded, blade) in 1866.

➤ The hockey stick, as noted, was perfected by the Mi'kmaq.

➤ Around the 1880s, posts began to be used to mark the goals and, according to Vaughan, in 1899, the Nova Scotia Box Net appeared.

➤ Shin pads were a Mi'kmaq invention.

➤ Padded gloves made their debut in 1904.

Of course, not all of these claims come without argument. The net, for instance, appeared at almost the same time in Montreal as it did in Nova Scotia, and many historians credit W. A. Hewitt (the father of legendary announcer Foster Hewitt), as the originator of the idea.

That Kingston Thing

Okay Mr. Cherry, you'd best flip to the next page now, because you're not going to like this.

Just as Albert Goodwill Spalding skewered the understanding of baseball history for almost 100 years by claiming, falsely, that Abner Doubleday invented the game in the 1840s, James Thomas Sutherland (a fine coach and innovator in the late nineteenth and early twentieth century and the man behind the Memorial Cup trophy for the top junior team in Canada), confused the issue for hockey by pushing his theory that Kingston, Ontario, was the birthplace of "organized" hockey.

Sutherland's propaganda was so good that the small city by the banks of the St. Lawrence River went unchallenged as the game's home until recent times.

Hockey in some form may have been played as far back as the 1840s on the frozen river by army troops, but the first recorded organized game at Kingston was in 1886, more than 10 years after James Creighton brought hockey west from Halifax to Montreal.

Sutherland, by the way, was a traveling shoe salesman by trade, so he came by his gifts honestly. He would push his theories until the middle of the twentieth century.

Aw, I Knew That!

Q. What was the best-selling brand of hockey stick from the nineteenth century until 1925?

A. MicMac sticks, made by Mi'kmaq craftsmen in Nova Scotia.

Aw, I Knew That!

Q. What important innovation in the game first appeared in 1872?

A. The rubber hockey puck.

Bienvenue à Montréal

You can argue until you're blue in the face about the origins of the sport, but hockey moved from infancy to its early childhood on the island of Montreal, Quebec. It was in the bilingual city (still under the firm grip of the Anglo population) that the first true club teams made their appearance after 1875, and where the first amateur leagues grew to prominence with clubs in the city and any community within easy reach.

And that growth traces back to one enthusiastic young man: James Creighton.

Creighton was 22 years old in 1872 when he left King's College in Nova Scotia for an engineering job in Montreal. He carried with him his luggage, books, train ticket, and a few hockey sticks. Other than the fact he may have had to walk naked down Rue St. Catharines if he'd forgotten the clothes, the sticks were the most important items that came with Creighton.

Montreal, writes Michel Vigneault, hosted an organized game of ice hurley as far back as 1837, and a Scottish version of shinny was also played there.

It didn't take long for Creighton to get a serious contest going among his new friends on the island. In March 1875, a game was played involving nine skaters a side at the Victoria Skating Rink, where eight-foot-wide nets were used, marked by poles, and again, no forward passing was allowed.

After that, the game exploded on the scene in a way it had never done in Halifax or Dartmouth. And Creighton led the way. With the game organizing nicely in Montreal, the young engineer took a job in Ottawa, where he put together "a team of public servants," says Vigneault, called the Rideau Rebels. That team included two sons of the Governor-General—Lord Stanley of Preston.

Aw, I Knew That!

Q. Where was the first indoor hockey game played?

A. Victoria Skating Rink, Montreal, 1875.

The first hockey tournament came in 1883, with two Montreal clubs and one from Quebec City competing at the Montreal Winter Carnival. McGill University was the winner.

Just four short years later, the first full-fledged league, the Amateur Hockey Association of Canada, began play with four Montreal clubs and one from Ottawa. Meanwhile, the first official hockey league was formed in Kingston.

And just six years after that, in 1893, Governor-General Stanley came up with the idea of presenting a cup in his own name to the winner of the Dominion hockey championship.

More on that in Part 2, "The National Hockey League."

First Steps South

The credited first game of hockey played by Americans came in 1895, when ice polo players went north to play a series of games in Montreal, Ottawa, Toronto, and Kingston—one game each of polo and ice hockey in each town. The Canadian hosts won all four hockey games and tied two of the polo games. More important, the Americans realized that hockey was a far better game than the one they played.

So, hockey it was.

All this is very well, except there is clear evidence that sportsmen in Boston, Massachusetts, first tried the game as far back as 1859, when a reporter for the *Boston Globe* was sent to do a story on sports in Nova Scotia and came back all aglow over the game of ice hurley, which was slowly being renamed hockey. The newspaper sent for a set of those solid Mi'kmaq sticks and introduced the game in Beantown.

Perhaps it was the interest in the parallel game of ice polo (regular polo played on frozen water and without the horses—lucky break for the animals), or that the attention of those in the northeast United States was somewhat taken by the insistence of the southern states to become uncivil and start a war, but hockey remained a novelty known by just a few until the 1890s.

Aw, I Knew That!

Q. One of the three teams to play in the first organized hockey tournament in 1883 stayed together long enough to win the Stanley Cup. What was the team called?

A. The Montreal Victorias.

Rules, Rules, Rules

The Hockey Hall of Fame in Toronto contains a summary of the rules that were originally published in the *Montreal Gazette* in 1877, probably written by James Creighton. They show how the game was already developing.

➤ Games would be started with a face-off, called a "bully."

➤ Players always had to be on their own side of the ball.

➤ Charging, tripping, collaring, kicking, and shinning (whacking a player's legs with a stick) were not allowed.

➤ If the ball went past the goal line, it came back 15 yards for another bully.

➤ If it went out at the side, a ball-in, much like a soccer throw in, was taken.

➤ Games had two umpires and a head referee.

The Least You Need to Know

➤ Hockey has a number of ancestors, including hurley, shinny, field hockey, and bandy.

➤ The first attempts to create a new game came at King's College in Nova Scotia.

➤ James Creighton brought the game west to Montreal in 1872.

➤ Kingston is not the birthplace of hockey.

➤ Hockey first tiptoed into the United States in 1859.

Chapter 2

Lord Stanley's Mug

In This Chapter

➤ Lord Stanley awards a cup

➤ Early Stanley Cup stories

➤ Montreal and Ottawa dominate the early going

➤ A long way from Dawson City

➤ Hockey spreads far and wide

As the last decade of the nineteenth century began, hockey was moving from baby steps to infancy with clubs, mostly formed by men with the money to buy equipment and build some kind of ice surface, organizing themselves into leagues and associations. What was needed, however, was some kind of binding force—a final goal for which to strive. It fell to an Englishman with royal connections, whose children had become hockey nuts, to provide that goal in the form of a $48 silver bowl that over 100 years later would still be the most desired prize in the game. In this chapter, we'll look at that prize and its early days, the way the game continued to grow and develop, and the seemingly endless arguments over who could play, where, against whom, and using what rules.

I Remember ...

In 1900, the Colored Hockey League of the Maritimes made its debut with teams in Africville, Dartmouth, Halifax, Truro, and Amherst, all in Nova Scotia. Later Prince Edward Island would have a club. Writer William Humber says the reasons for a separate league—whether racism or a need for community identity—have been lost to time. But the play was excellent, and crowds were large. The CHLM was also creative: It was the first organized league to allow goaltenders to leave their feet and fall to the ice to make stops rather than being basically glued in place. The Colored Hockey League survived until the 1920s, and individual teams were organized for tournaments and the like long after that.

Good Thing He Wasn't a Sailing Fan

His name was Lord Stanley of Preston, and by 1893 he was coming to the end of his stint as Governor-General of the Dominion of Canada. Even then, with the country's formation as an independent nation in 1867, the Governor-General's power had become somewhat neutered, but, as an honorary position, it was the best in Canada.

Among other things, the position came with a big house called Rideau Hall in the nation's capital of Ottawa. And on the front lawn of the hall, pushed by both his sons and daughters, a skating rink had been set up so everyone could play this new game of hockey. A photo taken in 1890 shows the rink on which, by the way, the first women's games were played, starring the Governor-General's own daughter, Isobel.

Aw, I Knew That!

Q. What teams were involved in the first women's game reported on by a newspaper?

A. The Ottawa Alphas vs. the Ottawa Rideaus, in the early 1890s.

But it was the enthusiasm of his two eldest sons for the sport that may have been the push needed to get the Governor-General to toss in a few guineas for a cup.

"I have for some time been thinking that it would be a good thing if there were a challenge cup which should be held from year to year by the champion hockey team in the Dominion of Canada," wrote Lord Stanley.

So off to a London, England, silversmith went a check and a request for a nice little bowl. Thus was born the Stanley Cup.

Lord Stanley never saw the bowl played for—he was called home a little early after the death of a brother. But he left a gift that became part of Canada's spirit and historic lore.

He also left the makings of a huge, running argument over who got to play for the cup and when.

A Lot of Noses Out of Joint

Sheriff Sweetland and P. D. Ross, a couple of sportsmen from Ottawa, were left with the silver mug and a set of instructions about who could play for it.

They might have said no, if they had known what was to come.

Stanley Cup Winners of the Era	
1892–1893	Montreal Hockey Club (AAA)
1893–1894	Montreal Hockey Club (AAA)
1894–1895	Montreal Victorias
1895–1896	Winnipeg Victorias (February 1896)
1895–1896	Montreal Victorias (December 1896)
1896–1897	Montreal Victorias
1897–1898	Montreal Victorias
1898–1899	Montreal Shamrocks
1899–1900	Montreal Shamrocks
1900–1901	Winnipeg Victorias
1901–1902	Montreal Hockey Club (AAA)
1902–1903	Ottawa Silver Seven
1903–1904	Ottawa Silver Seven
1904–1905	Ottawa Silver Seven
1905–1906	Montreal Wanderers
1906–1907	Kenora Thistles (January 1907)
1906–1907	Montreal Wanderers (March 1907)
1907–1908	Montreal Wanderers
1908–1909	Ottawa Senators
1909–1910	Montreal Wanderers

The Montreal Amateur Athletic Association was, in 1893, the just-crowned champs of the Amateur Hockey Association, and Stanley designated that club as the first holders of the new prize. This immediately left the Ottawa Hockey Club in a snit because they had won the Ontario championship and thought they deserved it.

Nothing to do but challenge the Montreal AAA to a game in Montreal.

Quote, Unquote

"[Weldy] so far forgot himself as to jump into the crowd and assault a fresh young supporter of the opposing team."

—Ottawa reporter on an incident in 1899 involving Weldy Young. Weldy forgot the fan might have friends, who promptly pounded him and tossed the star back onto the ice.

About 5,000 people thought it was important enough that they packed the arena (admission: 25 cents up to a dollar) on March 22, 1894, for the showdown. Important note: Ottawa was the nation's capital, but Montreal was the center of the Canadian universe in business and society at the time, so there was more than a $48 mug on the line here. This was for civic pride, baby.

The teams were still seven a side (goal, point, coverpoint, rover, and three forwards), there was no forward passing, and the goalie had to stay on his feet. After hacking and slashing their way through the contest, Montreal, led by Billy Barlow's two goals, polished off a 3–1 win.

That just made the Ottawa contingent, known as Bytowners (for Colonel By, who founded the city), even madder. They'd be back. But not for a while. In the first 10 years, covering 11 challenges, Montreal-based teams would win 9 times. Only the Winnipeg Victorias in 1896 and 1901 would head off that express train.

What Hath the Bluenoser Wrought?

Okay time travelers, let's go back to the late nineteenth century and wander over to an outdoor arena in Montreal or Ottawa to catch a hockey game. As Brian McFarlane would joke over 80 years later, don't bother trying to buy a seat, because chances are there aren't any—that's any chairs in the arena at all.

Standing room only, as it were.

Nobody faces off to start the game—the referee just puts the puck between two players and yells "Play." No one is wearing padded gloves, the goalie is maskless, the puck never leaves the ice, the goal is a couple of sticks in the ice, and some idiot down at the end waves a handkerchief like mad whenever the puck glides through the two sticks. You can't rebound, you can't pass forward … I mean, what is going on here?

Hockey, my dear fan. Taking its early steps.

Stories to Tell Your Great-Grandchildren (That Would Be You)

The early days of Stanley Cup competition may not have produced the most scintillating hockey ever, as Danny Gallivan, the famous Montreal broadcaster, might have said, but it sure produced some of the best stories.

Like the time referee Alex Martin called back a Montreal goal in a February 1896 series with the Winnipeg Victorias that, according to the local press, practically handed the Western interlopers the Stanley Cup. Montreal's Victorias would be so mad they'd make the unprecedented move of heading to Winnipeg the following December (who would go to Winnipeg in December on purpose?), where they won the mug back.

Like the 1899 game, when another referee, J. A. Findlay, called a penalty for a Montreal slash that was so violent that the Winnipeg club left the ice. So did the ref, who promptly took off his skates and went home. Someone talked him into coming back, but by that time many of the Winnipeg club were in Montreal bars having a beer and couldn't be found.

Or such as in 1903, when Rat Portage (a town whose name was soon changed to Kenora for obvious reasons) tried putting two goalies into the net at the same time because the rules didn't say they couldn't. The bumbling backstops kept bumping into each other, and the Thistles were trashed.

Or when the Thistles were playing the Ottawa Silver Seven in 1905, featuring a fast-skating club that had won game one going away. Ottawa rink attendants flooded the ice with an inch of water before the second game, nullifying the Kenora speed and handing the game to the Silver Seven. Kenora never recovered.

And in 1906, in the Ottawa Silver Seven, unbeatable for much of the decade, lost 9–1 in game one of a two-game, total goal series against the Montreal Wanderers. But by halfway through the second 30-minute half, the series was tied up 10–10, and Ottawa was on the way to another Cup. But then Lester Patrick got his mates together, smartened them up, and helped finally put the Silver Seven away with two quick ones of his own.

And then ...

Quote, Unquote

"The next step before death is refereeing."

—*Ottawa Citizen*, in a turn-of-the-twentieth-century attack on the officials.

Aw, I Knew That!

Q. What were the measurements of the Victoria Skating Rink in Montreal when the first organized game of hockey was played on March 3, 1875?

A. 200 × 85 feet. It has remained the standard measure of a hockey rink in North America ever since.

I Remember ...

Money was a major issue in hockey even back in its earliest days. It was understood that you had to be an amateur to compete for the Stanley Cup, but that didn't stop some leagues and their owners from slipping more than a few dollars to its players as inducement to jump organizations. The Ottawa Valley Hockey League was able to convince Fred "Cyclone" Taylor, the era's best player, to come on over. Taylor would make a habit of popping from this club to that as a proper mercenary. There was also money to be made in British Columbia and in Edmonton, Alberta. The first true professional league actually began, however, in Michigan (see Chapter 4, "Hockey by the Dawn's Early Light") in 1904.

Peter Puck's Favorite Story

Whose idea it was has become a little fuzzy, but somehow a bunch of guys in Dawson City, Yukon, came up with the idea of putting together a team and heading down to Ottawa to challenge the Silver Seven for Lord Stanley's spittoon. Wonderful idea, except that air travel was only a year old, this being December of 1904, and Ottawa was rather a long way away.

Aw, worth a try. So a bunch of the boys (and one real boy—17-year-old goaltender Albert Forrest) set out on a trek that would make Robert Service (the famous Yukon poet—see *The Shooting of Dan McGrew*) proud. They walked 30 miles in a snowstorm to catch a train to Alaska, then went by ship to Seattle, where they took a train to Vancouver, and then another across the country to Ottawa.

Aw, I Knew That!

Q. When did the red line between the goal posts first appear?

A. In 1903–1904 in the Federal League (Montreal Wanderers, Montreal Nationals, Ottawa Capitals, and Cornwall).

Twenty-three days. Twenty-three miserable days, only to have rat-faced officials in Bytown tell them they couldn't have a couple more days to rest and recover—they had to hit the ice the very next day. Actually, in game one, the Dawson boys didn't do too badly, coming up on the very short end of a 9–2 score. But hey, they were tired.

The following day, it was 23–2 for Ottawa as the Silver Seven followed the lead of One-Eyed Frank McGee and his 14 goals.

And the Dawson City boys' reward?

Another three weeks to get home.

Hockey: It's a Gas

Brian McFarlane called it the Era of Gaslight—the time when hockey got itself together and began to expand to other cities across Canada and into the United States, and when it became as important to the smaller towns and tiniest villages as it was to large centers.

The era began in 1875 with that first game at Victoria Rink in Montreal and ran to 1910.

Kingston, Ontario, boasts of the first hockey league, involving Queen's University, Royal Military College, and two local independent clubs around the early 1880s. That was but the start, however. Along came the Amateur Hockey Association of Canada (1886), a league in Toronto (1888), the Ontario Hockey Association (1890), and the Canadian Amateur Hockey League (formed in 1889 by unhappy AHA clubs including three in Montreal plus Ottawa and Quebec). Those clubs would win six of seven Stanley Cups in ensuing years.

But the game was definitely headed west at a propitious rate. McFarlane writes that by 1892, there were more than 30 teams in Winnipeg, and the game had made it all the way to the Pacific Coast, up to the Yukon and the Northwest Territories, and into the United States to Minnesota and Chicago.

Money, however, was becoming more of a factor wherever the game was played. True pro hockey was definitely on the horizon.

Stars of the Era

➤ Fred Higginbotham was both a tremendous hockey player and an accomplished musician who starred for the Winnipeg Vics in 1902. He lost his life in a family accident—snapping his spine when he ran into a clothesline while riding a pony with his children—that same year.

➤ One-Eyed Frank McGee, nicknamed because of his loss of sight in one eye, scored 14 goals in a Stanley Cup game in January 1905 and was one of the game's top performers in its early era. He scored five goals in a game seven times in his career, entirely spent with Ottawa clubs.

➤ Didier Pitre was the first French-Canadian star. A huge man for his time (200 pounds), Pitre had excellent skating speed and a cannon shot. He played in most of the important leagues, finishing with the Montreal Canadiens, for which he was the first player to be signed in 1909.

➤ Art Ross played for seven teams in his career, leading Kenora to the Stanley Cup in 1907 and the Montreal Wanderers in 1908. Ross was responsible for redesigning the goal net and the puck and would go on to become one of the key figures in the game's development in the United States.

The Least You Need to Know

➤ Lord Stanley presented the cup named for him in 1893.

➤ Early Stanley Cup games brought big arguments.

➤ Hockey spread quickly in this era throughout Canada and into the United States.

➤ Professionalism was becoming a factor for players and leagues.

Chapter 3

"National" Hockey Leagues (1910–1917)

In This Chapter

➤ The Montreal Canadiens

➤ National Hockey Association

➤ Birth and influence of the Pacific Coast Hockey Association

➤ Real war

On February 12, 1910, Fred "Cyclone" Taylor of the Renfrew Millionaires broke in on goaltender Percy LeSueur of Ottawa, pirouetted entirely (or accidentally stumbled), and scored one of the most famous goals in hockey history—that is, going backward. Whether it was designed or not (and Taylor, the era's greatest player, went to his grave without saying one way or the other), that score put the perfect capper on two decades of wild times and even wilder antics. It was time, however, for hockey to get itself truly organized, especially as ever more money was coming into it for owners and players. Over the next seven years, associations would form and fall by the wayside as the seeds for today's National Hockey League were sown. Two of the most significant of those seeds were planted in Montreal and far out on North America's west coast. In this chapter, we'll look at the events leading up to the birth of the NHL and the growth and importance of its keenest competitor, the Pacific Coast Hockey Association.

Les habitants

They are hockey's most famous, glorious team. Les habitants. Les glorieux. Le rouge, blanc, et bleu (The Red, White, and Blue—though they actually wore only blue and white for one of their early seasons).

The Montreal Canadiens were basically born because an anglo named Jimmy Gardner convinced another anglo named J. Ambrose O'Brien that the French half of the bilingual province of Quebec needed its own team to love, honor, and sway with their cheers. Since the beginning of hockey in Montreal, the game had mostly belonged to the English-speaking community, though there were many talented French-Canadian players, including a dynamic big fella named Didier Pitre.

No big-time team, however, had directly represented French Quebecers until Gardner, general manager of the Montreal Wanderers, and O'Brien approached Jack Laviollette, a city businessman, about putting together the Canadiens.

Back up a bit. A war in the Eastern Canadian Hockey Association swelled up when owners of the semi-professional loop wanted to kick out the Wanderers, who under owner P. J. Doran, were insisting on moving from their 7,000-seat digs into the new Jubilee Rink, which had a capacity of only 3,250 seats. That meant lower gate receipts for the league in general, so it set out to replace the Wanderers with another club that would operate out of the bigger Westmount Arena.

So, as writer Andy O'Brien points out, at the Windsor Hotel, the league simply voted itself out of existence and reformed as the Canadian Hockey Association, with teams in Ottawa, Quebec City, and three in Montreal. But no Wanderers.

J. Ambrose, meanwhile, was in the same hotel on that November 25, 1909, trying to get his Haileybury and Renfrew clubs (of the wild Temiskaming League) into the new CHA. The owners told him to buzz off. He buzzed a little way down the hall and ran into a despondent Gardner, who suggested J. Ambrose match his two clubs with the Wanderers and pick up a fourth team by getting Laviollette to put together a team for the French. And they could get a fifth from Cobalt of the Temiskaming loop.

Quote, Unquote

"To you with failing arms, we throw the torch, be yours to hold it high."

—Line from John McCrae's famous World War I poem, "In Flanders Fields," adopted by the Montreal Canadiens as their rallying cry.

Quote, Unquote

"Well, now. I don't want to spoil someone's story."

—Cyclone Taylor's regular response whenever anyone asked if he really did score going backward.

It was that simple. Five teams. Four of them owned by the same guy. And the cost for J. Ambrose to own the Canadiens? How about nothing down and $5,000 to guarantee player salaries. Within two years he turned the club over, for free, to the "French sportsmen in Montreal."

Tell It to the Judge

One of the first things the Canadiens did was sign right wing/defenseman Didier "The Cannonball" Pitre, a 5'11", 185-pound slab of iron (that was huge for 1909), to a contract that would match him with Edouard "Newsy" Lalonde, another superb player. Pitre had been in professional hockey since 1903 and had tallied an amazing 41 times for the American Soo Indians of the International League in 1905–1906. He was a star, and the fact that Pitre had already signed with the Montreal Nationals of the rival CHA for 1909 didn't sway J. Ambrose O'Brien one bit.

The Nats threatened to sue. They threatened to have Pitre clapped in irons. They went to court and eventually lost.

Pitre was a Canadien, and would stay so until the end of the 1922–1923 season, when he retired after 20 years of pro.

Sidenote: Pitre had a contract with the Nats for $1,100. Laviolette, acting for O'Brien, offered him $1,700 and told the player he could keep it if the courts made him go back to the Nationals and the other league. Makes you wonder if Pitre might have thought losing the case would have been a better idea.

Quote, Unquote

"$2,000 fine and sixty days jail for Pitre if he plays."

—Headline in the *Montreal Star*, January 5, 1910. Trouble off the top, just before the Canadiens play their first game.

A Bunch of Pirates

All of a sudden, money was flying all over the place as the two leagues went to war (and yes, you are invited to see parallels with the NHL vs. World Hockey Association battle that would break out 70 years later). As Bobby Hull's signing by Winnipeg of the WHA would do in more modern times, so did Cyclone Taylor's inking of a contract in late 1909 by Renfrew (which had already grabbed a number of other players from different leagues) set the tongues of media and officialdom wagging.

Aw, I Knew That!

Q. What year did linesman and referees start dropping the puck between players rather than placing it?

A. 1914.

As Eric Zweig points out, Taylor's mark of $5,250 for a 12-game season was the richest in all team sports at that time on a cost-per-game basis. All those rich Renfrew contracts (including those of Frank and Lester Patrick and Fred Whitcroft) led the club to be nicknamed "the Millionaires."

With the CHA now struggling, the NHA went after its rival's two best franchises: the Ottawa Senators and the Montreal Shamrocks. The Canadian Hockey Association couldn't handle that loss and folded amidst much bitterness. Of course, if they had let the Montreal Wanderers stay in the league in the first place, none of this would have happened.

It was their own fault.

Renfrew, trying to buy a Stanley Cup, obtained Newsy Lalonde from the Habs, but they couldn't take the 1910 cup. It went to the Wanderers.

This story continued to be pot-boiling. O'Brien gave up the Cobalt and Haileybury teams, the Quebec Bulldogs came in, and George Kendall took over the Canadiens. A salary cap was brought in pegged at $5,000 a team (end of big salaries—not that all the teams actually followed the cap, but it did drop overall earning potential for players).

With no other leagues as strong as the NHA at that time, the Stanley Cup would go to this group's champions.

Aw, I Knew That!

Q. What was the actual name of the Renfrew club nicknamed the Millionaires because of the large salaries they paid their players?

A. The Creamery Kings.

But that ending of big salaries would be a huge influence on the future of hockey in both Canada and the United States. Frank and Lester Patrick found they were unable to come east from British Columbia and play for the lower rate (they had their dad's lumber business to worry about). So with nowhere else to play, the brothers decided to start their own league, which would wind up costing the NHA owners a lot of money and heartache.

The Bluest Skies You've Ever Seen ...

The most significant event of this era did not happen in Eastern Canada, it took place on December 7, 1911, in Vancouver, British Columbia—out where the lumber seemed to go on forever and the sky disappeared over the Pacific horizon.

Enough young men and women had gone west that the Pacific Northwest of North America was flourishing and could well support its own quality professional hockey league—if they could get the players. Money would take care of that.

Lester Patrick would become such an important figure in United States hockey that after he died, a trophy was created in his name that honors a significant contributor to hockey in America each year. But he and his brother Frank were Canadians who grew up in British Columbia as the strapping and talented sons of a lumber baron named Joseph who himself made a killing in the wood business.

Not wanting to go back east to play in the now cheap NHA, the Patricks set up a meeting on December 7 and formed the Pacific Coast Hockey Association with teams in Vancouver (another group of Millionaires), Victoria (Aristocrats), and New Westminster (Royals).

Check out the names. They mean money, right? Right.

Lester took over the Victoria Aristocrats team as player-coach-owner, and Frank settled in with Vancouver.

The Patricks also built a beautiful new rink, the Denman Arena in Vancouver, which opened in 1911 with 10,000 seats, artificial ice (the first ever), and a large 200 × 85-foot surface.

And the PCHA brought in some innovative rule changes (more on this coming up), and opened up the United States as a source for big-league hockey, soon putting teams into Seattle (Metropolitans) and Portland (Rosebuds, transferred from New Westminster).

Now, they just needed players.

Quote, Unquote

"Why not build a couple of rinks out here, and start a hockey league?"

—Frank Patrick hits his father and brother with an idea. The Pacific Coast Hockey Association is born.

I Remember ...

The NHA and PCHA agreed to bury the hatchet long enough to compete for the Stanley Cup, with the first series set for the spring of 1915, between the Ottawa Senators and the Vancouver Millionaires. Splitting the games between seven- and six-man hockey, Vancouver took the best of three in two straight contests, marking the first time a PCHA club would win the cup. Frank Nighbor, Cyclone Taylor, and Mickey Mackay were the stars for the winners.

More Pirates

The NHA had started life by raiding the CHA for players. Now, in 1911, they were under attack, and this time it came from the Left Coast.

Frank and Lester wasted no time. With opening day set for January 2, 1912, there were a lot of brand-new uniforms waiting for warm bodies to fill them. By the time Lester was done, his entire starting lineup for Victoria was made up of former NHA players, including Bobby Rowe, Bert Lindsay (father of Ted, a future Detroit Red Wing star), Don Smith, Tom Dunderdale, Skinner Poulin, and Walter Smaill. Frank set his sights even higher, going after Newsy Lalonde. New Westminster grabbed a bunch for itself.

I Remember ...

Making American teams eligible for Stanley Cup competition was not as simple as just putting Seattle, Spokane, and Portland franchises into the Pacific Coast Hockey Association. When Lord Stanley had given the cup, he had specified to the trustees that it was for a Canadian winner. But he also gave the trustees wide powers to do what they felt was best with the competition. In 1915, with Portland in the Pacific loop, the trustees announced that American clubs would be able to claim the cup.

Aw, I Knew That!

Q. What was the first American-based team to challenge for the Stanley Cup?

A. The Portland Rosebuds, 1916, who lost to the Montreal Canadiens in five games.

Before the second season began, the NHA, in a fighting mood, lured Lalonde back east. On the westbound train, however, was Cyclone ("I'll play anywhere for a buck") Taylor, who would be the greatest player in PCHA history.

It would be 1915–1916 before the Pacific league went back on the attack, needing to fill the roster of the expansion Seattle Metropolitans. They came up with five solid NHA stars, including Jack Walker, Frank Foyston, Cully Wilson, Ed Carpenter, and Hap Holmes. But four PCHA stars went back east that year as well.

That would be the last year for Victoria. Suffering bad attendance, the club moved to Spokane, Washington, to become the Canaries, a team that itself would only last two seasons.

Much attention, however, was being taken up by a different war. When Austria's Grand Duke Franz Ferdinand was assassinated in Sarajevo in the summer of 1914, two angry groups of allies dropped the puck and faced off for four years of blood and misery.

It's War, Boys

While the United States sat on the sidelines to await developments, Canada went to war as a member of the British Empire and Commonwealth team. A number of players who answered the call wound up playing for military hockey teams, basically entertaining the troops both in Canada and Great Britain.

War meant shortages, and for hockey that meant shortages of good players, as not only the pro ranks, but the senior (over 20) and junior clubs (20 and under) found themselves desperate for men to perform on the ice.

Some of the military clubs, playing in regular leagues, did superbly, including the Winnipeg 61st Battalion, which went to France in 1916 after winning the Allan Cup (given to the senior champs of Canada and originally donated by Sir Montague Allan, a Montreal sportsman and financier). The senior Winnipeg Falcons decided to join up as a group and wound up in the trenches in 1917. Three of their group (Olie Turnbull, George Cumbers, and Buster Thorsteinson) paid with their lives.

Aw, I Knew That!

Q. Who still holds the record for most goals by a defenceman in one game?

A. Frank Patrick, Vancouver Millionaires, six goals, March 1912.

I Remember ...

William Brown writes of a bitter brawl between the Canadiens and Wanderers when the two Montreal teams played an exhibition game in Toronto during the 1914–1915 season. Quoting writer Henry Roxborough: "It was the roughest, toughest game ever played in Toronto ... instead of winning converts, [they] almost killed each other." Odie Cleghorn collided with the Habs' Newsy Lalonde, and both went down. Odie's brother Sprague then came up and clubbed Lalonde on the head with his stick. Police arrested Sprague and Newsy and tossed them in jail. When Toronto Arenas owner Charlie Querrie went to bail the combatants out, however, he found them happily sitting on the floor, shooting dice.

In Toronto, the Sportsman's Battery (including a young Lieutenant Conn Smythe) was put together by newspaperman Gordon Southam. They made it to Europe in time to be tossed into the long, bloody Battles of the Somme, where Southam was killed in the early going. Scotty Davidson of the Stanley Cup champion Toronto Blueshirts (1914) also lost his life.

Both the United States, which got into the conflict in the spring of 1917, and Canada would lose a superstar. For America, it was Hobey Baker (see Chapter 4, "Hockey by the Dawn's Early Light"). For Canada, it was a man who had set the record for goals in a Stanley Cup game.

With Both Eyes Wide Open

Frank McGee was 32 when he joined up. This was the same Mr. McGee who had earned the nickname "One-Eyed" because he was practically blind in one of them. How he got into the army with one eye is a matter of speculation, but somehow he found a way to pass his eye exam and was accepted.

McGee was wounded in December 1915 and spent nine months in an English hospital. As Trent Frayne writes, rather than take a safe position far back of the lines, he insisted on returning to the front, where he wound up in the cauldron of the Somme in 1916. On September 16, a German bullet fatally pierced his famous body. Frank McGee died in Flanders Fields.

Rules, Rules, Rules

In 1910, the National Hockey Association finally dumped the two 30-minute halves and went to three 20-minute periods. It also introduced numbers on the back of players' uniforms, something the PCHA quickly adopted as well. And the NHA dropped the rover positions and went to six players a side (five skaters and a goalie). The PCHA tried it, too, didn't like it, and kept the seventh man until 1922–1923, when the league was on the verge of death.

Stanley Cup Winners of the Era	
1910–1911	Ottawa Senators
1911–1912	Quebec Bulldogs
1912–1913	Quebec Bulldogs
1913–1914	Toronto Blueshirts
1914–1915	Vancouver Millionaires
1915–1916	Montreal Canadiens
1916–1917	Seattle Metropolitans

The PCHA introduced bluelines in 1913, dividing the rink into three equal playing areas. They also allowed the forward pass in the neutral zone (the forward pass in the offensive zone wouldn't be introduced until the late 1920s). Both leagues finally allowed goalkeepers to flop around, something the Colored Hockey League had done back in 1900.

Stars of the Era

➤ Clint Benedict was one of the era's great goalkeepers, playing on four Stanley Cup–winning teams, getting the mug three times with the Ottawa Senators and once with the Montreal Maroons. He also would go on to become the first goaltender to wear a mask (one period) in a pro game. Played 17 seasons, until 1929–1930.

➤ Frank Foyston was a member of the first American team to win the Stanley Cup (Seattle), his second as a player. He played with Seattle for nine seasons. Over his career, which ended in 1927–1928, he would win three cups.

➤ Edouard "Newsy" Lalonde (as a boy he worked in a newspaper printing plant in Cornwall, Ontario) was one of the era's superstars. Played for Renfrew and Toronto in the NHA, Vancouver in the PCHA, and the Montreal Canadiens and New York Americans in the NHL. Had 441 goals in his career.

➤ Joe Malone scored 379 times as a professional, playing with the Quebec Bulldogs, the Montreal Canadiens, and the Hamilton Tigers. Begun in 1908, his career lasted until 1924.

➤ Fred "Cyclone" Taylor played pro from 1906–1923, playing for Ottawa and Renfrew before jumping to the Pacific Coast Association in 1912. He led Ottawa to a Stanley Cup in 1909 and did the same thing with Vancouver in 1915. Scored 32 times in just 18 games in 1917–1918.

The Least You Need to Know

➤ The Montreal Canadiens were born.

➤ The National Hockey Association rose, and the Canadian Hockey Association died.

➤ Frank and Lester Patrick formed the Pacific Coast Hockey Association.

➤ Big-time pro hockey made it to the United States (Portland and Seattle).

➤ Hockey players left their leagues to fight in a real war.

Chapter 4

Hockey by the Dawn's Early Light

In This Chapter

➤ Boston leads the way

➤ Ice polo vs. ice hockey

➤ First pro league anywhere

➤ Roots of college hockey

➤ Hobey

Before the turn of the twentieth century, before the telephone was popularized and air travel had closed the huge gaps between faraway communities, relations between certain areas of the United States and Canada were stronger than those areas' relations with other parts of their own country. The Maritimes with New England. Saskatchewan and Alberta with the Dakotas. British Columbia with Washington and Oregon. It was this regional closeness that sped the introduction of hockey into the United States. As soon as one area in Canada became enamored with the game, its close American neighbors would inevitably pick it up, too. In this chapter, we'll look at the beginnings of hockey in the United States—its high points and low points—and at the most significant individual in hockey's early American years—a young man so shy of the attention paid to him that rumors persist he may have taken his own life in order to avoid the spotlight.

Bluenosers and Beaneaters

Perhaps it was the influence of Thomas Chandler Haliburton, "the Father of American Humor," whose character Sam Slick and his sharp sayings were hugely popular in the United States and Canada in the nineteenth century (by the way, Haliburton was Canadian, born and raised in the birthplace of hockey, Windsor, Nova Scotia), or the closeness of the relationship between New England and Eastern Canada, but hockey was actually being played in Boston, Massachusetts, before the game made it to the rest of Canada.

As early as 1859, writes Garth Vaughan, the *Boston Evening Gazette* was reporting on the game in Nova Scotia, and sticks had been brought to the New England city so the citizenry could try it out. They loved it, and Massachusetts became a hotbed of the new sport in the United States.

Quote, Unquote

"It was pretty generally agreed among us as a result of that trip that the Canadian game was better than ours."

—Alexander Meikeljohn, a participant in the polo-hockey exchange of 1895.

Courting a New Game

Writer Kevin Allen, among the best American hockey historians, points to that summer afternoon in 1894 when the college kids from the two countries were playing a tennis tournament in Niagara Falls as "one of the most important events in American hockey history."

With tennis over, the two sides were rapping about what they liked to do in the winter—the Canadians loved hockey, the Americans a form of the game called ice polo, which used a ball rather than a puck.

They bragged. They needled. They argued. They set up some games to settle the issue once and for all.

Move to the winter of 1895, when the polo and hockey enthusiasts played eight games, four of each style. The Canadians won all four hockey games and tied two of the polo matches. More significantly, the American kids fell in love with hockey and decided to ditch ice polo and take to the new sport.

A Perfect Job for a Dentist

His name was J. L. Gibson, and by trade he was a dentist from Ontario who had gotten himself into some trouble in 1897–1898 for having the temerity to actually pay some of his players in the Ontario Hockey Association.

Noticing that the wilds of northern Michigan were going through a mining boom, which meant lots of money around and nowhere to spend it, Dr. Gibson packed up his dentistry tools (who, other than hockey players, would need a dentist more?) and went to the United States with an idea—the world's first fully professional hockey league.

It was called the International Professional Hockey League (IPHL), and when the puck was dropped in 1904, the loop featured teams in Calumet-Larium, both Sault Ste. Maries (Ontario and Michigan), Pittsburgh, and Houghton.

Cyclone Taylor, who would play anywhere there was money, spent a year there, as did many other men who didn't mind taking money over the table (as opposed to all those in Canada taking it under the table while technically staying amateurs).

The league died in 1907, but its existence convinced many in Canada that it was time to become legitimately professional.

Aw, I Knew That!

Q. One of the first players to regularly wear a helmet in games was one of the greatest early stars in American hockey. Who was he?

A. Moose Goheen, St. Paul Athletic Club.

C. M. of AP Builds the St. Nick

Along for the ride when the Americans took on the Canadians in ice hockey and ice polo was C. M. Pope, a reporter for the Associated Press who was so taken by hockey that he went back to New York City and raised money to build St. Nicholas Ice Rink. Kevin Allen calls it "America's hockey center," and it seemed to work that way.

In 1896, the American Amateur Hockey Association was formed.

Collegiate hockey had its first recorded game in the United States in February 1896 when Yale and Johns Hopkins dropped the puck and immediately kissed their sisters by playing to a 2–2 tie at Baltimore. Hopkins jumped in with both feet by joining a league in Baltimore one year later.

I Remember ...

Hockey in the United States was still just a baby when the game wound up in court for the first time. Thanks to a disputed referee's decision on a goal in a 3–2 overtime victory by the University of Maryland over the Maryland Athletic Club in an 1897 championship game, the MAC decided to protest to the league, which upheld the protest and ruled the game to the MAC. As Kevin Allen writes, the Terrapins then sued, hired three big-time lawyers, and wound up seven months later in front of Justice Bailey. He ruled that the "umpire's decision on the question of goals should be final." Trophy to the college boys. There's nothing like higher education.

Out west, meanwhile, college hockey in Minnesota was taking seed, thanks to the close ties between that state and the province of Manitoba.

These were early steps, and as Allen points out, college hockey would not take off until after World War II. But you need a foundation to build on. By the early years of the twentieth century, that foundation had been poured.

Hobey

The basics on Hobey Baker are these:

Hobart Amery Hare Baker was born on January 15, 1892, in Wissahickon, Pennsylvania. His Hockey Hall of Fame biography states simply that "somewhere, very early in life, Hobey learned the arts of effortless skating and stickhandling." That, according to those who saw him play hockey, was putting it mildly.

Baker was such a natural athlete (he was a college star in football as well) that despite hockey's recent introduction to the United States, the youngster took to it. He quickly became, by all accounts, one of the most talented players of the era—no mean feat when you consider the advantages Canadian athletes had over their American counterparts in hockey—well-organized leagues, better coaching, etc.

Baker enrolled at Princeton University in 1910 and performed with great skill in hockey, football, golf, track, swimming, and gymnastics. A classmate of F. Scott Fitzgerald, it's said the famous American writer based a character in his novel *This Side of Paradise* on his handsome, hockey-playing friend.

I Remember ...

There were many who said that Francis Xavier Goheen was as fine a hockey player as Hobey Baker. Known as "Moose," Goheen was born in White Bear, Minnesota, in 1894 and played with equal excellence in football and baseball as well as hockey. The St. Paul Athletic Club was his home in the year before the United States entered World War I, a call that Goheen could not ignore, joining the army and fighting in Europe. A member of the first U.S. Olympic team in 1920, he turned pro with St. Paul when that team went professional in 1925–1926. A successful businessman, Goheen turned down the chance to play for the Boston Bruins (and later the Toronto Maple Leafs), preferring to stay at home and concentrate on his career. Moose was inducted into the Hockey Hall of Fame in 1952.

Baker was the perfect embodiment of the media ideal for the "All-American Boy"—tall, blond, strong, quiet, perfectly mannered. The media, especially in New York, took him to heart, building the legend of Hobey Baker into mythical proportions.

Despite the adulation, which included having a huge (for the day) contract offer of $3,500 from the Montreal Wanderers of the National Hockey Association (forerunner of the National Hockey League), which he turned down, Baker was an unhappy soul.

He despised the attention, as Kevin Allen writes, constantly trying to credit teammates after games when the press only wanted to talk to him.

Baker shunned the pros and joined the St. Nicholas amateur club in New York, leading them to two straight championships. But a different battle called for him. Europe was in the throes of World War I, and Baker almost joined the British army before being dissuaded by friends (which, considering the fate of many Canadian players in Europe, including Frank McGee, who was killed at the Somme, was a smart move on their part).

By 1917, having learned to fly on his own, Baker was sent to France as a member of the famous Lafayette Escadrille: a group of American volunteers flying for the French before the rest of the United States got into the war.

There, Hobey Baker found true freedom. Freedom from the press. Freedom from pressure. Freedom from the expectations of the public. Freedom in the air.

He would never return.

December 21, 1918

Kevin Allen of *USA Today* has done considerable work on Hobey Baker and the events leading up to his death four days before Christmas 1918.

While Allen does not state explicitly that the plane crash that took Baker's life was anything but an accident, there is enough in his story that could lead conspiracy-prone readers to the conclusion that the young star may well have taken his own life.

Six weeks after the War to End All Wars came to a bloody conclusion, Baker, with three kills to his credit during the fighting and the honor of

Quote, Unquote

"Here he comes!"

—Princeton fans' cheer whenever Hobey Baker got ready for one of his end-to-end rushes.

Quote, Unquote

"If it is possible to say of any man that he was beautiful, it may be said of Hobey Baker because he was beautiful of body, soul and spirit."

—Al Laney, *New York Herald Tribune*, writing in the 1950s.

France's Croix de Guerre medal on his chest, came to the French airfield where his American squadron was about to be disbanded and took up an aircraft for one last little spin. It was a last spin that killed him—the engine died at 600 feet, and instead of nursing the machine into the nearest field for a safe landing, Baker tried to make it back to the strip and wound up pancaking into a plowed field, smashing his head into the front of the cockpit.

He died of head injuries on the way to the hospital.

An accident? Very likely. But there are some strange circumstances surrounding the whole affair:

➤ Baker's biographer, John Davies, writes that the young athlete told friends after he left Princeton that "I realize my life is finished. No matter how long I live, I will never equal the excitement of playing on the football field."

➤ In a letter to his parents at the end of the war, Baker told his parents the same thing about life in World War I.

➤ Allen writes that when the war ended, Baker seemed "more saddened than pleased."

➤ Already ordered home, Baker broke a standing superstition about pilots taking a "last flight." For too many of them, it often was their last.

➤ Baker chose a just-repaired Spad aircraft from among a group of perfectly serviceable machines, another thing a veteran pilot would never do.

➤ Instead of picking a handy field to easily set down in, Baker tried to make it back to the airfield itself, another error that seemed, to some, unlikely for such a talented pilot.

Aw, I Knew That!

Q. Who was the first American to play in the new National Hockey League, 1917–1918?

A. Gerry "Duke" Geran, of Holyoke, Massachusetts. He played one game with Montreal Wanderers (some records have it as four) and later 33 games with Boston Bruins. Geran's debut with Montreal came just weeks before Raymie Skilton of Cambridge, Massachusetts, played his one game in the NHL.

The true case will never be known, but following his death Baker was honored by Princeton, which built an arena bearing his name in 1922. And in 1961, the Decathlon Athletic Club of Bloomington, Minnesota, instituted the Hobey Baker Award, given each year to the top player in NCAA college hockey.

A headline at the time of his death probably said it all: "Hobey Baker Was America's Ideal Athlete."

Stars of the Era

➤ Clarence Abel was just one of a number of talented Americans trained during this era. A native of Sault Ste. Marie, Michigan, he played for the Michigan Soo Wildcats from 1918–1922, followed by a stint with the St. Paul Athletic Club before turning pro. He spent three seasons with the New York Rangers and five with the Chicago Blackhawks of the NHL from 1926–1934, scoring 18 times in 333 games.

➤ Hobey Baker starred on the Princeton hockey team and later on the St. Nick's amateur club in New York City, which he led to two Eastern region championships. Baker was killed in a flying accident in France in December 1918. Posthumously elected to the Hockey Hall of Fame in 1945.

➤ Francis Xavier Goheen, nicknamed "Moose," played for the St. Paul Athletic Club in the years before and after World War I. Helped his club to two McNaughton Trophy championships, emblematic of the United States Amateur titlists. Elected to the Hockey Hall of Fame in 1952.

➤ Mickey Roach, born in Boston, started his amateur career in the United States Amateur Hockey Association with the Boston Arenas, the New York Crescent, and the New York Wanderers from 1914–1918. He went on to a 211-game career in the NHL with the Toronto St. Pats, the Hamilton Tigers, and the New York Americans. Roach was part of the 1925 playoff revolt in Hamilton that saw the entire team refuse to play after finishing first in the regular season, causing the team to move to New York.

The Least You Need to Know

➤ Boston was the site of the first hockey games in the United States.

➤ A series of games with Canadian college kids convinced American college kids to drop ice polo and switch to ice hockey.

➤ College hockey in America put down its roots in this era.

➤ Hobey Baker emerged as the most famous American player of the generation.

Over the Big Frozen Pond

Many fans growing up in North America are under the impression that hockey in Europe is a relatively new phenomenon, starting a few years before the Canada-Soviet series in 1972 and flourishing from there. Even the better informed tend to trace the game's European roots in their minds only back as far as the post–World War II era, when the Soviets took up the game seriously and changed the hockey world. This was hardly the case. The first true hockey game (as opposed to those played in the well-organized sport of bandy) took place well before the turn of the twentieth century. In fact, if the Great War of 1914–1918 had not rolled across the face of Europe and killed so many young men, the game of hockey may well have grown at a much faster rate and the Canadian dominance ended much earlier on the world scene. In this chapter, we'll look at hockey's early years in Europe.

Catching Up with the Stanleys

When Lord Stanley, the Canadian Governor-General who donated that silver bowl with his name on it, packed up the family and went home to England in the early 1890s, hockey was not left behind with the furniture at the Governor-General's residence.

Writer Igor Kuperman gives much of the credit for hockey's growth in Great Britain and Europe to his lordship's sons, especially Arthur, who was the young man who formed the Rideau Rebels club in Ottawa in 1888.

Bandy was popular in Great Britain, but the Stanleys were determined to introduce their favorite sport to the cricket- and rugby-mad nation. Okay, they didn't exactly dent the growing influence of Association Football (soccer) with their fellow Brits, but they did set the groundwork for what would eventually grow into the International Ice Hockey Federation.

Quote, Unquote

"The game is very entertaining and requires strong arms and legs, as well as nerves, determination, and speed."

—Report on the new game of ice hockey in *Suomen Urheilulehti,* a Finnish newspaper, in 1899.

In 1895, Kuperman writes, the Stanleys challenged a team of royals that included the future King Edward VII and the future King George V to a game at a frozen-over Buckingham Palace. The Stanleys whipped 'em.

After five more years of exhibition games, the Stanleys dropped out of the game, but not before inspiring a man who would be known as the Founding Father of the game in England—Major B. M. "Peter" Patton. He would form a team, the Princes, that would develop over 10 years and eventually win the first indoor international tournament, beating Germany and France in 1908.

Patton stayed in the sport until 1931, helping to oversee the formation of the first international association and the first official European Championship, in Switzerland, 1910.

Everywhere at Once

Perhaps because of the influence of bandy, which produced skills (skating, stickhandling) that could easily be adapted to the game of hockey, there were a number of countries that suddenly found themselves with hockey programs within a short time of the British.

Belgium had the game by the early twentieth century, as did Austria. Bohemia (now the Czech Republic) picked it up in 1905. The Germans had their first official game in 1897 and the Slovakians even before that. The Swiss were in the door as early as 1902 and the Yugoslavs by 1906.

Along with Peter Patton, however, there was one other man who would have a significant effect on the development years of hockey in Europe.

George's Game

George Meagher was a hockey-mad lad from Canada who moved to Paris in 1894, packing his clothes and other possessions with him on the steamer for France. While he may not have known it, the most important things he brought, other than himself, were a hockey rulebook and one of the first coaching manuals printed.

Armed with this ammunition, Meagher set about introducing the French to hockey from the ground up—drills, drills, and more drills. Under Meagher's influence, a small group of hockey nuts started to spread the word. It took nine years before the first official game took place in France, the boys from Lyon losing 2–1 to the Parisians, and the first official club, Patineurs de Paris, was formed.

France was actually the second European nation to have a national championship (1904), behind England, and it would be a Frenchman, Louis Magnus, who would be the international association's first president.

Aw, I Knew That!

Q. What unusual location was the site for the first game in Germany 1897?

A. The Berlin Zoo. Critics always said hockey players were animals.

Bohemian Rhapsody

Ruck Anderson was another Canadian who found himself working in Europe in the early years of the twentieth century. In Prague by 1905, he hit upon the idea of doing a little demonstration for the Bohemians.

Bohemia, the forerunner of Czechoslovakia, had seen its first bandy game in 1890 courtesy of Josef Rossler-Orovsky and had taken to it right away. So when Mr. Anderson made the scene, there was already a good group of players who knew how to skate, handle a stick, and put the puck through the posts.

The irony—Bohemia didn't have the long winters and endless frozen ponds, lakes, and rivers that Scandinavia had, but it was still well ahead of the Swedes and Finns in discovering the world of hockey.

A Little Organization, Please

It occurred to the Europeans early on that they needed an organization to look after international games, so in October 1908, Louis Magnus of France stood and declared the first meeting of the Ligue Internationale de Hockey Sur Glace open for business.

I Remember ...

When Japan hosted the Olympic hockey tournament at Sapporo in 1972 and at Nagano in 1998, outside observers saw the country as a latecomer to the game. Actually, it was one of the first non–North American countries to be introduced to Canada's game, thanks to a couple of Englishmen who showed off their skills at the beginning of the twentieth century in Japan's northern regions. The game was a hit in the cold climes of the north islands, but it wasn't until 1929 that the Japan Ice Hockey Federation was formed. Japan joined the IIHF in 1930.

Of today's European hockey powers, only one, the Czechs (as Bohemia), were in on that first meeting. The forerunner of the International Ice Hockey Federation (IIHF) was made up of four countries: France, Belgium, Britain, and Switzerland, with Bohemia joining officially shortly afterward. Or, depending on which researcher you go by, it was France, Britain, Switzerland, and Bohemia, with Belgium along shortly afterward.

It was Great Britain that took the first official European title in the winter of 1910, but it was the Belgians who surprised everyone by winning the bronze medal and tying the Brits 1–1 in their round-robin game.

In whatever combination the first five countries wound up in the new association, the sixth team in were the Germans (1909), and they came up with a silver in their first official European championships and were never out of the medals right through 1914, hosting the tournament three times over that span.

But it was the Bohemians, led by their inspirational leader Jaroslav Potucek, who dominated the early going, winning the title in 1911, 1912 (gold medal taken away due to a rule technicality), and 1914.

The forerunners to the Czech Republic Olympic champs of 1998 made their mark early.

Aw, I Knew That!

Q. What did the United States Navy have to do with the birth of hockey in Australia?

A. In 1907, a group of players in Melbourne played a challenge match with a team from the U.S. battleship *Baltimore* in front of a capacity crowd. The United States won. World War I, meanwhile, would end Australian hockey for nearly 40 years.

I Remember ...

Finland was not one of the early members of the Ligue Internationale despite being one of the first nations in Europe to pick up the Canadian game. Igor Kuperman writes that in the late 1890s, a Finnish professor, Leonard Borgstrom, held practices on the frozen harbor of Helsinki. Unfortunately, it was an effort that would go for naught as far as setting off a frenzy of interest in the game, however, as it would be almost 30 years—1927, to be exact—before bandy players, unhappy with having to share the huge fields necessary for the game with speed skaters trying to practice their own sport, turned back to hockey. An inauspicious start for what would be one of hockey's great nations.

A Slight Interruption

Apparently upset over their inability to break through and win the European Hockey Championships in five tries, the Germans rallied behind coach Von Schlieffen in August 1914 and tried a different breakthrough that took them all the way through Belgium and on into France before a combined French and British team stopped them almost at the gates of Paris.

A world war (well, a Western world war) had begun.

Four mindlessly bloody years later, no one had much energy left to dig the sticks and skates out of the closet (those sportsmen still living after the horrible carnage of the western front) and pick the game up right away.

European Champions from 1910–1914	
1910	Great Britain
1911	Bohemia
1912	Bohemia (medal removed on rule technicality)
1913	Belgium
1914	Bohemia

But with the Ligue Internationale, now the IIHF (since 1911), the hockey-playing nations of Europe (minus the Germans, who were serving a six-year misconduct penalty that would last until 1926) put out an invitation to the Canadians and Americans, asking them to come play in the first Olympic ice hockey tournament.

The Summer Olympics, that is.

Stars of the Era

➤ Peter Patton was 21 when he took up hockey in 1897, and he would still be playing for fun at age 55. The captain of both Britain's entry in the first indoor international ice hockey tournament (1908) and of its gold medal–winning 1910 European tournament club, Patton was a leading figure in the European game through the 1930s. He was the founder of the British Ice Hockey Association.

➤ Max Sillig was a key player in Swiss hockey's early years. As a player, he was a member of the 1904 club that traveled to Lyon, France, and surprised the hosts by splitting a two-game series with the more experienced French by identical 3–1 scores. He went on to lead Switzerland into the Ligue Internationale in 1908 and would be an early president of the IIHF in the 1920s.

The Least You Need to Know

➤ Britain was the birthplace of hockey in Europe.

➤ Four nations got together in 1909 to form the forerunner of the International Ice Hockey Federation.

➤ Bohemia (later Czechoslovakia) dominated the early years of European hockey.

➤ World War I put an end to hockey development in Europe for nearly 10 years.

Part 2
The National Hockey League

The NHL was created as the answer to a basic human problem: hatred. Because the owners in the National Hockey Association despised one of their own members, the old league was dissolved in 1917, and a new one set in its place. At this time, the league that would grow to be the world's most important professional hockey organization was struggling just to survive, featuring only three teams for a while. The 1920s became the wildest era in league history for a number of reasons. The professional game itself was an often bloody, sickening affair. Rules had to be straightened out. Franchises rose and fell, and by mid-decade, the NHL would expand to the United States. By the end of the Roaring '20s, it looked as though the loop was on its way to financial success. Then the Great Depression hit, and mere survival once again made its way to the top of the owner's to-do list. The so-called Original Six era would cement a half-dozen clubs in the minds of hockey fans, but the league became provincial and limited, so owners turned to expansion, which would continue almost unabated right to the end of the century. The league would also survive its most serious challenge from an outside organization. Across all the peaks and through all the valleys, the NHL would continue to feature the most competitive hockey in the world—no matter what country its players called home.

Chapter 6

Robbing the Cradle (1917–1932)

In This Chapter

➤ Eddie

➤ Influenza

➤ New teams, old teams

➤ The end of the Wild, Wild West

➤ The NHL discovers Boston, New York, Chicago, and Detroit

➤ Howie

➤ Two solitudes

Back in 1909, the Canadian Hockey Association told Montreal Wanderers' manager Jimmy Gardner to take a hike, which caused him to meet up with J. Ambrose O'Brien and form the National Hockey Association. You might think that would have taught the latter men something about civility, but rather, it taught them how to be even more hard-nosed as businessmen. All of which would lead to the formation of the National Hockey League in 1917, when the NHA pulled the same trick on someone those owners didn't like. The 1920s would be a key period for hockey because it brought in the establishment of the game as a big-league entity in the northeastern United States. But it also saw the end of big-time pro hockey in all but two Canadian cities. In this chapter, we'll look at those issues and at how the good times of the Roaring '20s could not prepare the game, and the league, for the tragedy of the Depression.

A Guy Named Eddie

It's important to remember that everybody hated Eddie Livingstone. The "everybody" in this case being the other members of the National Hockey Association, which by 1917 featured the Montreal Canadiens and Wanderers, the Quebec Bulldogs, the Ottawa Senators, and the Toronto Shamrocks.

It was that last team that was the problem, as far as the NHA was concerned, because Mr. Livingstone came attached as the owner.

Old Eddie was a former sports writer (which in itself was enough to put him at loggerheads with the big money owners of the other clubs), who bought the Ontario franchise in the NHA that was looking for a home and brought them to Toronto as the Shamrocks. That gave Hogtown two teams, the other being the Blueshirts, Stanley Cup champs in 1914.

Eddie was no dummy, and he saw two teams in the city as bad for business, so he bought up the Blueshirts and annexed them into his own club, which sent the other owners into a screaming frenzy.

Remember, when the NHA came into being in 1910, J. Ambrose O'Brien had owned four teams in four different cities, which apparently was okay. But that goose wasn't going to let Eddie the gander get away with multiple ownership in the same city. Thanks to the Pacific Coast Association, however, things settled down a while because the Westerners basically raped the Blueshirts for all their players, leaving Eddie with nothing to add to his own club.

Aw, I Knew That!

Q. Joe Malone scored 44 goals for the Canadiens in 1917–1918. Who were the next players to score 40 in a season?

A. Cooney Wieland (43), Dit Clapper (41), and Howie Morenz (40), in 1929–1930.

But everyone was still so mad at Eddie (who was mad right back at them) that a plan was hatched to dump Mr. Livingstone out of their midst—start another league.

Thus, on November 22, 1917, the owners met at the Windsor Hotel and declared the National Hockey League to be born—minus Eddie.

With the Quebec franchise choosing to sit out a season due to money problems, the new league would begin with the Wanderers and Canadiens, a new Toronto franchise (the Arenas), and the Ottawa Senators.

Actually, the Wanderers, Montreal's team for the English-speaking community, barely got out of the gate. On January 2, 1918, the Westmount Arena burned to the ground in a convenient fire that let the struggling franchise slip away, leaving a huge debt behind it.

Poor Old Joe

"Cully Wilson of Seattle fell to the ice complaining of dizziness and fatigue, and Montreal's Bad Joe Hall, also very ill, could not continue playing. He was rushed to the hospital with a temperature of 105 degrees."

Writer Brian McFarlane summed up the influenza incident of 1919 quite succinctly in that one paragraph. That was all the fans gathered in Seattle for game five of the Stanley Cup final series between Wilson's Seattle Metropolitans and Hall's Montreal Canadiens actually saw of what would be one of hockey's most tragic moments. But it's probably fair to say they all knew what was happening.

Let's back up a bit. When all the boys came home from Europe following World War I, they brought with them a terrible Black Flu epidemic that swept North America and killed tens of thousands of people. There were no antibiotics. There were no flu shots. There was just death. And hockey would not be spared.

The series, second for the National Hockey League up against the PCHA since the new loop's birth (the Toronto Arenas won the first in the spring of 1918), was 2–1 in Seattle's favor with one game tied when game five faced off. Most of the players were down sick, though they continued anyway.

But after Wilson and Hall went down, officials called the game, and the series, off. The Habs went home to Montreal, but not with Hall, who was bedridden in a Seattle hospital where he died six days later. He was 37 years old and had played 17 years of pro hockey, including a Stanley Cup during 7 years with the Quebec Bulldogs.

One of hockey's toughest, meanest players had been felled by the flu. Canadiens owner George Kennedy (who, according to writer William Brown, was really a French Canadian named Georges Kendall—the name change was to make it easier to move among the Anglo business community of Montreal), seemed to recover from his own illness at the time, but he would be dead within two years of complications from the Black Flu. The Habs would be sold to Leo Dandurand, Joseph Cattarinich, and Louis Letourneau for all of $11,000.

Aw, I Knew That!

Q. Corbett Denneny of Toronto and Cy Denneny of Ottawa both scored six times in different NHL games in 1921—the only brother combination to record such a feat. What was truly unusual about the scoring outbursts?

A. They were both against the same goalie: Howard Lockhart of Hamilton.

Franchises West and East

By the early 1920s, the NHL was thinking about setting up shop in the United States. Before that could happen, though, there was some sorting out to do with its Canadian franchises.

The Quebec Bulldogs were officially members of the NHL from the get-go, but financial problems kept them out of action until season three. In that 1919–1920 season, the club, now an expansion unit for all intents and purposes, won a scintillating 4 games out of 24 and wound up transferring to Hamilton as the Tigers. That club would stay in Canada's Steeltown for just four years (more on them in a bit).

Montreal's Wanderers died early, leaving the city with just one NHL club, the Habs. That would remain the case until 1924, when the Maroons were born as representatives of Montreal's English community (more on that to come).

Out west, a new league appeared to challenge the Pacific Coast Hockey Association. The Western Canada Hockey League started in 1921 with teams in Calgary, Edmonton, Regina, and Saskatoon. The Stanley Cup's guardians in Ottawa decreed that the PCHA and WCHL champs would have to play off for the right to play the NHL winner for the silver mug.

Quote, Unquote

"They were the greatest personal factors in twentieth-century hockey."

—Elmer Ferguson, *Montreal Gazette*, on Lester and Frank Patrick.

It wouldn't take long for the two western loops to get together. As soon as the PCHA finally dumped the seven-man game, writes Eric Zweig, the western leagues began playing an interlocking schedule and playoffs, giving the NHL what looked like a serious league to challenge it as the best in the nation.

But what of the other nation? That one south of the border whose northeastern states had fallen in love with the game of hockey in the early part of the century?

Howie

When Wayne Gretzky was traded from Edmonton to Los Angeles in the summer of 1988, his entrance onto the Southern California scene was so huge that the formation of two new franchises—the San Jose Sharks and the Mighty Ducks of Anaheim—was directly credited to his power as a superstar.

In the mid-1920s, the same was said for another superstar, one Howie Morenz.

Morenz was the ultimate star of the era, a player whose speed, talent with the stick (which he didn't use to whack others over the head—something that happened all too often in those times), and nose for the net would earn him 270 goals in 546 regular season games—unheard of totals.

He *was* the Montreal Canadiens, which is saying a lot for a club that featured goal-tending legend Georges Vezina, Aurel Joliat, and the pugnacious (and often dirty) Sprague Cleghorn.

Born in Stratford, Ontario, Morenz almost didn't become a Hab. In fact, if a backroom attempt by the Toronto franchise to obtain his services by stirring up Stratford fans had been successful, he might have gone down as the greatest to play for the St. Pats/Maple Leafs.

Montreal wanted the young star-in-the-making in the summer of 1923, and to seal the deal they tossed $850 in small bills at Morenz, which, the story goes, he threw on his bed and rolled in—a strange bit of work for such a quiet, self-effacing man. Suddenly, Morenz was under great pressure from townsfolk to welch on the deal and sign with Toronto instead. The Habs prevailed, even after Morenz went to Montreal and shed tears in front of Canadiens' owner Leo Dandurand, begging him to tear up the contract.

Morenz would lead Montreal to three Stanley Cups, but his influence would go much deeper than that.

Quote, Unquote

"Morenz is some wild wind, that number 7 of the Canadiens. To me, he's just a blur … 7777777777777777!"

—Roy Worters, on Howie Morenz.

I Remember …

In late March 1926, goaltender Georges Vezina walked into the Montreal Canadiens' dressing room, sat in his familiar corner, and cried. Ravaged by tuberculosis, the man who had played 367 career games for the Habs was just days from death. He had played for the last time the previous November 28, pulling himself out of a game against Pittsburgh due to chest pains and dizziness. As Michael McKinley writes, this was a man who knew pain—he had watched 22 of his 24 children die in infancy. But nothing seemed to hurt more than staring at those goalie pads one more time, knowing he could never play again. When Vezina died, Habs' owners dedicated to his memory the Vezina Trophy, which forevermore would be awarded to the NHL's best goaltender or goaltending duo.

Charlie's Boys

Hockey had first been played in the United States over 70 years before, when the *Boston Globe* imported sticks from Nova Scotia. So it was altogether proper, writes Stan Fischler, that the city should be the first with an NHL team.

Millionaire Charles Adams wasn't sure if he wanted to move from amateur hockey to the NHL, but some friends talked him into seeing the 1924 Stanley Cup finals between the

Great Games

April 7, 1928: Montreal Forum

In game two of the cup finals between the New York Rangers and the Montreal Maroons, Ranger goalie Lorne Chabot suffered an eye injury and could not continue. Montreal refused to let the visitors grab a goalie out of the stands who played for another club, so New York coach Lester Patrick, 44, strapped on the pads and handled duties himself. The former star defenseman played 46 minutes and gave up just one goal as the inspired Rangers won the game and went on to take their first Stanley Cup.

Aw, I Knew That!

Q. Who was the first NHL goalie to record 10 shutouts in his career?

A. Clint Benedict, Ottawa Senators, who got his tenth in March 1921.

Montreal Canadiens and the Calgary Tigers. One look at Howie Morenz and Adams was convinced. One blink was enough for the other league owners to welcome Mr. Adams and his money to the national league as the Boston Bruins.

The Bears' first season was hardly memorable—6 and 24—but with Art Ross at the helm as coach and general manager and a beautiful new arena in the hub—Boston Madison Square Garden (built with New York money, though very soon the building would simply known as the "Gah-den")—it only took three years for the team to become competitive.

Among the key signings were Harry Oliver, Duke Keats, Perk Galbraith, and Harry Meeking. But, as Stan Fischler writes, by far the most important was a tough, occasionally cruel, hard-nosed defender named Eddie Shore. Found playing for Edmonton in the WCHL, Shore would transform the Bruins and lead the club to its first Stanley Cup, beating the New York Rangers in 1929.

He would also have a hand in the most despicable incident in league history.

Deep in the Heart of Tex Rickard

Andy O'Brien writes that Tex Rickard, the man behind building Madison Square Garden in New York, "remained supremely indifferent to what he regarded as a purely Canadian game," as he put the finishing touches on his beautiful new building. Heck, an ice plant wasn't even in the plans for the Garden.

All that changed when Tex saw Howie Morenz.

Tom Duggan, a slightly shady Montreal racetrack owner, talked his friend Big Bill Dwyer, a very shady bootlegger during America's prohibition era, into convincing Rickard to come up to Montreal and get a look at Morenz, and hockey in general.

Tex came along, bringing famous sports writer Damon Runyon with him, and fell in love with Morenz' talents and the game itself.

The NHL wanted desperately to put down roots in New York City and was quite willing to bend over backward, sideways, or fully forward to get Rickard to go for it. What Tex wanted was an established team, and one just happened to be available.

Why Hamilton Isn't in the NHL

Hamilton, Ontario, has been trying to get an NHL team since the early 1980s, even going so far as to build a state-of-the-art arena (Copps Coliseum) even though it didn't have a club to play in it (and still doesn't). The fact was, however, that Hamilton was one of the earliest members of the National League, until a combination of owner cheapness, a bad labor idea by the players, and the NHL's desperation to get to New York did the city out of its Tigers.

In 1924–1925 (Boston's rookie season), the Tigers (formerly the Quebec Bulldogs) were the best club in the loop, winning the regular season and making themselves favorites for the cup. But the players, angry that they were being nickled and dimed by ownership, went on strike just before the playoffs began, looking for $250 each in bonuses before they'd keep going.

The league simply kicked the Tigers out. Duggan, the Montrealer, immediately talked Dwyer, the bootlegger, into putting up $75,000 for the Hamilton franchise, transferring as the Americans.

Tex had his club for his big new rink, and he didn't have to pay a cent for it.

Broadway Blueshirts

Hockey was rolling on Broadway with the New York Americans playing out of the new Madison Square Garden (built by Tex Rickard through the good graces of a large group of investors known as the "600 Millionaires"), and ol' Tex thought it would be good for MSG to own its own team rather than just rent the building to the Amerks.

Garden president Colonel John S. Hammond liked the idea, applying for and getting a new franchise to be known as the Rangers, set to begin in the fall of 1926.

Aw, I Knew That!

Q. How many consecutive games had Georges Vezina played when he collapsed in the Montreal net in November 1925?

A. 328. He would die of tuberculosis four months later.

Quote, Unquote

"He would take the puck away from the enemy with the guile and smoothness of a con man picking the pockets of yokels at a country fair."

—Dink Carroll, *Montreal Gazette*, on Frank Boucher of the New York Rangers.

I Remember ...

Violence was so much a part of the game in this era that it was accepted as everyday. William Brown tells of one incident in 1929 in which Eddie Shore of the Bruins hit Babe Siebert of the Maroons in the throat with his stick while the latter lay on the ice back of a net. Revenge was swift. By the end of the game, Shore "had a broken nose and a concussion, and was missing four teeth." He tried to keep playing but collapsed and was taken to hospital. The Bruins vowed they'd get the Maroons back. Every team, in every year, could tell a handful of stories like that.

Hammond hired Conn Smythe (whom we last saw as a member of the Sportsmen's Battalion in World War I), to put the club together, and he did a masterful job, hiring such future stars as Ivan "Ching" Johnson and Clarence "Taffy" Abel—the latter a huge American from Sault Ste. Marie, Michigan, who had Cherokee heritage—as a bruising defense pairing. He also got future stars Frank Boucher and two brothers, Bill and Bun Cook, to play up front. All three would be Hall of Famers.

But Smythe and Hammond couldn't get along. Hammond thought the team would stink up Broadway, while Smythe was convinced they would be great. They argued. Smythe was fired during the first training camp and was so mad he bought the Toronto St. Patricks franchise, renamed it the Maple Leafs, and set the groundwork for what would be hockey's second-most-famous franchise (behind the Canadiens).

Smythe turned out to be right, of course, as the club he built went 25–13–6 in that first year and made the playoffs, winning the Stanley Cup at the end of year two.

The Smythe firing opened the door for Lester Patrick to begin a long reign running the Rangers. That the co-founder of the Pacific Coast Association was available to take the job was another part of what had to be a very happy summer for the NHL, at the end of which there would be two more American franchises for the loop.

Picking the Bones of the Dead

Frank and Lester Patrick's Western Hockey League (the combination of the PCHA and the WCHL) had gone belly-up by the end of the 1926 season. Faced with heavy travel costs for teams from the coast to hit the prairies and vice versa, and tired of batting their heads against the wall, the Patricks gave in.

But not without pocketing a little change for their efforts.

First to get a call was Major Frederic McLaughlin, a playboy millionaire coffee tycoon in Chicago. For a couple hundred grand, the major could have the Portland Rosebuds of the WHL to put straight into the NHL with a lineup already intact. So, getting a few dozen good friends with money together, McLaughlin did just that, calling the new team the Blackhawks, after the 85th Blackhawk Division in which he had commanded a machine gun battalion in World War I.

As Stan Fischler writes, the team's history would have "touches of a Marx Brothers comedy, *The Three Stooges*, romance and a melodrama that Paramount scriptwriters would have trouble duplicating."

That was all for the future, however. There were now five NHL teams in the United States for the 1926–1927 season, as the Rangers were coming in as an expansion club with the Pittsburgh Pirates, owned by fight promoter and former boxer Benny Leonard.

Eric Zweig points out that the Pirates had but three weeks to get ready to play; despite that, with Canadian legend Lionel Conacher (a multi-sport performer of such skill he was named the country's male athlete of the first half-century) as coach and organizer, a team was hacked out in a hurry by picking the bones of the Western league, and it finished 19–16–1 in the new American division in its first year.

And still the NHL's good luck hadn't run out.

Bob Duff writes that there were fully five groups in the spring of 1926 clamoring for an NHL franchise for the motor city, but it was finally a large group that included former goaltender Percy LeSueur (the man Cyclone Taylor did, or did not, score on going backward back in 1910), that got it.

Great Games

April 5, 1931: Chicago Stadium

In game two of the cup final between the Hawks and the Canadiens, three important incidents took place. Behind the Montreal bench, Dick Irvin Sr. was coaching in what would be his first of 16 cup-final series. In the stands, the largest crowd in NHL history to that point, more than 18,000, watched on as the teams went to overtime, tied 1–1. And then they went to a second overtime, before Johnny Gottselig came up with the winner for Chicago at 4:40.

Hawks 2, Canadiens 1

Once again, looking for players, the Patricks had a proposal—$100,000 for the roster of the Victoria Cougars, 1925 Stanley Cup champs. So the Detroit Cougars joined the NHL. After a rotten first year, Jack Adams, a leader on the Ottawa Senators Stanley Cup–winning team, took over the club as general manager and coach. And by 1927, the Detroit Olympia, a beautiful new building, was open.

Quick math: In two years, the NHL went from no American franchises to six. So many, in fact, that the New York Americans had to play as part of the Canadian division, which now counted Toronto, Ottawa, and two clubs in Montreal as members.

Oh, those two clubs in Montreal …

Two Solitudes

Canadian author Hugh McLennan called them *Two Solitudes*. They are the French and English of Quebec, separated not just by language, but by culture and, for much of the twentieth century, by money and opportunity—most of which fell in the Anglo's lap.

French Quebec had its first professional team for which to cheer in L'National, which played in the old Canadian Hockey Association in the 1900s. But it wasn't until 1909 when the Canadiens were born that the French really felt they had hit the big time.

English Quebec had a number of teams—the Montreal AAA, the Montreal Victorias, the Quebec Bulldogs, and the Montreal Wanderers—for which to cheer. By 1920, however, they were all gone, and the only team in Montreal was the Habs.

Ironically, as William Brown would point out in his history of the Maroons, a new club was formed to fill a new hockey building—the Montreal Forum—by a group of English businessmen and one Frenchman, Donat Raymond.

Quote, Unquote

"Never mind the goddam puck, let's start the game!"

—Red Dutton, Montreal Maroons, 1926. He didn't care that the ref had forgotten to bring the puck to center ice.

When the club was announced in 1924, to enter with the Boston Bruins as an expansion unit that fall, the city of Montreal went wild. The Forum, which would be forever tied in with the history of the Canadiens, actually was the Maroons' home almost exclusively for two seasons after the first game. The Maroons would bring a host of strong players into the game, including Nels "Old Poison" Stewart, goaltender Clint Benedict (eventually the first goaltender to wear a mask in a game, he wore it for five games to protect a shattered nose), Babe Siebert, Lionel Conacher, and more.

And they would win two Stanley Cups.

But from 1924 until the late 1930s, the best would be saved for the rivalry with the Canadiens, when the Forum would rock, the players would bash heads, and hockey's wildest rivalry would flourish.

Conn's Building

With the Habs, Rangers, Bruins, Blackhawks, and Cougars (soon to be Red Wings) in place, hockey awaited one more team that would become part of what, after World War II, would be erroneously (and ridiculously, given all the team movement) the "Original Six."

Conn Smythe bought the Toronto St. Patricks for $160,000 and immediately renamed them the Maple Leafs in time for the 1926–1927 season. In order to build a decent team, he needed a star, and he got one in 1930 in Francis Michael "King" Clancy, bought from the Ottawa Senators for $35,000 (most of which Smythe got by betting a huge sum on one of his own horses, Rare Jewel, a noncontender who somehow found the legs to win a big stakes race when it counted the most).

I Remember ...

Foster Hewitt's "Hello Canada, and hockey fans in the United States and Newfoundland" was the most famous introduction in hockey broadcasting, invented by the most famous man to call a game. A cub reporter at the *Toronto Star* in 1923, Hewitt was sent down to the Mutual Street Arena to call a senior game for the newspaper's experimental radio station. He would carve out a career that would last into the 1970s and become the hockey voice of the Toronto Maple Leafs for English Canadians from coast to coast, and for hundreds of thousands of American fans living in border areas.

Next, Smythe needed a building. When the Depression hit, it looked like he was toast. But he talked the T. Eaton Co. department store chain into donating land at Carlton and Church streets in Toronto, got the labor unions to take some of their wages in building stock, and talked a bank and life insurance company into fronting him the money to build Maple Leaf Gardens in just six months in 1931.

Smythe had his building.

On the Eve of a Nightmare

The stock market crashed at the end of 1929, and for a while it looked as though the National Hockey League might weather the storm.

That was wrong. Pittsburgh, which had struggled along with its head above the waves for three seasons, had suddenly turned rotten on the ice by 1928–1929, winning just 9 times in 44 games. Few cities were hit by the Depression as hard as the steel city. No one was building anything, so there was no call for steel.

The 1929–1930 season was even worse (five wins), and finally team ownership gave it up and moved the club to Philadelphia, where it became the Quakers (a highly unusual choice for a team that played in such a violent sport). It hardly seemed possible that the Quakers could be any worse than the Bucs had been, but they were—4 wins in 44 games and the end of the line for the franchise.

Ottawa's Senators, by far the most dominant team in the 1920s (four cups and seven trips to the finals), also ran into a financial wall by the spring of 1932 and took a year off to pull together. Two more difficult seasons after that, the Sens quit for good, transferring the franchise to St. Louis as the Eagles. That didn't work either, and after 1934–1935, they were gone.

Stars of the Era

➤ Aurel Joliat joined the Montreal Canadiens in 1922 and would play 654 games over 16 seasons as a left winger. He scored 270 goals and 460 total points. During his career, Joliat suffered six shoulder separations, three broken ribs, and five broken noses. He played on a line with Howie Morenz.

➤ Joe Malone, "the Phantom," already had nine pro seasons under his belt when he left the Quebec Bulldogs to play with Montreal Canadiens in the NHL's first season of 1917–1918. He also played in the NHL with Quebec and Hamilton, retiring from the Habs in 1924. He scored 143 goals in the NHL.

➤ Frank Calder, a former sportswriter in Montreal, rose to become president of the NHL, serving in that role for 26 years. The league's rookie of the year trophy is named in his memory.

Stanley Cup Winners of the Era	
1917–1918	Toronto Arenas
1918–1919	No winner (influenza)
1919–1920	Ottawa Senators
1920–1921	Ottawa Senators
1921–1922	Toronto St. Patricks
1922–1923	Ottawa Senators
1923–1924	Montreal Canadiens
1924–1925	Victoria Cougars
1925–1926	Montreal Maroons
1926–1927	Ottawa Senators
1927–1928	New York Rangers
1928–1929	Boston Bruins
1929–1930	Montreal Canadiens
1930–1931	Montreal Canadiens

➤ Cecil "Babe" Dye won three scoring titles in the NHL for the Toronto St. Pats. Known as a "magical" stickhandler, he was sold to Chicago in the summer of 1926. A serious leg fracture in the 1927 training camp cut his effectiveness, though he played until 1931.

➤ Clint Benedict was one of the two best goalies, with Georges Vezina, of the era, playing 12 seasons with the Ottawa Senators and another 5 with the Montreal Maroons. His NHL goals against average was 2.30 with 58 shutouts. He was the first goalie to wear a mask in a league game after having his nose shattered by a shot in 1930. He took it off after five games. The nose injury would end his career. His up-and-down style would force the NHL to officially allow goalies to go down to stop the puck.

The Least You Need to Know

➤ The NHL was formed in 1917.

➤ An influenza epidemic killed Joe Hall and ended the 1919 Stanley Cup series.

➤ The NHL expanded heavily to the United States in this era, adding five teams.

➤ Howie Morenz was the era's best player.

➤ Lester Patrick began a long relationship with the New York Rangers.

➤ The Pacific Coast/Western league folded in the mid-1920s.

A Depressing Era (1933–1945)

When Marty McSorley of the Boston Bruins two-handed Vancouver's Donald Brashear across the temple with his stick in February 2000, those who had watched hockey during the pre-war years might have been forgiven for jumping up in their easy chairs, overcome by a sense of déjà vu. Media types at the turn of the twenty-first century were pointing to an incident a year ago, three years back, etc., to show how violent the game had become. But before the war, this type of thing happened all the time.

It was a regular occurrence! The most famous incident of violence in NHL history occurred on December 12, 1933, when one of the era's stars was almost killed by an on-ice incident. The 1930s were also a time when most teams struggled terribly due to the Depression, and then Adolf Hitler had to start a world war that would make things even harder. What the game needed by the end of the era was a new star—someone to help bring hockey back to health … In this chapter, we'll look at all of these points.

Ace and Eddie

Eddie Shore wasn't actually mad at Ace Bailey. The Boston Bruin captain and star was furious with King Clancy of the Toronto Maple Leafs when he picked himself off the ice on December 12, 1933, at the Boston Garden, and went looking for No. 7. He found No. 6—Bailey—and wound up almost killing him.

A little background: Clancy and Shore had been in a running feud for a number of years by this point, and neither missed an opportunity to get the other when possible.

On this night, the Leafs were killing a two-man disadvantage when Clancy raced into the Boston zone with the puck. Losing it, he hit Shore with a solid bodycheck, knocked him down, and took off up the ice again.

Quote, Unquote

"We didn't see each other coming."

—Ace Bailey, who had his back turned, on the collision with Eddie Shore that ended Bailey's career in December 1933.

Furious, Shore got up, looked for the long-gone Clancy and instead went after the first Leaf he saw: Bailey. Ace, one of the most gifted goal scorers of the era, had his back turned when Shore came up from behind him and blindsided the forward with no warning (and the puck at the other end of the ice). Bailey went down backward and hit his head on the ice with a thud heard 'round the rink.

His skull fractured in two places. It took surgeons in Boston hours to save Bailey's life. They couldn't save his career.

The National Hockey League held an all-star game, the league's first, later in the season to raise funds for Bailey, who had now lost his livelihood, and the Leafs hired him to work in the office and as a timekeeper in Maple Leaf Gardens, a job he held for over 40 years.

I Remember ...

Eddie Shore's tenacity, on and off the ice, is the stuff of NHL legend. During one game in Boston, Shore was cut on his ear so bad that his doctor thought only surgery would save even a portion of his ear. Instead, Shore had him sew the separated portion back on—without any anesthetic. In a scene right out of *Batman* with Jack Nicholson as the Joker, Shore then demanded a mirror from the terrified doctor. "I want to be sure you sewed it on right," said Shore.

And what did Shore get for almost ending a man's life in a cowardly attack? Suspended for a month. Bailey even forgave him, shaking Shore's hand at the all-star game in front of the Toronto fans, which defused any possible acts of retribution from the angry home audience.

Note: Brian McFarlane tells a story about Bailey's father, who, when he heard of the incident in Toronto, grabbed a gun and boarded a train for Boston, determined to shoot Shore. Fortunately, Leaf officials in Beantown were warned, met him at the train station, took him to a bar and got him drunk, and then piled him back on the train to Toronto.

No Money for Food, Housing ... or Tickets

Montreal Wanderers ... Quebec Bulldogs ... Hamilton Tigers ... Pittsburgh Pirates ... Philadel-phia Quakers ... Ottawa Senators. The NHL was used to losing franchises as it sorted out the good towns from the bad ones, the supporters from the pretenders.

But to lose two teams in cities considered the home of hockey in their respective countries—New York and Montreal—that was too much.

Montreal's Maroons, born as the team for the city's Anglo fans, had won two Stanley Cups, the most recent in 1935. They had brought a wonderful, swaggering style to the game, both on and off the ice, and their intra-city rivalry with the Montreal Canadiens had produced some of the most exciting and intense hockey of the era. The S-Line of the great Nels Stewart, Babe Siebert, and Hooley Smith had been one of the league's best combinations.

As William Brown writes, however, Montreal was one of the hardest hit cities by the Depression, and the fan base just couldn't support two clubs. As a matter of fact, it was the Habs that almost disap-peared first, before Montreal buyers stepped up and bought the team from Leo Dandurand and his group.

But the Maroons were running out of money and out of time. Both ran out at the end of the 1938 season, when the Canadian Arena Company (builders and owners of the Montreal Forum, which housed both city teams) asked the league to suspend the franchise for one year. There were also rumors of a St. Louis group wanting to try again in that city.

All for naught. The Maroons died, and Donat Raymond, the man who had helped build both the Maroons and the Forum, would take over the Canadiens, and the city would have one club— one superb club—forevermore.

Quote, Unquote

"Reg would drink a case of beer the day of the game. His breath would knock you down."

—Red Dutton, on former Mon-treal Maroons teammate Reg Noble, who finally retired in 1933 after 16 seasons in the NHL. He would play one more year with the Cleveland Indians of the Western League.

The New York Americans lasted until 1942 before suffering the same fate.

America's second NHL franchise had struggled in the early years, missing the playoffs nine times in the first decade and earning a better-than-.500 record just once in that time as a pretender in the "Canadian Division." At the same time, the Rangers, born one year later, were among the league's elite, winning two Stanley Cups and never missing the playoffs.

Great Games

March 24, 1936: Montreal Forum

The Detroit Red Wings and Montreal Maroons opened the semi-finals that year in what most thought would be a close, tough series. Game one certainly bore that out. The teams went scoreless through almost six full periods before Mud Bruneteau beat Lorne Chabot at 116:30.

Detroit 1, Montreal 0

If you live by the sword … well, you get the idea. You see, Bill Dwyer, Big Bill, had made his money through rum-running in prohibition, and the government was out to get him. They got him through the tax bill, and when Bill lost a court case that saw him owe almost four million dollars (an absolute fortune) in 1937, he was dead broke.

Red Dutton, now running the team as playing coach and general manager, kept the club afloat as long as he could thanks to a personal fortune. Realizing that most of the club's fans came from Brooklyn (whereas the Rangers drew from Manhattan), Dutton even changed the club's name to the Brooklyn Americans for the 1941–1942 season.

What finally did the Amerks in was World War II. As most of the players were Canadian, when that country went to war in September 1939, most of the players signed up, so that by the final year, as Stan Fischler points out, 14 of 16 Amerks had gone to the Canadian Armed Forces.

The spring of 1942 marked the end of the New York/Brooklyn Americans.

The Good, the Bad …

While the other five clubs that would eventually comprise the post-war misnomer the "Original Six" certainly had their ups and downs, none could match the strange existence of the Chicago Blackhawks, either in this era or in the one to come (more in a bit).

In New York, the Rangers settled into a happy 13-year run that saw them win two Stanley Cups and make the finals four times while settling in on Broadway. With Lester Patrick firmly in charge, the club built a strong farm system (the New Haven Ramblers, the New York Rovers, the Lake Placid Roamers, and a very good team in Philadelphia) and got a strong president in General John Reed Kilpatrick and a terrific group of players led by Patrick's sons Muzz and Lynn, plus Bill and Bun Cook, Bryan Hextall, and Phil Watson.

In Detroit, Jack Adams (the man for whom the word "parsimonious" was invented) went through the 13 seasons with 3 Stanley Cups, and it could have been 4 if the club hadn't blown a 3–0 lead in games to Toronto in the 1942 cup final. Now known as the Red Wings, thanks to a name change in the summer of 1932 (owner James Norris had been in the Montreal Amateur Athletic Association, known as the Winged Wheelers, as a kid, and the wing was attached to an automobile wheel to create the Detroit logo), the club would go on to dominate the late 1940s and early 1950s, thanks to the strong scouting and minor league system Adams set up.

Over in Boston, the Bruins, under Art Ross and led by Eddie Shore until 1940, won two cups of their own (1939 and 1941), and put out clubs that featured superb players such as forward/defenseman Aubrey Clapper, known as Dit, Lionel Hitchman, goaltender Tiny Thompson, and more. Near the end of the era, the Kraut Line (okay, it wasn't a time of great understanding) of Milt Schmidt, Bobby Bauer, and Woody Dumart became one of the league's best trios.

Ah, Montreal. Home of the true hockey fan. Nest of the bleu, blanc, et rouge. Having to share fans with the Maroons didn't help the club at all in the 1930s. Neither did being uncompetitive. After winning the cup in 1930 and 1931, the Habs went 12 seasons, their longest drought ever, without another sip from Lord Stanley's mug. Losing Howie Morenz (more later) was a blow, and with money short it was hard for the Canadiens to build back to a contender. That would change near the end of the war, however, with the signing of one very special Quebeçois.

And in Toronto, where Conn Smythe ruled with an iron fist, the Leafs, helped by the radio broadcasts of Foster Hewitt, had become Canada's Team—everywhere but Quebec, that is. After a cup championship in 1932, Leafs fans from Newfoundland to Vancouver Island had to endure an excruciating nine-year wait during which their boys lost in the finals six times. Cups came in 1942 and 1945, as the Leafs did a better job than most of finding replacements for all those men who went to war (including Major Smythe, who put together another Sportsmen's Battalion and then almost got killed in France just after D-Day).

Stars included Hap Day, King Clancy, Ace Bailey, and the Kid Line of Charlie Conacher, Joe Primeau, and Busher Jackson.

Quote, Unquote

"Turk Broda didn't have one nerve in his whole body. He could tend goal in a tornado and never blink an eye."

—Jack Adams of Detroit on Walter "Turk" Broda, Toronto goaltender.

Quote, Unquote

"Give me five Milt Schmidts up front and your grandmother in goal and we'd never lose."

—Red Storey, Toronto, on Milt Schmidt, Boston's future Hall of Famer.

Great Games

April 2, 1939: Boston Garden

There's nothing like overtime in game seven of a playoff series. In 1939, the New York Rangers and the Boston Bruins couldn't decide the issue after seven full games and went to the three extra periods. Finally, at 8:00 of the sixth period of the night, Mel Hill scored to give Boston the game and the series. The Rangers were so mad they came back the following season and won the cup.

Boston 2, New York 1

Aw, I Knew That!

Q. In 1939–1940, the Boston Bruins nabbed the three top spots in the scoring race. Who were the players, all members of one line, who pulled the feat?

A. Milt Schmidt (52 points), Woody Dumart (43), and Bobby Bauer (43). Together, they were the Kraut Line.

... and Chicago

Perhaps it was the Curse of Muldoon. At the end of Chicago's first season in 1927, coach Pete Muldoon got into a verbal brawl with the team's owner, Major Frederic McLaughlin, over the club's performance, which had been pretty good. As Stan Fischler writes, Muldoon warned his now ex-boss, "I'll hoodoo you. This club will never finish in first place."

It was 40 years before the Hawks would finish first in the regular season.

Or perhaps it was just the Major himself. Chicago won the cup in 1934 and 1938, but kept finding ways to make it onto the front pages for nonhockey reasons.

➤ Somehow, McLaughlin found a way to get himself kicked out of the Chicago Coliseum in 1929 while his new Chicago Stadium still wasn't finished, forcing the club to play in Fort Erie, Ontario.

➤ In 1931, he fired the respected Dick Irvin as coach and hired an unknown named Godfrey Matheson who had no experience at the top levels. Disaster ensued.

➤ In 1932, he got into a brawl with James Norris, soon-to-be Detroit owner, when the latter wanted a second club in Chicago. The Major eventually won, but he couldn't play out of the Chicago Stadium for a while because Norris' American Association club, the Shamrocks, had the lease on the building.

➤ McLaughlin set out to create an all-American lineup for 1936–1937. It was a good idea on one hand, but hardly responsible on the other, given the relative handful of U.S.-born players in the NHL at that time. He only had four Americans for most of the season, but according to Kevin Allen, by the end of the year five more were added and the team finished its last five games 1–4, outscored 27–14. None of the late additions played again.

But thanks to some strong goaltending from Charlie Gardiner, who would die tragically of a brain hemorrhage in the summer of 1934, and later, American Mike Karakas, the Hawks found ways to be competitive at times.

The 1938 win was highly unlikely. Fischler says they were considered 100–1 shots that year and at 15–25–9, had the worst record of any playoff club. But they pulled it off, beating Montreal in the quarterfinals, the New York Americans in the semis (where Karakas broke a big toe in the last game and was replaced with unknown Alfie Moore at the last minute), and then the Leafs in the final.

Coach Bill Stewart, an American who spent the summers as a Major League Baseball umpire, had pulled off a miracle.

Unfortunately, the Major didn't believe in building a minor league system, or in paying for a scouting team, or investing in the future at all—all of which would come back to bite fans in Chicago, who were about to go through one of the worst slumps in hockey history.

How Can You Mend a Broken Heart?

January 28, 1937: Montreal Forum. Canadiens vs. Chicago Blackhawks. St. Catherine Street (Rue Ste. Catherine) end of the rink. Babe Siebert the defender. Howie Morenz with the puck.

Fans in Montreal would have given anything if they could have frozen that moment in time. But time marches on, and so did Morenz, now back in Montreal to finish his brilliant career after spending time in Chicago and with the Rangers. He had totalled 270 regular season goals by this, his 546th regular season game.

The now mostly bald man tried to go around Babe Siebert, the former Montreal Maroons star, but the defender got a little piece of him, sending Morenz into the boards, feet first. One skate got stuck under the boards, and the rest of him came overtop, causing a double fracture. Off to the hospital went Morenz, in intense pain.

Six weeks later, just hours after some teammates came to visit, Morenz died of a cardiac arrest. Writer Brian McFarlane speculates that the great forward, realizing his hockey career was over, simply died of a broken heart.

"We didn't know that the next time Howie would be seen out at his beloved center-ice spot would be in a coffin, with the famous of hockey as pallbearers and with, for the last time, a capacity crowd drawn by the magic of the name," wrote Andy O'Brien.

One of the immortals was no longer of the mortal world.

Aw, I Knew That!

Q. In December 1940, a game between the Chicago Blackhawks and the New York Rangers featured four sets of brothers. Who were they?

A. Muzz and Lynn Patrick, Neil and Mac Colville for New York; Bob and Bill Carse, Doug and Max Bentley for Chicago.

War Again

Douglas Hunter, in his study of hockey in World War II, sees the years 1939–1945 as a transition between the upheaval of the Depression and the post-conflict time when the National Hockey League would experience its most stable years.

Sort of like the world in general, without the killing, maiming, or threat of nuclear war.

It wasn't only the top pro level that would experience shortages of players and officials, of course—that effect would be felt all through the minor pro, senior amateur, and junior ranks. And, despite the fact the United States would not "officially" enter the war until the Japanese bombed Pearl Harbor on December 7, 1941, the game would be seriously disrupted simply because the majority of its players were Canadian—and Canada got involved just days after Adolf Hitler's forces blitzkrieged their way into Poland on September 1, 1939.

Things got rather messy in Canada, thanks to a Conscription Act passed in 1940 that required men drafted to serve only in Canada itself, not overseas.

A lot of players liked that idea.

But many went, most famously Conn Smythe's Sportsmen's Battalion, an anti-aircraft unit of which he was the commanding officer.

Aw, I Knew That!

Q. What goaltender tended the net for Toronto in the 104:46 of overtime win over Boston in 1933, and the 116:30 of overtime loss for the Montreal Maroons in 1936—together the two longest games in NHL history?

A. Lorne Chabot.

Though many other players wanted to serve overseas, Hunter says, most were shuffled off to safe jobs, such as physical training officers. Many others found themselves on military teams, two of which won consecutive Allan Cups (Canadian senior title). Eventually some bad publicity put an end to the "shadow NHL" clubs.

The NHL got by with players who were too young, too old, or too infirm for military duty. Same situation as in Major League Baseball—there was the same drop in quality. The Canadiens, though, found a loophole by putting many players in essential "war industries" and thus kept them out of military service.

All was not happy between the NHL and the Habs for other reasons. William Houston says the club was struggling financially, cut-rating their tickets, and the Forum was fast becoming a wreck. The league wanted much better management for the club. It would get it in Frank Selke Sr.

Boston and the New York Rangers took the war hardest, losing so many good players and struggling through with lousy attendance. Others did much better, thanks to fans' need to find something to take their minds off the war.

One interesting development did come out of the war years, however—the center redline, which opened up the game because players could pass the puck over any line on the ice, as long as the pass didn't go over two of them.

Three excellent NHL prospects paid with their lives on the battlefields: Red Garrett died when the corvette escort ship on which he served took a torpedo; Canadian Joe Turner joined the U.S. Marines and was killed in action; Red Tilson died in Europe as a Canadian infantryman.

The Rocket's Black Stare (Part One)

Joseph Henri Maurice Richard. Born August 4, 1921, Montreal. Size: 5'10", 170 pounds. Superb with the stick. Nose for the net. Black, glowering eyes that scared the athletic supports off defenders for 18 seasons, during which he scored 544 regular season goals and 82 more in playoffs. First player to score 50 goals in one season. Won the scoring title five times. Helped win eight Stanley Cups.

"I can't figure what Canadiens saw in me to offer that first pro contract," Richard once told Andy O'Brien during a train ride. "It seemed I was always on my ass or in the hospital."

He always seemed injured. When he applied to join the army, Richard was turned down because of chronically bad ankles—both having been broken within the last two years, the second after he'd played 16 games as a rookie for the Habs.

Aw, I Knew That!

Q. What player holds the dubious distinction of leading the NHL in penalty minutes for eight straight seasons, a league record?

A. Red Horner, Toronto Maple Leafs, 1932–1933 to 1938–1940.

Aw, I Knew That!

Q. Who was the first defenseman to score 20 goals in one season?

A. William "Flash" Hollett, 20 for Detroit in 1944–1945.

Richard was actually offered to the Rangers in a trade (oh, how life would have altered on Broadway!), but Montreal finally kept him. Paul Haynes, the Montreal senior amateur coach, had an idea—make the natural right winger a left winger, because of the way he liked to cut across the ice while keeping his strong backhand as a constant weapon. Better to keep him from getting killed by switching him.

Paul Haynes. Disappeared into history, but what he did for the history of the game …

Teamed with Toe Blake and center Elmer Lach by coach Dick Irvin, the man shortly to be known as The Rocket (pinned on him by teammate Ray Getliffe) was an instant success, scoring 32 times in 1943–1944. But there was something brewing inside of Richard that people couldn't quite put a finger on.

Something they would discover as the next era of hockey began.

I Remember ...

In a hockey life of 65 years, which began in the cradle as the son of legendary coach Dick Irvin, Dick Irvin Jr. has seen almost every great player, and may have seen more games played by the great Maurice Richard than anyone. In 1942–1943, as a youngster, he was sitting in the crowd at the Forum with his mom, beside the Montreal doctor, watching the rookie Richard. After scoring twice, Richard was crunched by Boston's Johnny Crawford. Before even leaving his side, the Habs' doctor turned to the young Irvin and said: "That young man, Richard, has a broken leg." He would miss the season, but come back the next year to score 50 times in 50 games.

Stars of the Era

➤ Howie Morenz played 14 seasons in the NHL, 12 with the Montreal Canadiens. He scored 270 goals and 467 regular season points. Twice he won the scoring title and three times was most valuable player. Died of a heart attack in 1937 after suffering a double fracture in his leg.

➤ Eddie Shore was the epitome of tough and mean in an era of tough and mean. A Saskatchewan native, he joined the Bruins in 1926, winning four MVP awards and two Stanley Cups. Eventually went into coaching.

➤ Aubrey "Dit" Clapper made the junior Oshawa club at just 13 when he was still 8 years younger than many of the men he was playing against. Starred in Boston for 20 years. Clapper scored 228 times.

➤ Charlie Conacher, brother of Lionel, played 12 years with Toronto, Detroit, and the New York Americans, netting 225 goals and taking 2 scoring titles.

➤ Nels Stewart, called "Old Poison" for his slow skating style and lighting-quick shot, was the first player in NHL history to hit 300 goals, playing for the Montreal Maroons, the Boston Bruins, and the New York Americans.

➤ Aurel Joliat only weighed about 135 pounds, but as a left winger with the Montreal Canadiens he notched 270 goals. He was so tough that as an aged man in 1963, he got into a fight with another senior, Punch Broadbent, over a dispute they had on the ice as players 40 years earlier.

Stanley Cup Winners of the Era

1931–1932	Toronto Maple Leafs
1932–1933	New York Rangers
1933–1934	Chicago Blackhawks
1934–1935	Montreal Maroons
1935–1936	Detroit Red Wings
1936–1937	Detroit Red Wings
1937–1938	Chicago Blackhawks
1938–1939	Boston Bruins
1939–1940	New York Rangers
1940–1941	Boston Bruins
1941–1942	Toronto Maple Leafs
1942–1943	Detroit Red Wings
1943–1944	Montreal Canadiens
1944–1945	Toronto Maple Leafs

The Least You Need to Know

➤ Ace Bailey almost died as a result of an attack by Eddie Shore, an act that epitomized the violent era.

➤ The Depression killed a number of NHL teams.

➤ Howie Morenz died of cardiac arrest six weeks after breaking his leg in a game.

➤ World War II emptied the NHL of much of its talent for the duration.

➤ The war years saw the debut of Maurice "Rocket" Richard, who would be one of the most dominant players of the next era.

Post-War Baby Booms (1946–1967)

In This Chapter

➤ Leafs at the front and back

➤ Winning the Norris House League

➤ Rocket-powered Canadiens

➤ On Broadway

➤ Bobby and Stan break the curse

➤ The luckless Bruins find a shiny penny

➤ Stuck on an endless bus ride

It has been called by most, including a number of writers and journalists who should know better, the era of the Original Six. From the end of the war to the spring of 1967, the Montreal Canadiens, the Toronto Maple Leafs, the New York Rangers, the Boston Bruins, the Detroit Red Wings, and the Chicago Blackhawks *were* the NHL. Of course, only one of those clubs was actually an original—the Canadiens—and despite the pleasant dreaming of those who miss it, this era was filled with defensive hockey played in a parochial league locked into the northeastern United States and Central Canada, followed south of the border only by those fans living in the four cities that had clubs. At one point, half the teams were owned by the same family. But despite its shortcomings, the NHL at this point also featured some of the most famous names— and most bitter battles—in league history. In this chapter we'll look at those teams, those battles, and a handful of men who transcended the game itself.

Aw, I Knew That!

Q. Maurice Richard scored 50 goals in 1944–1945. Bernie Geoffrion scored 50 in 1960–1961. Who had the most goals in a season in the years between those two marks?

A. Gordie Howe, 49, Detroit Red Wings, 1952–1953.

Great Games

April 23, 1964: Detroit Olympia

Down 3–2 to the Detroit Red Wings in the semi-finals, Toronto absolutely had to win this game to stay alive. Enter Bobby Baun, the tough Leafs defenseman, who had left the game earlier with a suspected fracture of the smaller, nonweight-bearing bone in his leg, an injury that should have ended his season. Baun came back during the third period and scored the winner in overtime on a shot from the point.

Toronto 4, Detroit 3

C'monnnnnnnn Teeeeeeeder!

For 11 years—from the time Bill Barilko scored the Stanley Cup winner in 1951 (just a month before he would die in a plane crash on a fishing trip in Northern Ontario) to the time they knocked off the defending champion Blackhawks in 1962—the Toronto Maple Leafs lived through a mostly forgettable, frustrating time. Fortunately for the proud franchise, the beginning and end of the era were a wonderful dream.

Unless you were in ownership (see the following section).

The Leafs of the five seasons from 1946–1951 won the cup four times, led by the inimitable Ted Kennedy, who had the winning goal in game six of the 1947 final against Montreal. Other stars included Syl Apps and goaltender Turk Broda. Coached by Hap Day, overall this club would pick up five cups in eight seasons, going back to the war years.

Barilko's goal came in game five of the 1951 final tilt, with Toronto leading the series 3–1 and the game into overtime. The Leafs scored with the goalie out to send the contest to extra time and Barilko came in from the blueline to backhand the winner past Gerry McNeil for the cup at 2:53 of sudden-death.

After that, the Leafs would make the final just twice in 10 years, losing both times to Montreal. But a new coach and general manager would put Toronto back on top.

Who's Minding the Mint?

Conn Smythe had owned the Leafs since 1927 and had run them with an iron fist, a nasty temper, and, as Jack Batten writes, an acid tongue. He basically scared the pants off anyone who came near him, and that included league president Clarence Campbell, whom Smythe once told to shut up in a league meeting. Campbell proceeded to do just that.

But in the 1961–1962 season, Smythe sold his beloved Leafs to a group that included his son Stafford,

Harold Ballard, television and radio magnate John Bassett, and four minority investors. In the local press they were known as the Silver Seven.

The new owners did everything to increase the profitability of their arena: tore down the Queen of England's portrait to put up new seats; tore down the balcony the military bands used to play in to put in new seats; made the wide seats themselves much thinner to fit in new seats. Batten says the elder Smythe would later claim he thought he was selling just to his son, but it seems obvious he knew Stafford didn't have enough money.

Before long, legendary writer and broadcaster Dick Beddoes had bestowed a new nickname on Maple Leaf Gardens—the Cashbox on Carlton Street.

Punch Punches In

George Imlach punched the clock as Maple Leafs' coach and general manager after firing then-coach Billy Reay just 20 games into 1958–1959.

Imlach was a mass of contradiction. He could be funny or cruel. He was cool under intense pressure or blew his top at almost nothing. He could hold a grudge (he hated Frank Mahovlich—the feeling was mutual—and he went so far as to refer to his star left winger as "Maholovich"), show an almost egg-like shell, and clasp his fingers to the purse strings with a death grip.

But he won. A lot.

From the time he took over through the Leafs' last Stanley Cup (right up to this printing) in 1967, his clubs won four cups, including three in a row.

Aw, I Knew That!

Q. In the 1964 intra-league draft, Toronto picked up two aging future Hall of Famers. Who were they?

A. Dickie Moore, forward, from Montreal, and Terry Sawchuk, goaltender, from Detroit.

Gordie Joins the Norris House League

Gordie Howe was nearly a New York Ranger, and how that would have altered the history of the NHL over the next four decades one can only speculate. But, as Jim Vipond writes, a homesick 15-year-old at a Ranger try-out camp in Winnipeg decided not to sign with the Broadway Blueshirts and go home to Saskatchewan instead.

Detroit would get him, and Howe (first season 1946–1947), with teammates such as the superb goaltender Terry Sawchuk (a troubled man who is considered among the top three at his craft ever), center Alex Delvecchio, defenseman Red Kelly, and a winger named Terrible Ted Lindsay, would go on to help the Wings dominate the early to middle period of the era.

Run by Jack Adams, who like most other bosses of the era believed in keeping his charges in line by terrorizing them, Detroit took the cup in 1950, 1952, 1954, and 1955 under

Quote, Unquote

"You ever smelt half-boiled octopus? It ain't exactly Chanel No. 5 you know."

—Pete Cusimano, who tossed an octopus on the ice in Detroit in 1952 to start a Red Wing tradition.

coaches Tommy Ivan and Jimmy Skinner. Pete Babando in 1950 and Tony Leswick in 1954 scored overtime goals to wrap up championships.

But somehow, the club fell apart. Many writers credit a pair of deals that together saw 15 players change teams, including Sawchuk, who went to Boston. It didn't work. Then there was Adams' fight with Lindsay over that player's involvement in an attempt to start a players' union in 1957. Angry, Adams sent Lindsay to Chicago with goalie Glenn Hall—a key move in the turnaround of the Blackhawks.

As Bob Duff writes, even when Adams traded to get Sawchuk back, he had to give up John Bucyk, who would only go on to score 556 goals in his Hall of Fame career.

The Wings hit rock bottom.

A Norris for Every Occasion

Follow the bouncing Norrises.

In 1952, James Norris Sr., who had owned the Red Wings since 1932, died of a heart attack. He had already seen to it that James Jr. ("Little Jim" as he was called) was running the Chicago Blackhawks as team president, since that team was co-owned by the Norrises and Arthur Wirtz. Norris Sr.s daughter, Marguerite, "a graduate of exclusive Smith College," as Brian Kendall writes, took over as president of the Wings, becoming the league's first female executive. She would be replaced by her brother Bruce in 1955. And the Norris family owned majority interest in New York's Madison Square Garden at that time, which meant they were the landlords of the Rangers.

Oh, and the Norrises happened to have a big old barn of an arena in St. Louis that they would eventually unload on the Salomon family as the home of the Blues when expansion came in 1967.

No wonder writers referred to the NHL as the Norris House League.

Big Gordie Perseveres

The Wings went in the toilet for the 1957–1958 season, finishing dead last. They had a succession of coaches, some successful, like Tommy Ivan (two cups), and others less so, like Jimmy Skinner. Sid Abel, formerly a key member of the Production Line with Howe and Lindsay, led the team back to respectability, losing the semi-finals and finals over the next two seasons. Back they went to the bottom again, only to resurrect once more.

But with Abel behind the bench, four trips to the finals in six years from 1961–1966 still resulted in four losses, the last one coming when Henri "The Pocket Rocket" Richard scored in overtime by sliding headfirst into the net with the puck crooked under his right arm to beat Roger Crozier for one of the most controversial winning goals in cup history.

Through it all, Gordie Howe just kept on doing what he always did—scoring, hitting, intimidating (he once beat tough guy Lou Fontinato in a long fight in the late 1950s and never had to fight again because no one would touch him).

Never did he reach the 50 goals in one season mark, but his amazing consistency saw him score never less than 23 times, and over 40 on five occasions including 49 in 1952–1953.

By 1967, he had put 20 years into the NHL, and still had 11 years of pro ahead of him.

Aw, I Knew That!

Q. Maurice Richard scored his 325th career goal in 1952. Whose NHL record did that goal allow him to pass?

A. Nels Stewart, 324 goals.

Great Games

May 5, 1966: Detroit Olympia

The game but aging Detroit Red Wings, backed up by young goaltender Roger Crozier, won the first two games in the cup final against the Montreal Canadiens but then lost the next three in a row and found themselves in overtime of game six, tied 2–2. Then one of the most controversial plays in hockey history occurred when Henri Richard slid into Crozier's crease with the puck cradled in his elbow. The Habs' center slid toward the goal, the puck wound up in the net, and the goal counted.

Montreal 3, Detroit 2

The Rocket's Black Stare (Part Two)

Maurice Richard, he of the frighteningly intense black-eyed glare, came into the post-war era as the first player to score 50 goals in a season—in 50 games during the 1944–1945 season. Some suggested he had been able to achieve that mark because of the watered-down talent pool still in effect that year, but he would show the talent in his hands by netting 45 in 1946–1947.

I Remember ...

Rocket Richard was notorious for taking advantage of an opponent's error. In the early 1950s, at Maple Leaf Gardens, a young defender made the cardinal mistake of trying to complete a "powder puff" pass over the middle of the ice. As Sid Smith tells it, Richard jumped on the pass, came right in, and scored the winning goal. At the train station a few hours later, Richard saw Leaf coach Joe Primeau and called out, "Don't give that kid shit, Joe. I do that stuff [taking advantage] all the time."

There was something different about Richard—something new. He was a man filled with fierce pride for Quebec, determined to help young French Canadians feel that pride as well. It was a long way from the time when owner Georges Kendall felt compelled to anglicize his name in order to get along in the Montreal business community.

Writer Mike Ulmer says of him that he had "a natural rage," and an incredible ability to overcome all obstacles put in his way: "He poured resentment toward his bosses into his play, and regarded the shadows who followed his every move as necessary stagehands for his greatness."

When Richard died in 2000, the event became a major national news story as the entire province of Quebec went into mourning. He lay in state in the Molson Centre, as Howie Morenz had done in the old Montreal Forum, and was given a state funeral.

Led by Richard and his linemates Toe Blake and center Elmer Lach, Montreal won cups in 1944, 1946, and 1953, all under coach Dick Irvin. The best—really, the greatest—was about to come.

But not without a time-out for a little civil disobedience.

Quote, Unquote

"It's funny, but until I made that decision, I was never acknowledged as the head of the NHL."

—Clarence Campbell, NHL president, on his 1955 suspension of Maurice Richard.

The Riot

Spring 1954. Richard has been weekly criticizing Clarence Campbell, the league president, in a ghost-written column printed in a small French newspaper in Montreal. The NHL boss got manager Frank Selke of the Canadiens to shut him down.

Go forward a year, and Richard strikes a linesman during a game, drawing a heavy fine (he was the most-fined player in league history to that point). Campbell is getting really mad. Richard is even madder.

Enter Hal Laycoe of the Bruins, who hits Richard over the head with his stick (no helmets, remember), touching off an on-ice melee during which the Rocket whacks Laycoe across the defenseman's back (which he would have likely gotten away with, given the fact that kind of violence was A-OK in those days). Unfortunately, he also punches linesman Cliff Thompson in the head.

Campbell suspended him for the rest of the season and the playoffs. The city, Anglos included, went nuts.

So ... the next game happened to be at the Forum, March 17, 1955, and Campbell thought he'd show his toughness and refusal to back down to thugs by showing up (with his wife) and sitting in his regular seats. Eggs, programs, and garbage rained down on him (and his unfortunate wife), and a tear-gas bomb went off, emptying the arena and cancelling the game.

Coach Dick Irvin said he'd seen the Rocket fill up a lot of arenas, but "that's the first time I've ever seen him empty it."

Out on the street, a large group of (mostly) young punks started to riot up Rue St. Catherine, smashing windows, beating up the innocent, and generally acting like morons.

Rocket, realizing things were out of hand, went on French and English radio and asked for calm, which was restored.

There were 137 people arrested.

In all of the mess of that spring, the Canadiens made a significant decision that would affect the next 15 years of the league's history—they hired Toe Blake as coach.

Toe's Boys

Toe Blake, former linemate of Maurice Richard, took over the club in the summer of 1955 and began an incredible string that would see the Habs win eight cups in his 13 seasons behind the bench, including five straight from the spring of 1956 to 1960, when the Rocket hung them up for the last time.

Other wins would come in 1965, 1966, and 1968.

Toe's boys were, together, the best team in league history (though there is some argument, of course, for the Edmonton Oilers of the 1980s).

Next to the Rocket, they had a startling lineup of wonderful players:

➤ Jacques Plante, who would play 17 seasons in the NHL and miss the playoffs just once, and who would be the first goalie to wear a mask regularly during games (starting a trend).

➤ Doug Harvey, voted by a star-studded *Hockey News* panel as the sixth best player of all time, right behind Richard, was a standout on defense.

Quote, Unquote

"It's hard to put into words how we felt about Jean. It's just that we were so damned proud to have him as our captain."

—Ralph Backstrom on Montreal captain Jean Beliveau.

➤ Jean Beliveau (nicknamed Le Gros Bill), was seventh on the *Hockey News* all-time list. He was such a beloved star in Quebec City that the Canadiens had to buy the entire Quebec Senior League in order to get him on their roster.

➤ Henri "The Pocket Rocket" Richard, Maurice's younger brother, was twenty-ninth on the all-time list. He played 20 seasons starting in 1955 and scored 358 times.

➤ Dickie Moore, number 31 on the *Hockey News* list, a hard-working winger so stubborn that he once quit the team rather than allow himself to be traded.

➤ Bernie "Boom Boom" Geoffrion, the second player to score 50 times in a season and number 42 in the *Hockey News* poll.

That's 8 players in the top 50, folks. They were incredible.

Add that to an up-and-coming face in the front office named Sam Pollock (more on him in Chapter 9, "Keeping Your Head Up [1969–1980]"), and the Canadiens were set for decades to come.

The Pony Line and a Whole Lot of Nothing

How bad were the Chicago Blackhawks from 1946–1958?

So bad they missed the playoffs 12 times in 13 years. So bad the league stepped in and asked other teams to send a few useful players their way to help out. So bad they were dead last on nine occasions.

I Remember ...

Phil Esposito, who always played tons of minutes in his prime, was frustrated as a young player in Chicago by his lack of ice time. One night, with the Hawks miles behind, coach Billy Reay, who had said he was going to break the youngster in "slowly," finally went to Espo and sent him in. The center leaned over the bench and asked, "Billy, do you want me to score the winner, or just tie it up?"

The era didn't start out that way. Led by the Pony Line of Max and Doug Bentley and Bill Mosienko, the Hawks were competitive, finishing third in the first season after the war, a year in which Max won the scoring championship. Then, management lost its collective heads after one tough season and traded Max to the Leafs for an intact forward line of Gaye Stewart, Gus Bodnar, and Bud Poile.

Down into the toilet went Chicago.

A change of ownership to James Norris Sr. and Jr. and Arthur Wirtz in 1952 brought a small improvement, and the club made the playoffs. Down they went again, however, and stayed there most of the remaining years of the decade.

But ownership started to invest money, brought in Tommy Ivan as manager from Detroit, and, as Stan Fischler writes, started to build a decent minor league and junior system that was centered in St. Catharines, Ontario, home of the junior TeePees.

That club would develop Stan Mikita, Pierre Pilote, and, among others, a blond-haired, Adonis-bodied young man with the hardest shot in league history.

The Golden Jet

His name was Robert Marvin Hull. He began his hockey career as a toddler in 1942, taking his Christmas gift of a new pair of skates 50 yards out the front door onto the Bay of Quinte, on Lake Ontario, near the city of Belleville, Ontario. He was noticed first by Bob Wilson, a scout for the Blackhawks, who put the young Hull on the team's negotiation list, locking him to the club forever.

Hull was 12. He left home to play in the low junior ranks at 13. He was in the NHL at 18, joining Chicago for the 1957–1958 season.

He was an instant hit, with a shot so hard that Jacques Plante said, "When it hits you, it feels like a piece of lead."

It was Hull, with the amazing (and, before almost every game, physically sick) goaltender Glenn Hall, Mikita, and Ed Litzenberger, who led the Hawks out of the wilderness. They may not have broken the Curse of Muldoon right away by finishing first in the regular season, but after two straight playoff appearances they captured the Stanley Cup in 1961.

It was Chicago's first cup in 23 years. They haven't won since.

The Bad Luck of the Irish

Boston, with its large Irish population, should know something about luck. In the Boston Bruins' case, it was mostly bad.

Quote, Unquote

"Someday, his bucket should be in the Hall of Fame."

—Unidentified teammate on Glenn Hall's penchant for throwing up before, during, and after games.

From 1946 to 1959, the Bruins missed the playoffs only twice, four times making it to the finals, where they lost each time—always to the Montreal Canadiens. Under coach Milt Schmidt, a former member of the Kraut Line, they were run over 4–2 and 4–1 in consecutive cup finals in the late 1950s. Bad timing.

Tops among the performers were the Uke Line of Bronco Horvath, Vic Stasiuk, and John Bucyk, and defenseman Fern Flaman. After a playoff appearance in 1959, the club missed the playoffs eight straight years up to 1968.

However, there was one incredibly bright light. You see, in 1960 a Bruins scout stumbled upon a 12-year-old, 5'2", 110-pound defender at the Ontario provincial Bantam championships. They never lost track of the youngster from Parry Sound, signing him two seasons later at 15.

The kid's name?

Bobby Orr.

The New York Strangers

If it hadn't been for the Blackhawks, the Rangers would have easily been the worst team of the era. In 22 seasons from 1946–1967, the Broadway Blueshirts missed the postseason 15 times. On 19 occasions, they finished with a less-than-.500 won-lost mark.

Awful.

Wiped out by player losses during the war, facing a weird situation that saw the circus take over Madison Square Garden at playoff time each year (forcing the club to play the few postseason games they did get in on the road), and hurt by a rotten minor league and junior system, New York couldn't do anything.

They did produce a few young players of note, especially Harry Howell, Andy Bathgate, and goalie Gump Worsley (real name Lorne—no one ever used it), but it wasn't enough to make much of a difference.

A turnaround, of sorts, came in 1964 when Emile "The Cat" Francis replaced Lester Patrick's son Muzz as general manager. He started to turn things around in the Big Apple. The club would make the playoffs 9 years in a row, but the team that last won the Stanley Cup in 1940 wouldn't sip from the old mug for 54 straight seasons.

Aw, I Knew That!

Q. The Conn Smythe Trophy for most valuable player in the play-offs actually went to a player on the losing team in 1966. Who was that?

A. Goaltender Roger Crozier of the Detroit Red Wings.

Aw, I Knew That!

Q. Doug Harvey of the Montreal Canadiens won the Norris Trophy as best defenseman seven times in the eight seasons between 1954–1955 and 1961–1962. Who was the only other man to win it during that time?

A. Tom Johnson of the Montreal Canadiens.

On the Buses

In the spring of 1967:

American Hockey League: Hershey, Baltimore, Quebec, Springfield, Providence, Pittsburgh, Rochester, Cleveland, Buffalo.

Western Hockey League: Portland, Seattle, Vancouver, California (San Francisco), Victoria, Los Angeles, San Diego.

Central Professional Hockey League: Oklahoma City, Omaha, Houston, Memphis, St. Louis, Tulsa.

International Hockey League: Dayton, Fort Wayne, Toledo, Des Moines, Port Huron, Muskegon, Columbus.

Eastern Hockey League: Clinton, New Jersey, Johnstown, Long Island, New Haven, Nashville, Charlotte, Greensboro, Knoxville, Florida.

At around 15 players per team, that's 585 professional hockey players who were unable to find a home in the National Hockey League by that spring. The six-team NHL itself employed about 120 athletes, most of whom (if they weren't stars) were just a bus ticket away from being back in the minors.

And don't think coaches didn't use that as a hammer over players' heads to keep them in line. Question one thing an organization was doing, and you could be back in Nashville.

Of the 120 players in the NHL at that time, 119 were Canadians. The lone American was Tommy Williams of Duluth, Minnesota, who toiled for the Boston Bruins. Pro hockey was being played all over the United States and Canada, but only six teams lived in the NHL parish.

Fortunately for hockey, that was all about to change.

Stars of the Era

➤ Maurice Richard. The Rocket. He played 18 seasons with Montreal, scoring 544 times and adding 421 assists for 965 regular season points. He added 126 more in the playoffs. First player to 50 goals.

➤ Gordie Howe. Mr. Hockey. Played 26 seasons in the NHL (Detroit, Hartford), 6 more in the WHA. Scored 801 NHL goals and 1,049 assists for 1,850 points. Had 160 points in playoffs.

➤ Jean Beliveau. Le Gros Bill. Played 20 seasons, to 1971, scoring 507 times, all with Montreal. Considered the classiest player ever.

➤ Terry Sawchuk. Uke. Played 21 seasons as a goaltender (Detroit, Boston, Toronto, Los Angeles, New York Rangers) to 1970. Overall 2.52 average with 103 shutouts— still the record.

➤ Bobby Hull. The Golden Jet. Played 16 seasons in the NHL (7 in the World Hockey Association), scoring 610 times in the National League. Hardest shot in hockey.

➤ Frank Mahovlich. The Big M. Played 17 seasons (Toronto, Detroit, Montreal) as a left winger, scoring 533 times. Scored 48 times in one season on a defensive-minded Leafs team. Brother Peter (The Little M) played 15 seasons in the NHL.

➤ Jacques Plante. Plante played 834 games in goal for Montreal, the New York Rangers, St. Louis, Toronto, and Boston in a career that lasted 19 years and was interrupted by a three-year retirement. Made the mask a regular piece of equipment. Had a 2.38 GAA and 82 shutouts.

Stanley Cup Winners of the Era

1945–1946	Montreal Canadiens
1946–1947	Toronto Maple Leafs
1947–1948	Toronto Maple Leafs
1948–1949	Toronto Maple Leafs
1949–1950	Detroit Red Wings
1950–1951	Toronto Maple Leafs
1951–1952	Detroit Red Wings
1952–1953	Montreal Canadiens
1953–1954	Detroit Red Wings
1954–1955	Detroit Red Wings
1955–1956	Montreal Canadiens
1956–1957	Montreal Canadiens
1957–1958	Montreal Canadiens
1958–1959	Montreal Canadiens
1959–1960	Montreal Canadiens
1960–1961	Chicago Blackhawks
1961–1962	Toronto Maple Leafs
1962–1963	Toronto Maple Leafs
1963–1964	Toronto Maple Leafs
1964–1965	Montreal Canadiens
1965–1966	Montreal Canadiens
1966–1967	Toronto Maple Leafs

The Least You Need to Know

➤ Toronto dominated the late 1940s, Detroit the early to mid–1950s, Montreal the late 1950s, and Toronto the early 1960s.

➤ Montreal won five cups in a row, still a record.

➤ The NHL was a parochial league based in just six cities.

➤ Maurice Richard, Gordie Howe, and Bobby Hull were the era's superstars.

➤ The era ended with the announcement that six new teams would be added for 1967–1968.

Chapter 9

Keeping Your Head Up (1968–1980)

In This Chapter

➤ Six new teams are just the beginning

➤ Bobby Orr

➤ The World Hockey Association

➤ Bullies and more bullies

➤ First seeds of a European invasion

➤ Montreal shows how it's done

➤ From the rink to the courts

This was the wildest era in National Hockey League history. Not only did the league expand from 6 teams in the spring of 1967 to 21 by the spring of 1980, it also fought off a serious challenge by the upstart World Hockey Association, survived the dark cloud of bully tactics and bench-clearing brawls, found ways to stave off a slew of court cases against violent players, and, perhaps most significant for its future, finally opened the doors to European players—who not only brought new blood into pro hockey, but also began a change in the way the game was played. There must have been times in the mid-1970s when yet another ugly, brawl-filled game left many fans and officials wondering if the NHL would implode in on itself, but thanks to one team and its coach—the Montreal Canadiens and Scotty Bowman—a brighter future was ahead.

Six of One, a Half-Dozen of the Other

"Give us your tired, your lame ..."

Okay, it wasn't quite that bad for general managers of the six new NHL clubs when they came to the expansion draft table in the summer of 1967. But when the league announced in March 1965 that it was going to expand to a half-dozen new U.S. cities in the largest growth the league had ever seen at one time, the owners of the existing franchises had already determined they were going to make sure the new clubs got as few decent players as possible.

And for the 9,000 or so minor leaguers who were going to get a shot at the big time—many after years riding the buses—it was certainly the discovery of heaven.

As Douglas Hunter points out, the only reason the owners jumped quickly into expansion was the threat from the Western Hockey League (fairly close, but not quite the talent level of the NHL) that it would expand eastward.

Aw, I Knew That!

Q. Scotty Bowman coached the St. Louis Blues to three straight Stanley Cup finals in 1968–1970. Name the coach he replaced in 1967–1968, just 16 games into the team's expansion season.

A. Lynn Patrick.

Time to cut that off at the pass. So feelers went out to a number of cities (including Vancouver, which didn't make the first cut because of arguments over an arena), to find men with more money than sense to apply for membership in the NHL.

Eventually, the list was cut down to Oakland (Seals), Los Angeles (Kings), Philadelphia (Flyers), St. Louis (Blues), Pittsburgh (Penguins), and Minnesota (North Stars).

Each paid two million dollars for the honor.

All but Philadelphia were cities with strong minor league hockey backgrounds and a solid core of fans ready to buy season seats.

Guess which one won the Stanley Cup first? Yep, Philly (1974).

Hunter calls the expansion "a near-disaster." While it might not have been quite that bad, there were serious problems. The established teams had big farm systems, the new ones none. The old clubs had long lists of protected players in junior, the new had none.

Under a plan set up by Montreal GM Sam Pollock, each old team would protect 11 skaters and 2 goalies with the others available for draft.

That didn't exactly leave a whole lot of scoring or goaltending for the new clubs, which often reached into the ranks of the retired to find warm bodies to fill their uniforms. But a number of players who should have been in the NHL but were stuck in the minors found their way onto the big-league rinks.

The biggest joke, of course, was the way the league was set up, with the Original Six in the Eastern Division and the new six in the West—guaranteeing that an expansion club would make the Stanley Cup final (which the St. Louis Blues did three years in a row, getting blown out each time).

The Ups and the Way Downs

So, who did well with expansion, and who didn't?

➤ Los Angeles and St. Louis began a string of more than 30 years without winning a cup—strings that continue at this writing.

➤ Pittsburgh would have to wait until the 1990s before winning two championships in a row, led by the incredible Mario Lemieux.

➤ Minnesota would not win a cup in the Twin Cities of Minneapolis/St. Paul, would survive with good and bad years until 1993, move to Dallas to become the Stars, and then finally take the cup in 1999.

➤ Oakland was a complete disaster (see the following section).

➤ Philadelphia, which played much of its first season on the road when part of the roof fell in at the Spectrum, would be the first expansion club to win the cup, taking two in the 1970s, but none since.

Aw, I Knew That!

Q. Bobby Clarke, a legend in Philadelphia, was the Flyers' second-round choice in the 1969 amateur draft. Who did the Flyers take in round one?

A. Bob Currier, a center from Cornwall of the OHA, who never played a game in the NHL.

Oops!

If you're going to expand at the speed the NHL did during this era, some mistakes are bound to be made. Adding the Vancouver Canucks and Buffalo Sabres (Buffalo won the coin toss and drafted Gilbert Perreault first overall—the league had gone to a universal draft in 1969—and under general manager Punch Imlach made it to the cup final in 1975) was a good choice for the league (though neither team has a cup win), but the same couldn't be said about some other cities invited into the fold during this era:

➤ The Oakland/California Seals/Golden Seals were the first mistake. Actually, the league had thought it was going into San Francisco for 1967 until it was pointed out, too late, that the new arena had been built across the Bay. Barry Van Gerbig owned the club at the beginning, and he was the one who went across the Bay. Attendance was bad, the team relied on old veterans and traded away top draft positions, and by year four missed the playoffs and would never make them again.

Charlie Finley, the flamboyant owner of the Oakland A's in Major League Baseball, changed the name to the California Golden Seals, gave them white skates, and still couldn't win. Another set of owners didn't work either, and the league actually took the team over. Finally, the club moved to Cleveland and became the Barons.

➤ The Cleveland Barons had their own arena problem. The Richfield Coliseum was 40 miles from downtown, and no one wanted to make the long trip to see a lousy team. Though owned by George and Gordon Gund (normally smart businessmen), the club lasted two years and was folded into the equally struggling Minnesota North Stars franchise.

➤ The Atlanta Flames joined the NHL in 1972 along with the New York Islanders. The latter club would go on to greatness. By 1980, the Flames would go on to Calgary. Though with a good general manager in young Cliff Fletcher (out of the St. Louis Blues organization though originally trained by the Canadiens), the team was hammered by World Hockey Association raiding and a nasty habit of losing in the first round of the playoffs. Main moneyman Tom Cousins lost most of his quiet financial supporters and wound up with 89 percent of the club, which he eventually sold to financier Nelson Skalbania, who in turn sold 50 percent to Calgary business interests. The loss of the Flames was a strange one—the city seemed to like them, but the money wasn't there to keep the club "away down south in Dixie."

➤ The Kansas City Scouts entered in 1974 with the Washington Capitals and lasted exactly two seasons. With the NHL offering next to nothing in the expansion draft and the WHA running off with tons of players, the Scouts had almost nothing to offer, says Stan Fischler. Led by smart general manager Sid Abel, the club wasn't bad for a rotten expansion club, but attendance stunk. The club moved to Colorado.

➤ Colorado's Rockies (not the baseball team—they would pick up the name much later) had a beautiful logo (mountains, purple majesties, the Colorado state "C" in the middle), and for a while a colorful coach in former Bruins' boss Don Cherry, and his sidekick Blue (that would be his dog). But still they struggled and couldn't attract fans. Owner Arthur Imperatore would sell the club to John McMullen in 1981, and it moved to New Jersey and became the Devils for 1982.

Kneecapping Bobby Orr

"There are stars, superstars, and then there's Bobby Orr."

Serge Savard, Hall of Famer and former Montreal Canadien, said it best in Craig MacInnis' book of writings on the Boston defenseman. Orr transcended the normal while he was transforming the game of hockey.

Prior to his arrival with Boston in the fall of 1966, defensemen tended to be just that—defensive. They would hold their ground at the blueline, stand-up their men, and finish their checks. Only the great Doug Harvey and a few others would think offensively.

Orr changed all that. Number 4 could go end-to-end with the puck, he could quarterback the powerplay in a way no one had before. He was fast, had excellent hands, and would dipsy-doodle around the fleetest opponent.

But he was also tough and would never back down, blocking shots and handing out heavy checks.

He was, in late-century parlance, the complete package.

Orr, remember, had been property of the Bruins since he signed as a 15-year-old in 1962. His agent, R. Alan Eagleson (see Chapter 10, "Wayne, Mario, and a New Reality [1980–2001]"), forced the Bruins to pay Orr a princely $25,000 a season, or he would sit out. Most rookies got $8,000.

Aw, I Knew That!

Q. Speaking of mistakes, name the two players drafted by Boston in 1970 who would eventually each score 50 goals in a season for Philadelphia.

A. Reg Leach, third overall, and Rick MacLeish, fourth overall.

All of this was tempered by one unfortunate fact: Bobby Orr had the worst knees of any athlete anywhere, with the possible exception of New York Jets' quarterback Joe Namath. They were tied.

In his rookie year, Marcel Pronovost checked him into the boards (cleanly) and Orr's left knee gave out. That resulted in the first of three knee operations in the youngster's first two seasons. About 10 years later, he had two more that left him with bone on bone in the knee. There were no tendons left.

Bobby Orr scored 270 times, added 645 assists, won two Stanley Cups and a Canada Cup (an international tournament staged every so often through the 1970s and 1980s—see Part 3, "International Incidents"). But by 1979, after playing just 26 times in 3 seasons following a free-agent signing with Chicago, Orr left the game. He had put in 13 seasons.

The *Hockey News'* panel picked him as the second best player in history behind Wayne Gretzky, though many thought the position should be reversed. Matters not.

Personal memory: In 1972 at Maple Leaf Gardens, the Bruins took a penalty and sent Orr out to help kill it. He didn't need any help. Picking up the puck off the faceoff, Orr moved back behind his own net and began playing a game of keep-away with the Leafs. He didn't give up the puck once in two full minutes.

Bobby Orr and the Animals

That's what *Sports Illustrated* called the Bruins, referring, as MacInnis writes, to their rock-star-idol air and their "flamboyant, chippy style."

The Bruins had been an unlucky club in the 1950s (mostly unlucky to be good when Detroit and then Montreal were overwhelming) and a simply horrible club in the 1960s.

But with the arrival of Orr, a vast improvement in their minor league and junior system, and one highway robbery–like trade, they became Stanley Cup winners by the spring of 1970.

Milt Schmidt, the club's general manager, somehow talked the Blackhawks into sending him forwards Phil Esposito, Fred Stanfield, and Ken Hodge for Jack Norris, Pit Martin, and Gilles Marotte in the summer of 1967. Okay, who can tell the future when you make any trade, but Esposito (the best player in the deal) would blossom from a 21-goal man the year before to a 35-goal machine in his first Boston campaign. That was just the warmup. Check this out: His next seven seasons would read 49–43–76–66–55–68–61!

That 76 was miles over the former record of 58, held by Bobby Hull.

Espo liked to stand right in front of the crease as an intimidating presence, picking up a lot of rebound and deflection goals that way—critics said he scored garbage goals—but no one then or since had ever done it better.

Add Esposito to Orr, with John Bucyk, John McKenzie, Ted Green, Ed Westfall, and everybody's favorite semi-counterculture figure Derek Sanderson as strong cast members, give the club great goaltending in Eddie Johnston and Gerry Cheevers, and you had a winning combination.

But the Bruins had something else as well—style. It was Sanderson (who would eventually drink himself out of hockey, become a recovering alcoholic, and enter his 60s as a successful businessman and person), who set the tone with his long hair, sideburns, and an air of invincible arrogance. The whole team picked up on it and would intimidate opponents with their looks, their toughness (some said chippiness and violence), and their belief that no one could beat them. In 1970, they beat St. Louis in four straight for the cup and repeated the trick in 1972, this time over the New York Rangers.

Bud Poile, GM of the Philadelphia Flyers, said when the puck was dropped the Bruins went after it "like a piece of meat." He added, "I'm afraid my guys will desert the place some night."

Remember that, kids. It's going to be important.

Aw, I Knew That!

Q. There are three goaltenders whose names are on the Stanley Cup for Montreal's 1969 victory. Name them.

A. Gump Worsley, Rogie Vachon, and Tony Esposito, who played 13 games in the regular season for the Habs before being claimed that summer by Chicago in the intra-league draft.

The Color of Money? Blue!

Doug Michel, who would own the Ottawa Nationals in the World Hockey Association's first season, coined it best in the title of his book on the experience—*Left Wing and a Prayer*.

The Prayer was usually invoked either by owners, hoping they could come up with enough money to continue for a while longer, or the players, hoping they'd actually get paid that week.

The left wing was Bobby Hull.

But we digress here.

Lawyer Dennis Murphy and salesman Gary Davidson, two Californians with a good idea, founded the American Basketball Association in 1967 based on some practical strategy. Because there was no free agency in North American sports, teams owned your butt for life. If you created a rival league, players would be very interested in jumping if the price was right.

Thus: You could start a new league, pack it with great talent, get franchise fees from a lot of rich business guys who wanted in on the pro-jock thing, and then force the established league to take you in by merger.

Worked like a charm in basketball, and the pair thought they'd try it with hockey.

And you know, for the four clubs that survived the WHA experiment—Hartford Whalers, Edmonton Oilers, Quebec Nordiques, and Winnipeg Jets—it all worked out fine. There was the matter of the two-dozen or more other franchises that came and went over the seven seasons the league lasted, of course.

But remember the idea—get some good players, make money on franchise fees, force a merger. Hey, for Murphy and Davidson, it worked, too.

So the pair started looking for money and wound up in bed with a very smart business-man from Edmonton named William "Wild Bill" Hunter, who wanted to get a franchise for himself and as many as he could for the western Canadian prairies.

I Remember ...

One frigid winter day, the Minnesota Fighting Saints of the WHA were practicing at a local rink in Winnipeg that had an indoor swimming pool attached to the complex on the other side of a glass wall. At the end of practice, remembers coach Harry Neale, Mike "Shaky" Walton, one of the most talented players he says he ever had, was seen bounding on the end of the diving board—in full equipment. He jumped in, but the weight of his equipment weighed Walton down and he couldn't get off the bottom of the pool. Some team members dragged him out, spluttering. Then Walton had to walk to the team bus in the freezing weather, and by the time he got there he was a "human icicle." The guys on the bus broke up in laughter.

In November of 1971, the new league announced 10 franchises, and after a little bouncing around (San Francisco and the Miami Screaming Eagles never got off the ground), launched in 1972 with 12 clubs: New England Whalers, Cleveland Crusaders, Philadelphia Blazers, Ottawa Nationals, Quebec Nordiques, and New York Raiders, all in the Eastern Division; and Winnipeg Jets, Houston Aeros, Los Angeles Sharks, Minnesota Fighting Saints, Alberta Oilers, and Chicago Cougars in the West.

It also featured the short-lived debut of the blue puck (there was also a red one, but that lasted only a game or two itself), which television loved and the players, especially goaltenders, just hated.

Still, it was something creative. And creativity was something the WHA had in abundance.

Bobby and Gordie

The WHA needed something right away to get both the media and the fans' attention. They got it in one Robert Marvin Hull. The Golden Jet became a Winnipeg Jet in 1972 (the nickname turned out to be perfect, didn't it?), when the league got together to jointly pony up $2.75 million over 10 years, making the Chicago left winger by far the highest paid player in the game.

Suddenly, all sorts of guys started bolting their NHL clubs as established owners just couldn't make themselves reach into their fat wallets to pay and keep them.

Aw, I Knew That!

Q. Name the rookie Boston goalie who tied an NHL record by recording 14 straight wins in February of 1975.

A. Ross Brooks.

And there were other surprises. One was Gordie Howe, who had retired after 1971 but decided to give it another run when the Houston Aeros signed both of his sons—Mark and Marty—to pro contracts for 1973–1974. Gordie took the skates back off the hook and formed an all-Howe line with his youngsters, scoring 31 times that year in 70 games. He was 45 years old at the time—and still had six pro seasons ahead of him.

Dave Keon, Frank Mahovlich, Gerry Cheevers, Derek Sanderson (for a handful of games), J. C. Tremblay, and dozens more came the WHA's way as salaries skyrocketed. The NHL clubs that found a way to head off defections prospered. Those who couldn't, such as the Toronto Maple Leafs, floundered.

What Can You Say About a League ...

➤ That was the home of Steve and Jeff Carlson and their friend, Dave Hanson, who starred in the movie *Slap Shot* as the goon trio "The Hanson Brothers"?

➤ In which goalie Gilles Gratton of the Toronto Toros once "streaked" naked through a practice session?

➤ That had one ice surface—Cherry Hill Arena—that was actually tilted?

➤ That allowed both Robbie Ftorek and Claude Larose of the Cincinnati Stingers to wear number 8—at the same time?

➤ In which a coach, Jacques Demers, had to sign himself to a contract during a flu epidemic in order to ensure his Quebec Nordiques had the required 15 players on the bench?

➤ That invited daredevil Evel Knievel to put on a between-periods demonstration by taking penalty shots on Toronto goaltender Les Binkley? Knievel, a former minor-pro player, scored.

➤ That allowed Derek Sanderson to sign a million-dollar contract, play just eight games, and then bolt back to the NHL?

➤ In which the players on the Cleveland Crusaders wore black armbands to a 1976 game in protest of a move by owner Jay Moore that might have brought the Kansas City Scouts of the NHL to his own city?

➤ That had an arena in St. Paul, Minnesota, featuring see-through boards around the rink?

But as writer Murray Greig points out, there was a lot more to the league than just its highjinks.

Quote, Unquote

"In Biblical days I stoned people to death. So, now I am stoned by pucks as punishment."

—Gilles Gratton, oddball Toronto Toros goalie in the WHA. He was a firm believer in reincarnation.

A Little Legacy, Please

The WHA had some profound effects on the NHL—some good, some bad (especially if you were a cheap owner).

Player salaries during the opposing league's existence went up 400 percent.

Europeans, led in the WHA by Bobby Hull's linemates Anders Hedberg and Ulf Nilsson and their captain, Lars-Erik Sjoberg, all of Sweden, and Toronto's Vaclav Nedomansky of Czechoslovakia, began to pour into North America.

Cities without pro hockey were given a shot.

Because the league went after 18-year-olds with a vengeance, a lot of players who would be stars in the 1980s made their debut in the WHA.

Oh, and when the WHA finally merged with the NHL in 1979, there was one other minor detail. See, Nelson Skalbania, owner of the Indianapolis Racers, was looking for money in that last year of the league and he hit on the idea of selling his 18-year-old phenom center to the highest bidder. Two teams, Edmonton and Winnipeg, were willing to match his price so he gave the kid a choice—pick the one you want.

He picked Edmonton.

The youngster's name was Wayne Gretzky.

Bullies and Other Lesser Men

Meanwhile, back in the NHL ... Remember Bud Poile's comment about how scared his Philadelphia Flyers were to face the Big, Bad Bruins in the early 1970s? Well, one person who heard that loud and clear was new coach Fred Shero. Known as "the Fog" for his deep-thinking ways when it came to hockey, Shero and new general manager Keith Allen came up with a brilliant (though awful) plan for making his Flyers the "best" team in hockey—match intimidation with more intimidation.

I Remember ...

Fred Shero had a unique relationship with his Flyers. Just before the third period in game six of the cup finals, with Philly leading Boston three games to two and up 1–0 in the game, the Flyers were waiting for their coach to come in and give a rousing speech. And they waited. And waited. Finally, with three minutes left, the Fog came in, slowly walked around the room, and looked every player in the eye. He said absolutely nothing and then just left. "It was as if he was saying to us, 'It's all up to you now, boys. I've done all I can,'" remembers Terry Crisp. "We were so high we were two feet off the ground going out for the third." The Flyers hung on and won their first cup.

The idea was simple. They had drafted a true leader in 1969 when Bobby Clarke, a superbly talented player with the annoying habit of getting opposing players so upset with his stickwork that they'd want to kill him, was taken in the second round.

He had to be protected. And since they were protecting him, they could add some smaller, finesse players and protect them as well. And since the Bruins wanted to be big and bad, why not be bigger and badder?

And the Broad Street Bullies (named for the street that runs by the old Spectrum Arena in Philly) were born.

Mayhem ensued. You see, the Flyers only had to score two goals a game to win because they had the unbelievable Bernie Parent in goal, so they could spend much of the game pounding the opposition. Led by Dave "The Hammer" Schultz and Bob "Hound Dog" Kelly, Philly basically beat the bananas out of the opposition, often ganging up two or three players on one poor guy.

In a playoff series with the Leafs, Shero waited until five relatively soft Toronto players were on the ice, then sent out his goons to pound the opposition's best player, Borje Salming, to a pulp.

They were brutes. But they had enough talent hiding behind the brutes that two Stanley Cups followed, in 1974 and 1975.

Other teams felt compelled to get a goon or two of their own, which led to the introduction of some wonderful people like Bob Gassoff, Kurt Walker, Paul Higgins, and Randy Holt, the latter playing 395 games, scoring 4 times, amassing 1,438 minutes in penalties, including a record 67 in one game. He "performed" for Chicago, Cleveland, Vancouver, Los Angeles, Calgary, Washington, and, ironically, Philadelphia.

And if you think the NHL was dangerous, try the WHA, where some players who could barely skate—players such as Curt Brackenbury, Frank "Seldom" Beaton, Gilles Bilodeau, and Jack Carlson proved that if you could tie your own skates and drop your own gloves, there was a job for you.

Spurred by the media, the courts, at least those in Canada, started to catch on.

Great Games

May 20, 1975: Memorial Auditorium, Buffalo

Fog Night in Buffalo saw play in game three of the Stanley Cup final between the Sabres and the Philadelphia Flyers stopped a number of times due to fog on the ice. Players were forced to skate in endless circles to dissipate the fog. Rene Robert eventually scored the winner for Buffalo past Bernie Parent at 18:29 of overtime.

Buffalo 5, Philadelphia 4

In the Running (from the Law)

This era was, at times, gruesome, violent, and bloody. But some incidents stood out above the others.

On September 21, 1969, Ted Green of the Boston Bruins and Wayne Maki of the St. Louis Blues got into a brawl during an exhibition game in Ottawa. Neither dropped their stick, however, and both came up swinging with the lumber. Maki connected, fracturing Green's skull and putting him into the hospital for five hours of brain surgery and, ultimately, leaving him with a steel plate in his head. Both were arrested and eventually exonerated by the courts.

Ironically, Maki would die just a few years later of a brain tumor.

Things would get worse.

Jump ahead to April 11, 1976, and a WHA playoff between the Calgary Cowboys and the Quebec Nordiques. Marc Tardif, Quebec's superb winger (510 total goals, WHA and NHL, in his career) was minding his own business when Calgary's Rick Jodzio (17 career goals) jumped on the ice and skated right across the rink to deliver a disgusting cross-check to Tardif's face. Though his "opponent" was already unconscious, Jodzio started pounding him in the head with his fists.

The subsequent brawl took 20 Quebec police to break up. Tardif had a severe brain contusion and was out for the year. Jodzio was arrested, found guilty of assault, fined $3,000, and subsequently suspended for a year by the WHA. The surprise was that Jodzio, poster-boy for 1970s goon, was ever allowed to play again. Which he did, in both the World League and the NHL.

Also in 1976, Toronto vs. Philadelphia, playoff contest at Maple Leaf Gardens. This was where Borje Salming was jumped by five Flyers. In the penalty box, Don Saleski goes after a fan who had, allegedly, spit on him. Wrestling with a policeman for his stick, Saleski clocks a female usher on the head with the wood. Joe Watson and Bob Kelly got involved by swinging their own sticks into the fray. Ontario Attorney General Roy McMurtry steps in and charges Mel Bridgeman for assaulting Salming, Watson for assaulting a police officer, and Saleski and Kelly for simple assault.

Quote, Unquote

"Clarke makes the bombs, and I drop them."

—Reggie Leach on his relationship with Philadelphia linemate Bobby Clarke.

Charges against Saleski and Bridgeman are dropped, but Watson and Kelly plead guilty to lesser charges a year later and were fined.

Some rules were changed, including kicking out the third player in a fight (no more ganging up) and giving the first man off the bench in a bench-clearing brawl an automatic 10-game suspension, which kept the benches full.

What actually changed attitudes, and it would take more than a few years, was a combination of three things—the influx of European players, the appearance of one Wayne Gretzky in 1980, and, most important, the dominance of the Montreal Canadiens.

Chicken Swede

Borje (*Bor-ee-ah*) Salming and Inge Hammarstrom were not the first Swedish products to cross the ocean and join the NHL—Thomie Bergmann had that honor in 1972, joining the Detroit Red Wings. But he was a fringe player.

Hammarstrom was a good player who would last six seasons from 1973 to 1979.

Salming was a superstar and future Hockey Hall of Famer.

A defenseman, Salming came to the Toronto Maple Leafs in 1973 from Brynas IF Gavle of the Swedish League, and he immediately impressed with a number of talents—swift skating, huge reach, a patented dive to knock the puck off opponents' sticks, excellent passing and shooting skills and, perhaps as important, a seemingly endless capacity to take abuse from the almost-exclusively Canadian players out to prove he didn't belong.

Okay, it had only been the year before when Canada and Sweden played a dirty two-game exhibition series in Europe just before the second-half of the famous Summit Series with the Soviet Union, and many of those NHLers still harbored grudges against the Swedes.

But if anyone understood how Jackie Robinson must have felt when he broke baseball's color barrier in 1947, it was Salming.

He was called Chicken Swede so many times, while bravely standing up to everything dished out, that it became rather a sickly joke. But he endured. And with the coming of Anders Hedberg and Ulf Nilsson to the WHA in 1974, a trickle was about to turn into a flood.

Salming played 17 seasons in the NHL, amassing 787 points and a necessarily nasty 1,344 penalty minutes. He also was five times an NHL second-team all-star.

It's the considered opinion of both authors (life-time Leaf fans, admittedly), that if he had been from Kirkland Lake, Ontario, instead of Kiruna, Sweden, he would have been a multi-time winner of the Norris Trophy for best defenseman.

The Flowering of the Game

Sam Pollock was a brilliant man. Successful in business, successful in hockey. It was Pollock, as general manager in the 1960s and 1970s, who remade the Montreal Canadiens five times and won six Stanley Cups, including four in a row from 1976–1979.

Quote, Unquote

"Trying to move the puck past Keon is about as easy as shaking your shadow in the sunshine."

—Defenseman Bill Gadsby on elusive Toronto center Dave Keon, one of the best defensive forwards of all time.

Great Games

May 10, 1979: Montreal Forum

The Stanley Cup seemed to be in the bag for the Boston Bruins, leading 4–3 with less than two minutes to go in game seven of the semi-finals, until the Bears were penalized for too many men on the ice when a player took off too quickly on a line change. Guy Lafleur tied the contest on the power play (the most famous goal of his amazing career), and Yvon Lambert scored the winner at 9:33 of overtime. Boston coach Don Cherry wrote years later, "I died on May 10, 1979, at 11:10 P.M., to be exact"—the time of the winning goal.

Montreal 5, Boston 4

In 1969, the NHL abandoned the old system of clubs owning junior teams and signing players for life as early as 13 (à la Bobby Orr), going instead to a universal draft—the same year that Montreal last used its option to select the two best French Canadian juniors as a way of protecting cultural heritage.

Pollock adapted and proceeded to embarrass many other organizations by trading them old retreads for first-round draft picks. Especially bad was a trade in 1970–1971 with California that sent the overwhelmingly average Ernie Hicke and a draft choice to the Seals in return for their first pick, which would turn out to be Guy "The Flower" Lafleur.

And Pollock had a smart scouting staff. Check this out: 1971—Lafleur (1st overall), Larry Robinson (20th); 1972—Steve Shutt (4th), goalie Bunny Larocque (6th), Dave Gardner (8th), Bill Nyrop (66th); 1973—Bob Gainey (8th); 1974—Cam Connor (5th, and you can't win 'em all), Doug Risebrough (7th), Rick Chartraw (10th), Mario Tremblay (12th), Dave Lumley (199th).

And so on.

He also grabbed a young goalie named Ken Dryden in a trade with Boston (then waited while he went to Cornell University), who only won the Conn Smythe Trophy as best player in the 1971 playoffs after being called up with just 10 games to go in the regular season.

He was magic.

Add to that coach Scotty Bowman, at once the most hated and most respected bench boss in the league, and the Habs of the late 1970s were in place to dominate.

Led by Lafleur, Montreal was almost unbeatable at times, losing just once at home in 40 games in the 1976–1977 season. Bowman designed the club to be tough and mean when it had to be, but what the Habs liked to do best was play it straight, skate opponents into the ground, and show what skill and finesse could do.

Skill and finesse could kill.

It was the Montreal Canadiens who begat the next two dominant clubs, the New York Islanders and the Edmonton Oilers—clubs that could play it tough but that loved to win by playing beautiful hockey.

Ken Dryden writes that the turning point was a two-game exhibition series with the Philadelphia Flyers in the fall of 1975 when the first game on Saturday was

Quote, Unquote

"Don't forget, we've got a game in hand."

—Detroit goalie Jim Rutherford to his team, which was 78 points behind the Montreal Canadiens in the 1976–1977 season, just before a game with the Habs.

Quote, Unquote

"To deal productively with human beings, it's necessary to act like one."

—Unidentified Montreal Canadien on Scotty Bowman's taskmaster tendencies behind the bench.

rough and the second on Sunday night was an all-out war at the Spectrum, which the beefed-up Canadiens won on the scoreboard and in the alleyway, pounding the Philly goons in every fight. At that point, the Habs knew they would win the Stanley Cup. And they could do it the way they wanted to.

"We won the cup that night," said Steve Shutt, "it just wasn't official until next May. We knew we had them, better still, they knew it, too. And once you beat them at their style, you could impose your style on them, and we knew they could never skate with us."

Stars of the Era

➤ Bobby Orr played only 12 seasons (13 if you miss a full year out with injury) but changed the game of hockey by turning the defenseman into an offensive force. Scored 270 times and added 645 assists in just 657 regular season games. First player with more than 100 assists in a season—102 in 1970–1971.

➤ Guy Lafleur. "The Flower." After a slow start to his career, dominated the middle to late 1970s from right wing. Scored over 50 goals six times, including 60 in 1977–1978. Struggled with injuries later in his career, retired for one season, then finished with a year in New York (Rangers) and two in Quebec. Retired in 1991.

➤ Bobby Clarke came out of Flin Flon, Manitoba, to captain the Philadelphia Flyers to two Stanley Cups. Afflicted with diabetes, but never allowed it to be a factor. Reputation as a dirty player. The center scored 258 times and added 852 assists. Retired in 1984.

➤ Marcel Dionne was one of the greatest scorers in NHL history, playing mostly for an average Los Angeles Kings club. Six times with 50 or more goals, scored 731 times in 18 seasons with Detroit, Los Angeles, and the New York Rangers. Totalled 1,771 points. Retired in 1989.

➤ Phil Esposito was a superb pure scorer and team leader. Started with Chicago, traded to Boston, where he won two Stanley Cups, and then to the New York Rangers. Started a long career as a coach, general manager, and team president after retiring in 1981 following 18 seasons, 717 goals (76 in 1970–1971 and five times over 50).

➤ Gilbert Perreault was the first player chosen by the expansion Buffalo Sabres in 1970. Played 17 years, scored 512 goals and 814 assists. Five-time all-star. Centered the famous French Connection line with Rick Martin and Rene Robert.

➤ Darryl Sittler led a Toronto Maple Leaf resurgence in the 1970s. Played 11 years in Toronto, finished in Philadelphia and Detroit. Scored 6 goals and 10 total points on February 7, 1976, setting a record for the latter and tying Red Berenson of St. Louis for the modern record in the former category.

➤ Ken Dryden was unusual even for goaltenders. Came out of Cornell University and went up to the Montreal Canadiens with 10 games left in the 1970–1971 season, taking the Habs to the Stanley Cup over Chicago. Won six Stanley Cups. Sat out the

1973–1974 season to article as a lawyer (a move caused by a salary dispute) but came back to star again. Retired after eight seasons to pursue a law career. Eventually became president of the Toronto Maple Leafs and led them back to respectability. Career 2.24 goals against average.

➤ Bernie Parent was the best goalie in hockey during in the mid-1970s, backstopping the Philadelphia Flyers to two Stanley Cups. Played 13 seasons, mostly with Philadelphia, and 1 season in the WHA. Lifetime 2.56 goals against, including an amazing 1.89 in 1973–1974.

Stanley Cup Winners of the Era

1967–1968	Montreal Canadiens
1968–1969	Montreal Canadiens
1969–1970	Boston Bruins
1970–1971	Montreal Canadiens
1971–1972	Boston Bruins
1972–1973	Montreal Canadiens
1973–1974	Philadelphia Flyers
1974–1975	Philadelphia Flyers
1975–1976	Montreal Canadiens
1976–1977	Montreal Canadiens
1977–1978	Montreal Canadiens
1978–1979	Montreal Canadiens
1979–1980	New York Islanders

The Least You Need to Know

➤ The NHL expanded by 6 teams in 1967 and would be up to 21 clubs by 1979.

➤ Bobby Orr was the greatest player of the era and one of the top two ever.

➤ Many franchises struggled through the 1970s.

➤ The World Hockey Association rose and fell during the era.

➤ Fights and violence dominated the headlines in the 1970s.

➤ Europeans began to appear in the pro ranks.

➤ The Montreal Canadiens were the dominant franchise.

Wayne, Mario, and a New Reality (1980–2001)

The National Hockey League came out of the 1970s bruised and battered, needing something, anything, to pull it out of a funk. What it got was far beyond any expectations—the introduction to the NHL of a youngster who would transcend any offensive force yet seen in hockey. On his heels came a man-mountain from Quebec who would turn a losing franchise into a Stanley Cup winner. Off the ice, however, things were anything but calm as labor troubles, controversy around two successive league presidents, and infighting in the players' union itself would contribute to bad press and unhappy fans. But the league would survive and undertake its most aggressive expansion program ever. In this chapter, we'll look at those issues.

Islanders

May 24, 1980, Nassau County Coliseum, Long Island, New York. Overtime. Game six. Stanley Cup final. Bob Nystrom takes a pass from John Tonelli, races in on Philadelphia goaltender Pete Peeters and tips the puck into the net for the victory, bringing the Stanley Cup to the Island for the first of what would be four consecutive championships.

The Islanders' dynasty had begun.

This was a team that had won just 12 games in 1972–1973 as an expansion club and a mere 19 a year later. No longer a joke for being bad, New York, led by coach Al Arbour and general manager Bill Torrey, suddenly improved dramatically, making the semi-finals four out of the next five years. And they lost them all.

The Islanders were now known for putting their hands to their throats and squeezing for all they were worth.

But, after that goal by Nystrom, no more.

"We heard 'hapless' to describe us in our early days in this league and 'choke' in the past few seasons," said Arbour, quoted by Brian Kendall. "Thank heavens we won't hear those words now."

The Islanders were a tremendous team in the early 1980s. They were led by forward Mike Bossy, who would become the first player in league history to score 50 goals in seven straight seasons; Bryan Trottier, Bossy's linemate, who would score 524 times in his career; Clark Gillies, the type of hard worker every team needs to cut down opposing offensive threats and a 319-time scorer himself; defenseman Denis Potvin, a future Hall of Famer and superbly gifted; and goaltender Billy Smith, who was talented, tough, and not above falling down in the crease as if shot in order to draw a penalty from an opponent who came too close, or hacking said opponent in the ankles with his big goal stick.

Quote, Unquote

"Tell him he's Wayne Gretzky."

—Edmonton coach Ted Green to the Oiler trainer when told that stunned winger Shawn Van Allen couldn't remember his name.

Torrey also had a knack for making important trades for supporting players, the best of which was for center Butch Goring in 1980.

The team would continue to dominate the rest of the league until a group of talented kids came along to take their crown.

Simply for the Love of the Game

Peter Gzowski, who traveled with the Edmonton Oilers for a year to write his book *The Game of Our Lives,* described a scene in Toronto, some hours before a contest with the

Leafs, where an impromptu floor hockey game broke out in the hall outside the Oilers dressing room featuring Wayne Gretzky, Mark Messier, and numerous other teammates. They played hockey even when they didn't have to, simply because they loved it.

The Oilers, who took over from the Islanders as hockey's dominant club, winning four out of five cups from 1984 to 1987 and then another in 1990, had every reason to love the game. The cast, led by the greatest offensive player ever to lace on a pair of skates, was too good, and too young, not to enjoy it.

The Great One

Harry Sinden once said of Wayne Gretzky, "He sees a picture out there that no one else sees. It's difficult to describe it because I've never seen the game he's looking at."

Gretzky had that ability to see a play developing in ways no one else could, as though he were watching it from the press box up high instead of at ice level. It was a skill he seemingly always had.

Born in Brantford to a hard-working, blue-collar family, Gretzky first found himself skating on a backyard rink flooded by his telephone company employee father, Walter, or on the river near his grandparents' farm. He was superb right from the start, shattering minor hockey records wherever he went and actually scoring 378 goals in one season as an eight-year-old. At just 14, he was in junior hockey, and one year later the top-level Major Junior ranks in Ontario. By 17 he had signed with Nelson Skalbania's Indianapolis Racers of the WHA.

Shortly thereafter, Skalbania, as mentioned earlier, sold him to the Edmonton Oilers (fall of 1978), which put Gretzky in the NHL the following season after the merger of the NHL and World Hockey Association.

"Gretzky," wrote Douglas Hunter, years later, "had the potential not only to excel at the game the NHL played, but also to change it."

Led by The Great One, whose early nickname was The Kid, the Oilers dominated to such a degree that the entire league started to open up and play

Aw, I Knew That!

Q. Three members of the Ottawa Senators won major trophies at the end of the 1998–1999 season. Who were they and what did they win?

A. Jacques Martin, Adams Award for coach of the year; Magnus Arvedson, Selke Award for best defensive forward; Alexei Yashin, Hart Trophy for Most Valuable Player.

Quote, Unquote

"Gino is tougher than Saddam."

—Sign in Vancouver held up by a fan during the Gulf War, for winger Gino Odjick.

Great Games

May 15, 1990: Boston Garden

Game one of the best of seven finals between the Bruins and Edmonton Oilers became known as the blackout game II, after the lights went out, causing a huge delay. It was the second final in three years at Boston that had been delayed by bad wiring. Petr Klima came off the bench for only his second shift of the game at 55:13 of overtime to give Edmonton the win and send them off on a four-game sweep and their fifth cup in seven seasons.

Edmonton 3, Boston 2

run-and-gun. They featured such wide-open offensive hockey, with little regard for defense, that they would often give their excellent goaltenders, Grant Fuhr and Andy Moog, fits.

Gretzky not only broke records, he shattered them in a way no other player in professional sports ever had. He amassed a record 152 points in 1980–1981, was the first to 200 points in 1981–1982, the fastest to 1,000 points for a career, and won 9 Hart Trophies as Most Valuable Player through 1989. By the time he retired in 1999, The Great One led in all-time career goals, career assists, career points, most goals in a season (92), and had the 9 top single-season assists totals and 9 of the top 11 all-time goal-scoring years.

He was unstoppable.

The Boys on the Bus

Also a Gzowski turn of phrase. Despite his talent, Gretzky could not have turned the Oilers into a juggernaut by himself. Coach and general manager Glen Sather put together a startling supporting cast that could, and actually eventually did, win the Stanley Cup without The Great One.

Mark "The Moose" Messier played hard, scored prodigiously, and provided instant leadership even barely out of his teens. Paul Coffey would become one of the best offensive defensemen ever to play, breaking Bobby Orr's mark for most goals by a defender with 48 in 1985–1986. Jari Kurri, on Gretzky's wing, was an enormous talent out of Finland. Glenn Anderson was the third Oiler, behind Gretzky and Messier, to amass more than 100 points in 1982–1983 when the club was hitting its stride. And the brilliant Fuhr—and to a lesser extent Moog—was there to pick up the pieces when defense occasionally went out the window.

Despite their talents, despite the fun they had playing the game, by 1987, something dark and at the time undefinable, was on the horizon.

August 9, 1988

In the United States and across Europe, that date probably passed without too much notice—just another day.

In Canada, however, that day brought news that no one would have considered possible: Wayne Gretzky had been traded. It was like the Parliament Buildings in Ottawa had been turned into a Nissan dealership, or the CN Tower sold for scrap.

Edmonton owner Peter Pocklington, needing money in a bad way, had already begun taking his club apart the year before by trading Paul Coffey to Pittsburgh after the defenseman refused to ever play for the man again following what he considered a gross insult to his toughness.

But that was nothing compared to this. The Oilers had won the cup again that past spring and looked like they could do it almost endlessly for the next 10 years.

Then, Pocklington struck. Gretzky was traded to the Los Angeles Kings with Marty McSorley and Mike Krushelnyski in a deal that brought Jimmy Carson, Martin Gelinas, three first-round draft picks, and $15 million (U.S.) to Edmonton.

L.A. owner Bruce McNall had a franchise player (who, it would turn out, couldn't overcome the loss of those draft picks all by himself and take the Kings to a cup) and a man who would have such an influence on hockey in southern California that two other franchises—Anaheim and San Jose— would be born as a result.

Pocklington would get one more Stanley Cup, in 1989–1990, and the everlasting anger of Canadian hockey fans.

Quote, Unquote

"He's a good actor. I thought he pulled it off perfectly."

—Edmonton owner Peter Pock- lington, responding to Wayne Gretzky's tearful departure from the Oilers in August of 1988.

Three Bohemians and Three High School Brats

Agent Art Kaminsky was speaking about American-born players when he told Kevin Allen, "It wasn't as much anti-American as it was pro-Canadian. The GMs were all Canadian, the coaches were all Canadian, and the scouts were all Canadian. They just didn't believe there were better players than Canadian players."

He could have as easily been speaking about Europeans as this era got underway. It won't please Canadian readers much, but the fact is that even as late as 1979, Canadians got the first look.

That would change suddenly and dramatically on a dark night in Eastern Europe.

I Remember ...

Coach Scotty Bowman, never known as a patient man, used to drive bus drivers nuts with his shouted directions. In the early 1980s when he was with the Buffalo Sabres, he and the club went to Rochester for an exhibition game. Up in the overhead luggage rack, a huge container of water began to leak, with the liquid collecting in a very large puddle. Suddenly, Bowman shouted out "Stop" to the bus driver, which he did. The water instantly ran down the rack, out the front, and straight down on the coach's head. According to writer Jim Kelley of the *Buffalo News*, the players, knowing they couldn't laugh out loud, practically split their guts giggling as quietly as they could.

Marcel Aubut, president of the Quebec Nordiques, and the team's head scout, Gilles Leger, took a little trip to Europe in 1980 that changed the look of the NHL for the rest of the century. They found themselves in Austria, where the European Club Championships were going on. But they weren't there to watch hockey. They were there on a mission that would made a CIA agent's heart beat a little more quickly.

What they did was spirit brothers Peter and Anton Stastny, and Peter's pregnant wife, out from under the noses of Czechoslovakian security officials, away from their Czech club team, and out of Austria to Canada, through Amsterdam. The two brothers actually lost each other in Holland, which set off a scare, but finally made it out.

Peter would be the NHL's rookie of the year in 1981 and would score 450 goals in 15 years with Quebec, New Jersey, and St. Louis.

But with Peter and Anton safe, there was still the question of the third brother, Marian, who had been barred from playing anywhere by angry Czech authorities. The other brothers raised a $30,000 "transfer fee" (okay, so it was a bribe) and got Marian out from behind the Iron Curtain for the following season.

Now, with Swedes and Finns coming over in greater numbers, and Czechs finding a way out of their country, the European invasion was officially on. And because of what happened with the Quebec situation, the Czechs made a money deal with the NHL that would allow older players out.

The American Revolution

There was another, quieter revolution going on at the same time, however—the discovery that Americans could actually play hockey.

In the mid-1960s, Tom Williams had been the only United States–born and –trained player in the NHL. There were no others until 1980, after which American players began trickling into the pro ranks.

Lou Nanne had a long career with the Minnesota North Stars; Bill Nyrop, a defenseman, went to Montreal in the 1972 draft and had a solid career; Mark and Marty Howe (sons of a Canadian legend) played in the WHA and NHL, Mark for much longer and more effectively; and Rod Langway went to Montreal in 1977 and would be the first American to be voted top defenseman in the National League.

All this was nothing compared to what happened in 1981 and beyond. That season, Bobby Carpenter, an 18-year-old center out of St. John's Prep School in Massachusetts, was chosen third overall in the first round of the NHL draft by the Washington Capitals. This was beyond unprecedented. Understand that in Canada, high school hockey is not important because all of the best high school–aged players are in the junior ranks.

But in the United States, where there has never been a strong junior (16 to 21) program, high school hockey is where it's at in hot hockey areas like New England and Minnesota.

Carpenter, who would score 318 times in his career and be the first American with over 50 goals in a season, was followed in 1983 by Brian Lawton, out of Mount St. Charles High School in Rhode Island, who did Carpenter two better by being chosen first overall. Though his career didn't pan out that well (112 goals in 483 games of an injury-plagued existence), a youngster out of Acton-Boxboro High School in Acton, Massachusetts, taken fifth overall, made up for it.

Goaltender Tom Barrasso, chosen by Buffalo, would win two Stanley Cups with the Pittsburgh Penguins and would still be playing at the end of the century.

In that 1983 draft, 144 Canadians were chosen along with 63 Americans and 35 Europeans.

Some stats: In 1970, almost 100 percent of the players in the NHL were Canadian. In 1980, that number was down to 82.1 percent. By 1990 it was 75.5 percent, and it continued to fall.

The Magnificent One

When Mario Lemieux was a young junior player, the title of The Next Gretzky was plastered on his forehead. Which he didn't need.

It was totally bogus. Mario Lemieux was about to become, rather than the next anything, the first Mario. He was that good.

Though listed at 6'4" and 225 pounds, the Montreal native seemed so much taller and heavier than that. He was the first overall choice by Pittsburgh in 1984 after scoring an immense 133 goals and 149 assists for the Laval Titan in the Quebec Major Junior League.

That was in one season, by the way, not his career.

Lemieux was an instant impact player, scoring his first goal on October 11 and winding up with 43, 48, 54, 70, and 85 scores over his first five seasons. But the Penguins themselves were not winning. Add that to the fact Lemieux was so much different than Gretzky—quiet, introspective, almost painfully shy when a young player, and so effortless that it looked as though he wasn't putting out top effort all the time.

It was a crock, of course, but we do break down our heroes, don't we?

There was so much more to Mario Lemieux than just straight stats: 613 goals in just 745 regular season games and 70 more in 89 playoff appearances (as close to a goal-a-game mark as any player in league history has ever come); a brilliant one-night performance on December 31, 1988 that saw him score five times—power play, short handed, even strength, penalty shot, and empty net.

Quote, Unquote

"If John Ziegler were alive, this never would have happened."

—Chicago columnist Bob Verdi on the 1992 NHL players' strike. Ziegler, by the way, was alive.

His nationalism, at a time when Canada was facing a crisis of possible separation of Quebec from the rest of the country, was questioned. And yet, it was Mario who scored one of the most famous goals for Team Canada, winning the 1987 Canada Cup final against the Soviets.

His leadership was questioned. And yet, it was Mario, once the Penguins had built a solid supporting cast around him, including goaltender Tom Barrasso and winger Jaromir Jagr (debuted in 1990), who led the Penguins to consecutive cup victories in 1991 and 1992.

His courage was questioned. And yet, it was Mario who kept playing through horrible back injuries, and, in January 1993, when it was announced he had been diagnosed with Hodgkin's Disease, a form of cancer that kept him out two months for radiation treatment, who came back and won the scoring championship anyway.

He would miss the following season due to the effects of the cancer therapy.

And, after he retired in 1997, it would be Mario, owed $40-million himself in deferred payments, who would rescue the bankrupt Penguins by putting together an ownership group by himself and becoming the team president in 1999.

What more could the guy have done?

What more? How about an unbelievable comeback, rumored during the fall of 2000 and come to fruition in early January 2001. In just 43 games, Lemieux scored 35 times, added 41 assists for 76 points, was a plus-15 (goals on the ice for versus goals on the ice against), and played just under 25 minutes a game.

The NHL was so thrilled to have him back (ticket sales went through the roof in Pittsburgh, and he drew thousands more a game while on the road) they even relaxed rules against a team owner also being a player. The player-owner hadn't been seen since the old days of the Patrick brothers and the Pacific Coast Hockey Association. And Lemieux was planning on playing at least until 2003.

The Hunt for Reds by October

With Swedes, Finns, Czechs, and Americans now a regular feature of the NHL, there remained one group still to be heard from—the Soviets. Before the fall of the Iron Curtain in 1990, Soviet players had been effectively banned from playing in the league by their Communist rulers.

Some had gotten through. Viktor Nechayev was the first Soviet in the league, 1982–1983, allowed to come to North America because he had married an American woman, and because he wasn't very good. He had a quick three-game career with Los Angeles.

Calgary signed Sergei Priakin, another second-rate Soviet, in 1988, and rumors abounded that the Iron Curtain might be drawn back a bit to allow more veteran (meaning aging) players to come to the NHL.

That turned out to be true as Glasnost hit the hockey world in October 1989, when Vladimir Krutov, Igor Larionov, and Sergei Makarov (together the KLM line of Soviet fame) and defensemen Viacheslav Fetisov and Alexei Kasatonov all made their league debuts, the first two with Vancouver, Makarov with Calgary, and the last two with New Jersey.

Just months after that, the Berlin Wall fell and communism in the Soviet Union went as well as most of the states that made up the block declared independence.

The flood from Europe was set to turn into a deluge.

Great Games

April 18, 1987: Capital Center, Landover, Maryland

The New York Islanders and Washington Capitals couldn't decide game seven of their Patrick Division semi-final in regulation so they went to overtime. The Capitals dominated much of the play in the extra time, forcing Kelly Hrudey of the Islanders to make 73 total saves during the game. But it was the Islanders, on a shot by Pat Lafontaine that beat Bob Mason at 68:47 of overtime, that won it for New York.

New York Islanders 3, Washington Capitals 2

The End of the Old Guard

At the start of the 1992 season, something significant happened. Three events that in themselves were important had come together in the previous months to alter the power structure of the NHL in totality.

John Ziegler, who had been chosen as successor to Clarence Campbell as league president and always seemed to have a hard ride of it, was replaced by Gil Stein, who himself would have a controversial short reign and step aside for Gary Bettman. Ziegler was best remembered for always seeming to be out of the country when something important happened, which came to a head during the "Donut Incident" of 1988.

During the playoffs of 1988, New Jersey coach Jim Schoenfeld got into a huge argument with referee Don Koharski after a game with Boston, starting when the coach followed the official down the hall to the ref's dressing room. Schoenfeld yelled at Koharski: "Why don't you have another donut, you fat pig."

That cost him a game suspension that the Devils went to court to temporarily restrain, which in turn sent the referees into a tizzy. They refused to work the next game at the last minute and fill-ins from local college and minor ranks were found in New Jersey.

Because the linesmen had to wear yellow practice jerseys for the first period until proper striped shirts were found, writes Gary Mason, the night was forever known as Yellow Sunday.

Ziegler was nowhere to be found again (though to be fair, he was dealing with serious family business at the time—something that was never reported), and that made the board of governors angry enough to start thinking of a replacement.

Aw, I Knew That!

Q. The 210th player chosen in the 1975 amateur draft would go on to score 431 goals in 1,111 NHL games up to his retirement in 1994. Who was he?

A. Dave Taylor, 17 years with the Los Angeles Kings.

I Remember ...

Coach and humorist Harry Neale had his Vancouver Canucks in St. Louis in the late 1980s, where he had gotten to know the police officer who guarded the visitor's bench. Sending out the line of Stan Smyl, Thomas Gradin, and Curt Fraser to start the game, they instantly gave up a goal. On their next shift they gave up another goal. Neale quietly went to the security guard and talked him into giving up his revolver, which he then shoved right into Smyl's back, saying, "One more shift like that by you jerks and I'm using this on you!"

Then Bill Wirtz, who had been the doyen of league owners as the last of the old guard still standing, found himself on the outs. A new breed of owner, led by Kings' boss Bruce McNall (who himself would be on the outs by the end of the decade, as he found himself in jail for fraud), had grown tired of Wirtz' old ideas and helped remove him as head of the board of governors.

And then there was Eagleson. During the WHA days, Alan Eagleson had worked closely with the owners to come up with deals that would help protect jobs. They also helped limit free agency far longer than any other sports league. Eventually, the players became unhappy with what they saw as a too-friendly relationship with the owners and forced him to quit, replacing him in 1992 with Bob Goodenow.

R. Alan Eagleson, who had been so involved with international hockey for almost 30 years (more ahead), had a much larger indignity ahead of him.

Aw, I Knew That!

Q. They were called the Long Island Electrical Company, or the Trio Grande. Name them.

A. Bryan Trottier, Mike Bossy, and Clark Gillies.

Plucking the Eagle

This is a little more complicated than you might first think.

As Scott Morrison points out, there was a lot that R. Alan Eagleson did that worked out well for players and the NHL. He basically traded off free-agency rights to the owners in return for their co-operation with all the international ventures the league became involved in—1972 Summit Series, Canada Cups, and 1979 Challenge Cup—which then helped put money in the NHL players' association's retirement fund and opened up the league to European performers.

But there was something that wasn't right about the goings on, though no one could quite put a finger on it.

A succession of events came together to bring the Eagle down, and put him in jail.

➤ In 1980, Bobby Orr, Eagleson's, first client and the man with whom he built a reputation as an agent, fired him. It would turn out that Orr had retired basically penniless, and that the Eagle had purposely kept the details of an offer from the Bruins from his client in order to make sure he signed with Chicago.

➤ Later in the decade, a group of players hired Ed Garvey, formerly of the National Football League Players' Association, to look into Eagleson's dealings and write a report. It was damning, saying he hadn't done nearly what those in other sports had done to improve the players' lot in life.

➤ In November 1991, the FBI announced it was launching an investigation into financial conflicts of interest by Eagleson, and a month later he quit as head of the players' association.

➤ March 1994 found Eagleson indicted by a United States Grand Jury in Massachusetts for theft of union funds.

➤ In 1995, a group of former players launched a lawsuit in Philadelphia, basically charging the same thing.

111

➤ January 1998 found Eagleson agreeing to plead guilty in both Canada and the United States to fraud charges. He paid a $1 million fine and served five months in jail. The former tzar of hockey in North America also found himself kicked out of the Hockey Hall of Fame and Canada's Sports Hall of Fame.

The Eagle had turned into the man who fell to earth.

You Can't Get Me, I'm Part of the New Union

The players' association faced by the owners in 1991–1992 was a very different animal from the one the owners had been used to dealing with under Alan Eagleson. The players were angry and, in April of 1992, went on strike just days before the playoffs were to start.

Ten days later a deal was reached (better free agency, more control over licensing of the players' likenesses), and they went back to work. That was, by the way, the last of John Ziegler.

Round two came on October 1, 1994, when the owners hit back, locking out the players for 48 games, or 103 days, while everyone had a nice argument over unrestricted free agency, a salary cap, and a luxury tax (under which rich teams would have to pay a "tax" into a fund to help less-fortunate clubs for every dollar over a set spending cap). Finally, everyone called a halt, allowing hockey to avoid the mistake that baseball would make in missing an entire World Series.

Expanding the Waistline

Team movement and league expansion were other huge issues facing the league in the 1990s.

First in were the San Jose Sharks for 1991, inspired by the presence of Wayne Gretzky in California.

I Remember ...

In 1984, the desperate Vancouver Canucks hired junior hockey coach and inspirationalist Bill Laforge as their bench boss. After evening their season record at 1–1 with a win over Los Angeles, the players returned to the dressing room, where Laforge looked at Tony Tanti and Garth Butcher, two players he had coached before, and exhorted them to sing the fight song. Fight song? Dutifully, Butcher, and Tanti blared out, "We are Billy's Raiders ... Raiders of the Night ... All we want to do is shoot, skate, score, and fight ..." Goaltender John Garrett recalled years later that veteran Peter McNab looked at him and said: "I guess this is the NHL ..."

Then there were two surprise additions for 1992: the Tampa Bay Lightning and Ottawa Senators. Going to Florida certainly raised some eyebrows (the club was headed by Phil Esposito), but letting the Ottawa Senators back (the club had died in the 1930s) was even more surprising, as many had thought Hamilton, Ontario, would get the nod. The Sens had terrible ownership and arena problems in their early years that would finally be sorted out at the end of the century but not without a major heartache for Ottawa fans (more in a bit).

Next in were the Mighty Ducks of Anaheim (owned by Disney, named after a team in one of the company's movies) and the Florida Panthers (owned by Blockbuster Video), both for 1993. Big business was getting involved.

Gary Bettman was just warming up, but the next two "new" clubs were a surprise.

The truly unthinkable in Canada occurred in 1995 when the Quebec Nordiques, the most suffering of a group of teams north of the border under stress due to a rapidly falling Canadian dollar against the U.S. greenback, and aging arenas, finally gave up the ghost and moved to Colorado to become the Avalanche. Bad revenue streams, high taxes, and not enough support from the provincial government ended a proud franchise's run in Quebec.

One year later, the Winnipeg Jets, killed by the lockout, an old arena, and the dollar, joined them south of the border, this time in Phoenix.

Hartford's Whalers, tired of battling bad crowds in Connecticut, made their way to Carolina for 1997 as the Hurricanes.

And inspired by what some felt was an endless supply of good Europeans to fill out rosters, the league announced more expansion. The Atlanta Thrashers for 1999, to be followed a season later by the Columbus Blue Jackets and Minnesota Wild, the latter replacing the North Stars franchise that had moved to Dallas in 1993.

Too many teams, not enough good players, said many critics. But hey, those franchise fees looked good in the pocketbook.

L'Affaire Lindros

"It never ends, does it?"

That's what Eric Lindros said to a reporter following his successful defense of assault charges in 1992 stemming from an incident in an Ontario bar.

And it was true. But also true was that the bad publicity and difficulties of the big, rangy center many thought would be the next superstar had been going on for some years, much of it self-inflicted.

Aw, I Knew That!

Q. Who was the last on-ice official who had worked in the Original Six era to retire from the game?

A. Linesman John D'Amico, retired in March 1988.

113

Much criticism was pointed toward Lindros' parents, Bonnie and Carl (especially Bonnie), for pushing Eric's (and to a lesser extent his talented younger brother Brett's) career ahead of any team goals or needs. When drafted by the Sault Ste. Marie (Ontario) Greyhounds of the Ontario (Major Junior) Hockey League, Eric refused to report, forcing a trade to the Oshawa Generals.

When taken first overall by the Quebec Nordiques (despite his agent's warning that he wouldn't report), Lindros refused to go, setting off what was called L'Affaire Lindros. He sat out the season, playing in the 1992 Olympics for Canada.

Eventually Lindros was traded to Philadelphia, giving the Nords some key players in what would be a Stanley Cup victory (after they moved to Colorado). Lindros, big, a pure scorer, fearless with his body, could not lead the Flyers to the cup.

By the end of the decade, Bob Clarke, the Flyers' GM, and Carl Lindros, now Eric's agent, weren't talking, Eric was suffering from back problems and consecutive concussions (concussions had ended Brett's career with the New York Islanders at just 20), and more trouble was ahead.

A misdiagnosed concussion by the Flyers' training staff in 2000 led to a huge argument, accusations back and forth, Clarke stripping Lindros of the captain's C, and both sides at an impasse. Lindros missed most of the playoffs due to the effects of his concussions. He returned for game five of the conference finals and played well, but early in game six, Lindros took a jarring check (shoulder to head) from New Jersey defenseman Scott Stevens and went down, and out.

Speculation ran rampant that the big one's career was over, but all during the following season, 2000–2001, rumors swirled about a pending trade of Lindros. Toronto was where he wanted to go and a deal seemed to be set, but it fell through at the last minute. With Lindros' people limiting the teams Clarke could trade the player to and the Flyers' GM balking unless something good came back in return, the situation was still at an impasse by the summer of 2001.

Wayne Says Good-Bye

Wayne Gretzky skated off the ice at Madison Square Garden as a New York Ranger, and into hockey history, on April 18, 1999, following the final game of his twenty-first season. Injuries, doubts about his own ability, awareness that time was marching on, sick of flying (which he'd always hated)—it was time to say good-bye.

Over and over in his press conference he said, "I'm done," as though to convince us and himself.

The NHL immediately retired the number 99 permanently—no one would wear it again. And the Hockey Hall of Fame waived the waiting period for getting in and inducted him on November 22, 1999.

After a year in retirement, Gretzky announced he was getting involved again, this time as a part owner of the Phoenix Coyotes. The details of the club's sale took almost an entire season to work out, but in 2001, Gretzky began to exert his influence on hockey in the desert, firing general manager Bobby Smith and hiring Cliff Fletcher. He also accepted a job as general manager of Team Canada for the 2002 Olympics.

The Y2K Bug

Coming into the new century, the NHL had a lot going for it. There were stars from almost every hockey-playing nation on earth in the league: Brett Hull of the United States was closing in on his father's 608 goals for a career and would pass it in the spring of 2000; Jaromir Jagr and goaltender Dominik Hasek of the Czech Republic were among the best ever to play in the NHL; Russian brothers Pavel Bure, of Florida, and Valeri Bure, of Calgary, were both in the top 10 in scoring; the Slovak trio of Pavol Demitra, Michal Handzus, and Lubos Bartecko helped St. Louis to its greatest regular season ever; Nicklas Lidstrom of Detroit had an all-star year and was a finalist for the Norris trophy; Teemu Selanne had another 40+ goal season; and despite changing demographics, Canadian stars were still everywhere, including Paul Kariya, Chris Pronger (the league MVP), and Al MacInnis.

Aw, I Knew That!

Q. Coach Roger Neilson was head coach for seven teams in his NHL career, up to the year 2000. Name them, in order.

A. Toronto, Buffalo, Vancouver, Los Angeles, New York Rangers, Florida, and Philadelphia.

Hockey had made it into the U.S. Southeast, South Central, and Far West, and seemed set to stay around. A new television deal with ABC in the United States seemed to indicate even better days.

But bad things seemed to follow the league around in the 1999–2000 season:

➤ Ottawa captain Alexei Yashin, who had already held the Senators up for more money once, refused to play without a bigger contract. Senators' owner Rod Bryden refused to buckle and Yashin sat out the season, losing millions of dollars in contract money. The Sens went to court to challenge whether Yashin owed them another year on the contract in what could be a precedent-setting case for all sports. Yashin lost the case, and things were left up in the air: Would he play? Would he be traded?

➤ Canadian teams, especially Ottawa, were hoping for federal tax breaks and money help, and looked like they had it when the federal government announced such a package, which was then met with such a negative stream of publicity and public anger that the feds reversed themselves a few days later and withdrew the package.

➤ Marty McSorley clubbed Donald Brashear of Vancouver across the temple with his stick, putting the victim out for the rest of the season and earning the Boston winger a suspension for the rest of the year, a big fine, and an arrest by Vancouver authorities for assault. He was found guilty of assault and given a suspended sentence with a conditional discharge.

➤ Just a week later, Scott Niedermayer of New Jersey hit Florida's Peter Worrell over the head with his stick and got 10 games. Both incidents created a slew of bad publicity for the league.

➤ Bryan Berard of Toronto was accidentally hit in the eye by a wild follow-through from Ottawa's Marian Hossa and stood to lose his sight on the right side. He faced a future of operations and little hope for continuing his career. That brought the debate about facial shields back into the open. At the time of the injury about 10 percent of the league's players wore the protection.

➤ The Lindros affair near the end of the season brought more bad publicity.

While the league itself might not have been in trouble, the future looked cloudy for a number of teams, and the NHL, wanting good publicity especially in the United States, found itself in the sports news for many of the wrong reasons.

Stars of the Era

➤ Wayne Gretzky broke every offensive mark in the books during his 21 years in the league. Scored 50 or more goals 9 times, better than 100 assists 11 times, and won the Hart Trophy as most valuable player 9 times. Won four Stanley Cups.

➤ Mario Lemieux played just 12 seasons but scored 613 times, had better than 50 in a year six times and won 2 Stanley Cups. Missed a full season while recovering from Hodgkin's Disease.

➤ Brent, Brian, Darryl, Duane, Rich, and Ron Sutter set a mark that may never be broken—six brothers from Viking, Alberta, who all had long careers in the NHL. Brent had the most goals at 363 and the most points at 829. All had at least 100 goals in their career and between them piled up 77 seasons in the league. Twins Ron and Rich were the youngest.

➤ Joe Mullen, who, like his brother Brian, was a product of early playground roller hockey games in New York City, became the first American to score 500 goals in a career, reaching the mark in his final season, 1996–1997. He played 18 seasons in the league and won 3 Stanley Cups. He also represented the United States three times in Canada Cup tournaments.

➤ Scotty Bowman, the winningest coach in NHL history, passed the 1,000-victory mark in 1997 while at the helm of the Detroit Red Wings. Won five Stanley Cups with Montreal, one with Pittsburgh while filling in for Bob Johnson (who died shortly after the 1991 season) and two more and counting with the Wings.

➤ Jaromir Jagr came into the league in 1990 and scored more than 300 times up to the turn of the century. Dogged by injuries in later years, he was considered the best player in hockey in 1995–1996 when he compiled 149 points. Helped lead the Czech Republic to the Olympic gold medal in 1998.

➤ Mark Messier, the son of a minor leaguer, joined the WHA at 17 and went to the Edmonton Oilers at 18. Scored over 600 times in his career, winning 6 cups, including the 1994 victory in New York that ended the Rangers' 54-year championship drought. Was still going, with the Rangers, in 2000.

➤ Raymond Bourque played 20 loyal seasons as a defenseman for the Boston Bruins and was almost through his tenty-first when the club unloaded him to the Colorado Avalanche. With 400 goals and more than 12 times a first-team all-star, Bourque finally got what he really wanted—a Stanley Cup—in the spring of 2001.

➤ Jari Kurri's 601 goals over a 17-year career left him tops among European players in NHL history. As Wayne Gretzky's right winger, he won four Stanley Cups in Edmonton and then one more after The Great One had been traded to Los Angeles.

➤ Goaltender Dominik "The Dominator" Hasek won two Hart Trophies as the Most Valuable Player in the NHL, making him the first goalie to win even one since Jacques Plante in 1962. He also led the Czech Republic to the gold medal at the 1998 Winter Olympics in Nagano.

Stanley Cup Winners of the Era

1980–1981	New York Islanders
1981–1982	New York Islanders
1982–1983	New York Islanders
1983–1984	Edmonton Oilers
1984–1985	Edmonton Oilers
1985–1986	Montreal Canadiens
1986–1987	Edmonton Oilers
1987–1988	Edmonton Oilers
1988–1989	Calgary Flames
1989–1990	Edmonton Oilers
1990–1991	Pittsburgh Penguins
1991–1992	Pittsburgh Penguins
1992–1993	Montreal Canadiens
1993–1994	New York Rangers
1994–1995	New Jersey Devils
1995–1996	Colorado Rockies
1996–1997	Detroit Red Wings
1997–1998	Detroit Red Wings
1998–1999	Dallas Stars
1999–2000	New Jersey Devils

The Least You Need to Know

➤ The New York Islanders and the Edmonton Oilers dominated the 1980s.

➤ Wayne Gretzky dominated most of the era.

➤ The NHL added eight teams through expansion.

➤ Two Canadian teams moved to U.S. cities.

➤ Europeans and Americans began to come into the league in huge numbers.

➤ Soviet players made their appearance.

➤ Alan Eagleson fell from grace.

➤ The owners and the players' union had one short battle and one very long one.

Part 3

International Incidents

International hockey started, of course, in Europe, where national teams began playing each other shortly after the start of the twentieth century. Part of that was a result of needing more competition and part because everyone lives on each other's doorsteps on the European continent, so putting together an all-star national club to play someone else is no big deal. The really big deal early on, however, was to convince the North Americans (especially Canadians) to jump on board and come play. For many years it was no contest, but inspired by the quality of the Canadian play, European teams gradually improved until they could challenge the best from across the pond. Canada would no longer have its way with those in the "old country," nor, for that matter, would it with the United States. Through the Olympics, world championships, special series, Canada Cups, and the first World Cups, hockey spread its wings far and wide. Two incidents, however, would have special significance—one in 1972 and the other in 1980.

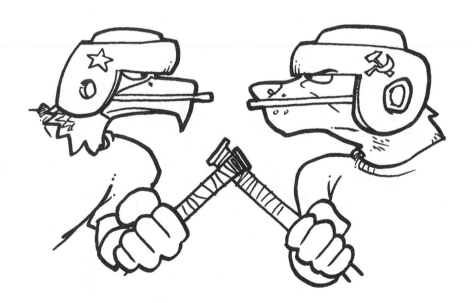

Olympic Hockey (Men's Division)

The Olympic hockey tournament began in 1920 before there was an official Winter Olympics, which was four years away. Instead, the tournament was played in the spring as an "attachment" to the Summer Games. Canada dominated the Olympics from the first puck, losing the gold medal only once before the Second World War, despite sending senior amateur teams—meaning less-than-the-best players in the country. In the post-war period, a ragtag bunch of "amateurs" out of the Soviet Union turned the hockey world on its ear for 30 years, stopped only by a pair of improbable American entries. Finally, the Olympic tournament would open itself to "professional" players, and then to National Hockey Leaguers. And a surprise winner would emerge from the pack. In this chapter, we'll look at these developments.

A Tournament Takes Flight

On April 3, 1920, a group of young men from Winnipeg, Manitoba, known as the Falcons boarded a ship and headed for Antwerp, Belgium, to help make a little history.

They packed everything they needed for the trip, forgetting only one thing: their sticks. Undaunted, the Falcons got the ship's carpenter to make them 20 out of some wood bought in Montreal (couldn't they have just bought some sticks at a sports store?) and took off on a jaunt that for many years would be looked at as simply a free trip to Europe for a little fun.

Aw, I Knew That!

Q. Who refereed the first-ever Olympic hockey game, in 1920 between Sweden and Belgium?

A. W. A. Hewitt, the father of Canadian hockey broadcasting icon Foster Hewitt.

In 1920, seven teams had been lined up: Belgium, Canada, Czechoslovakia (formerly Bohemia, and still Europe's best club), France, Sweden, Switzerland, and the United States (led by star, Frank "Moose" Goheen).

Some of the scores were a little embarrassing, to say the least. Canada beat the Czechs 15–0 and the Swedes 12–1. The United States skated Olympic rings around the Swiss, 29–0. Wow.

Against each other, it was a somewhat different story. Canada needed second-period goals by Frank Fredrickson and Connie Johannesson to subdue a competitive "American" club that had been put together as a combination of Americans in college programs and Canadians playing in U.S. towns.

Canada won the first four tournaments, but through it all there were indications that all would not go as planned forever.

This Time, for Real

The first true Winter Games (called the International Week of Winter Sport, until the IOC recognized it a year later as the first Olympics) were held in 1924 at Chamonix, France, with eight teams on hand to drop the official puck: Canada, United States, Great Britain, Sweden, Czechoslovakia, France, Belgium, and Switzerland.

Canada, represented by the Toronto Granites, won the tournament, played, as Andrew Podnieks points out, on a European-sized rink for the first time—longer and much wider than what North Americans were used to, which, in turn, called for a more wide-open style of play. The Granites, led by future NHL stars Dunc Munro and Hooley Smith, scored 110 goals in 5 games, still a record.

No other country could match them, not even the United States (with future NHLers Taffy Abel and Herb Drury in the lineup) could put up much of a fight, losing 6–1 in the gold medal game.

Thanks for Nothing, General

Money, or the lack of it, reared its ugly nose in 1928 when none other than General Douglas MacArthur, then head of the United States Olympic Committee, refused to let Augsburg College of Minnesota represent the country in hockey (no one else could raise the money to send an all-star club or another college club) because, writes Donald Clark quoted by Kevin Allen, it "was not representative of American hockey."

Great. The only country with even the remotest chance to heading off the Canadian juggernaut didn't go, and the boys from up north, represented by the University of Toronto Varsity Grads (coached by none other than Conn Smythe, who would run the Toronto Maple Leafs for over 40 years), walloped everybody by outscoring three opposition outfits 38–0 in the medal round.

Three in a row for Canada.

Aw, I Knew That!

Q. Who was the first goaltender in Olympic history to wear a mask?

A. Frank Farrell of the United States, 1932. He also wore glasses.

Almost Not Worth the Effort

The Depression hit worldwide in 1929, and by the time the youth of the world attempted to reconvene at Lake Placid, New York, on February 4, 1932, much of that youth was spending most of its time trying to figure out how to eat, let alone get to the United States. As a result, only four clubs competed in the Olympics: Canada, United States, Germany, and Poland.

The Canadians and the Americans picked this time to start a big row over eligibility that saw the Canucks accuse the Yankees of taking gate receipts from an exhibition game with the Boston Bruins of the NHL, in violation of Olympic rules. Canada didn't launch an official protest, however, and won the tournament again.

Actually, the Canadians had missed the real violation—the United States had sent professionals as part of their 1924 and 1928 teams, and it took an American journalist to admit it.

Missed that one.

The real big news in these Games was a 2–2 tie between Canada and the United States. The Canadians had been blooded for the first time.

Rule Britannia! (Sort Of)

The 1936 Games, in Garmisch-Partenkirchen, Germany (where "dogs and jews were not allowed"—how could the world have missed the signals the Nazis were putting up?), presented the largest contingent of countries yet: 15.

To make matters short, the British and Canadians got into a big argument over all the "ex-Canadians" in the British lineup, and two especially, whom Canada said were professionals. Those two were kicked out.

The Brits, fuming (and no one fumed more than one Bunny Ahearne: more on him later in this chapter, and in Chapter 12), went out and handed Canada its first loss, 2–1, and eventually took the gold after a very late rule change (pushed by Mr. Ahearne) that allowed the British to carry that win into the final round, even though originally the rules said no. The United States finished third with a win, loss, and tie in the medal round, losing 1–0 to Canada and tying the British 0–0.

Oh well, there was always 1940 in Germany. Unfortunately, the only view Canadian and American players might have had of that country from 1939–1945 would have been looking down from a bomber.

Flying in the Face of Logic

Canada, represented by the Royal Canadian Air Force Flyers, won the 1948 tournament in St. Moritz (Canada, Czechoslovakia, Switzerland, Sweden, Great Britain, Poland, Austria, Italy), but the best story revolved around the American team. Or both teams.

It was around this time that the new Amateur Hockey Association of the United States (AHAUS) organized, and that group took it upon itself to send a team to Switzerland for the Olympics, which made two clubs with USA emblazoned on their sweaters, because the Amateur Athletic Union (AAU) had already sent one, with the support of the U.S. Olympic Committee (USOC).

Except the International Ice Hockey Federation (IIHF) told the USOC and the AAU that the AHAUS club (which, by the way, had pros on it) was the recognized entity and if the USA didn't want to see the whole Olympic hockey tournament cancelled, they'd get in line PDQ.

So basically, the AAU and USOC were SOL. Except, after a protracted fight, the Americans played the tournament (that's the AHAUS team) as an "unofficial" entry. So the United States finished nowhere.

Enter a New Challenger

Sweden was a latecomer to ice hockey, having been reluctant to abandon its love affair with bandy—a love that would never really be completely expunged.

In 1952, the United States thought they had a team that could challenge Canada (the Edmonton Mercurys) for the gold medal. And indeed, they tied the Canadians 1–1 and finished with the silver. Minor miscalculation, however: The Swedes, led by Hans Oberg, Lars Pettersson, and a bunch of terrific skating teammates (the bandy influence), beat the United States 4–2 on February 21, taking away any gold medal chance for the Americans.

This same Swedish team had lost to Canada just 3–2 one day later, and it finished with the bronze medal after a special extra game with Czechoslovakia to break a deadlock.

First Soaking from a Red Tide

The Canadians (Kitchener-Waterloo Dutchmen), the Americans, the Swedes, and the Czechs all went to the 1956 Olympics in Cortina d'Ampezzo, Italy, thinking they had a team good enough to win the gold. None of them did.

Back in 1954, the Soviet Union, which hadn't really picked up on hockey until after the war, entered the world championships for the first time and destroyed the Canadians 7–2 to take the gold.

Had to be a fluke. Canada had won 5–0 a year later.

But it was no fluke.

The Soviets won both their preliminary round games and went 5–0 in the medal round, scoring 25 times and giving up just five games for the gold (see Chapter 16, "Teachings from the Tsar [1946–September 1972]").

The United States, thanks to a 4–1 victory over Canada in which it was outshot, won the silver, and Canada the bronze.

Everyone expected 1960 to be more of the same.

Everyone except an American coach named Jack Riley.

Quote, Unquote

"There is one area where the Russians have shown results bordering on the impossible and that area is ice hockey."

—*The New York Times*, 1956.

Call It a Minor Miracle on Ice

Kevin Allen, in *USA Hockey,* calls the 1960 U.S. hockey team's gold medal triumph "The First Miracle on Ice."

Perhaps. But when you take a look at the American lineup that year—the Cleary brothers (Bill and Bob), the Christian brothers (Roger and Bill), Tommy Williams (who would, in the mid-1960s, be the only American in the NHL), and goaltender Jack McCartan (who played two seasons for the New York Rangers at a time when the six National League clubs only used one goalie), among others, there was a lot of talent there.

And a lot of leadership—there were six players on the club who had played in the 1956 Games, and they had a determined, highly organized coach in Jack Riley.

This is the way it came down: The United States beat Canada 2–1 on February 25 on the outdoor rink at Squaw Valley, California, which was a big upset. Then they knocked off the Soviets 3–2, in another big upset. Then, in the game they needed for the gold, the Americans finally found the killer touch, exploding in the third period to come from behind and beat the Czechs 9–4.

Gold, finally, after 40 years of trying.

I Remember ...

One of the most famous stories to come out of the 1960 Games involved Soviet captain Nikolai Sologubov, who visited the U.S. dressing room when the club trailed 4–3 to the Czechs after two periods. Using hand signals, he got across the idea that the players should take oxygen before the third period. Eight of them did, and whether it really helped or not (Roger Christian didn't, and he scored three times in the third), it was a heck of a sportsmanlike gesture at a time when the Cold War was at its height.

Who's an Amateur?

The next two golds would go to the Soviets, with Sweden and Czechoslovakia in silver and bronze spots at Innsbruck in 1964, and the Soviets again, with the Czechs and Canadians behind them in 1968. The United States would be fifth and sixth, respectively.

For Canada, it was a fine achievement because the "amateurs" in Europe were beginning to put distance on the real amateurs from North America. Father David Bauer established a program at the University of British Columbia that would keep the team together for two years before each Olympics and give it a chance to gel while the players were attending school (on scholarships, by the way, which, technically, made them no longer amateurs).

I Remember ...

Psychological warfare has always been as important in Czech-Soviet/Russian games as scoring goals. In 1968 at Grenoble, the two teams were ready for their round robin game when the Czechs drew the referees' attention to the fact that seven Russians didn't have the required protective covering on the back of their skates. With none to be had, the Russians began calling around the rink looking for some, which were eventually provided by the Norwegian speed skating team that had come to the game to watch. Everything was delayed for 45 minutes and the Soviets were completely thrown off—especially goaltender Viktor Konovalenko. The Czechs then went out and won the game 5–4.

Canada should have had the bronze in 1964, but some trickery by Bunny Ahearne (again) changed the scheme for tie breaking while the third period of Canada's last game was still going on.

The bronze came in 1968.

Meanwhile, a much bigger controversy was brewing as the Canadians had had enough of losing big-time to the Soviets and Czechs, whom they knew (because a couple of Czechs had told them) were being paid to play—team members were ostensibly given jobs or put in the army, but they were really there for the hockey.

Canada sent an ultimatum to the IIHF—let us use our pros (minor leaguers, really, since the NHL wasn't going to shut down in the middle of the season) against your "amateurs" or we won't play. The IIHF called what they thought was a bluff, and Canada pulled out and would remain out for two Olympics.

An Incomplete Tournament

But the Olympic tournaments would go on. In 1972 at Sapporo, Japan, the Soviets won again, but this time the silver went to a courageous bunch of American college players and juniors. Led by Robbie Ftorek, Mark Howe, Henry Boucha (a Minnesota high-school star now in college), and Ron Naslund, they lost to the Soviets but beat the Czechs for second place.

But there were mumbles in the European fraternity that it would be nice to have Canada back.

Great Games

1976 gold medal game: Soviet Union vs. Czechoslovakia

The Olympics' greatest modern rivalry came down to one game for all the marbles, and the Czechs came out flying, building a 2–0 lead that they took into the middle of the second period. It looked like they could put the hated Big Red Machine away when the Soviets took two penalties in a row and the Czechs had a five-on-three advantage. But the Soviets didn't allow a shot on goal during the power play and then went about tying things up 2–2. The Czechs again went ahead, but back came the Red Machine, scoring to tie the game with 5 minutes left and getting the winner just 24 seconds after that.

Soviet Union 4, Czechoslovakia 3

In 1976, at Innsbruck, Austria, both Canada and the Swedes refused to play and the Soviets won again. Hockey was passing the Olympics by, especially with the success of the 1972

Soviet-Canada Summit Series, the 1974 Soviet-Canada Summit Series II, and with the upcoming inaugural Canada Cup, all of which would pit pros against pros.

But people were getting bored.

Gunther's Realm

In 1976, the International Ice Hockey Federation had a new boss in Dr. Gunther Sabetski, a forward thinker who had none of the backroom stench on him that Bunny Ahearne had carried for 40 years.

He set out immediately to get Canada back into the fold (and Sweden back on board), and before long he had worked out an agreement that would see NHLers eliminated from the playoffs eligible for world championships, and any pro reestablished as an amateur allowed into the Olympics.

Okay, we know, how can you ever be a virgin again? But at least they had a deal.

Aw, I Knew That!

Q. What assistant coach with the Canadian Olympic team in 1984 moved to the NHL as a head coach and won a Stanley Cup in his first year?

A. Jean Perron, Montreal Canadiens.

Surely something better would come out of the 1980 Games in Lake Placid, New York?

1980

Nothing much of importance happened in 1980. Twelve teams competed in the hockey tournament: Canada and the Swedes were back in; a few pros found their way into clubs; the Soviets looked unbeatable, coached by Viktor Tikhonov.

Oh, and the Americans upset the Russian bear on the way to winning the gold medal in what's now called the Miracle on Ice.

Pretty dull, really.

(See Chapter 14, "A Huge Upset on Ice.")

The End of the Red Menace

Over the next three Olympics, the Soviet Union would win two golds as themselves, one while masquerading as the Unified Team, and then exit the stage forever with the breakup of the USSR and the fall of the Berlin Wall.

The 1984 Games, in Sarajevo, Yugoslavia, saw a return to the old-time fights between Canada and the United States over eligibility. It was understood through the IOC that any players with 10 games or less NHL experience would be eligible to play. The Americans (and sorry, American readers, but this is a U.S. squad that had used pros for years back in the early days) claimed no pros should be allowed to play at all, and it started a huge fight—the Americans going so far as to threaten to remove the U.S. college scholarship of any player on the Canadian team who was registered with the National

Collegiate Athletic Association. Hockey Canada retorted by saying it would guarantee the scholar-ship money of any of its players so affected.

Nasty.

Under relentless American attack, the IOC reversed itself and declared that anyone with even one game NHL experience was ineligible. As Andrew Podnieks points out, that meant the Olympics were open to anyone who had played pro in the World Hockey Association or any of the high minor leagues. But not the NHL. Rick Cunning-ham, with 300 games in the WHA, was eligible.

Nuts.

Canada, angry, went out and beat the United States, 4–2, in the first game of the tournament and the Americans wound up seventh, a position they would follow up by taking seventh in 1988, fourth in 1992, and a humiliating eighth in 1994. The hockey gods were not happy.

The Soviets, by far the dominant team, beat the Czechs 2–0 on the final day to win the gold.

Alberta Bound

The Winter Olympics went to Calgary, Alberta, in 1988, where the Canadians were under a lot of pressure to do as well in front of their home fans as the Americans had done in front of theirs in both 1960 and 1980.

Sabetzki had announced two years earlier that all pros would be eligible, but that didn't mean the NHL was about to let everyone go. Actually, they let only a few fringe players go. But that didn't stop, for example, those in contract disputes with NHL teams from showing up. Enter goaltender Andy Moog, who was at an impasse with the Edmonton Oilers. Or Dr. Randy Gregg leaving the same team for a sabbatical. Seven NHLers, mostly third-stringers, played for Canada, which didn't help as much as everyone hoped because Canada was fourth behind the Soviets, Finland, and Sweden.

Two in Two

The IOC wanted to separate the Winter and Summer Games from each other, so in 1992 it declared that a special 1994 version of the winter festivity would be held.

Quote, Unquote

"The difference between a professional and amateur is not whether you're paid a salary, but whether you're paid a big or small salary."

—Carey Wilson, Canadian forward, on the 1984 dispute over the eligibility of pros.

Quote, Unquote

"Some of my players have told me they're surprised they don't have to show their passes at the blue-line when they backcheck."

—Simon Schenk, Swiss coach, on the tight security at the 1988 Games in Calgary.

129

In 1992, Albertville saw a strange hybrid from the now-broken-up Soviet Union—Team Unified, which basically meant Russia and most of the former Soviet states. No logo on the uniforms. No flag. No national anthem.

And they won anyway.

Canada had all sorts of disaffected NHLers, including goaltender Sean Burke and a young forward named Eric Lindros, who refused to report to the Quebec Nordiques, the team that drafted him (see Chapter 10, "Wayne, Mario, and a New Reality [1980–2001]"). The United States had an excellent club as well, including current or future NHLers Joe Sacco, Keith Tkachuk, Scott Young, Ted Donato, and Scott Lachance.

Great Games

1992 Quarterfinals: Canada vs. Germany

Canada was expected to destroy the Germans and sail on into the semi-finals at Albertville, but someone forgot to send the script to the Germans. Jurgen Rumrich and Dieter Hegen scored in the first to give the Germans a 2–1 lead into the break, but when Canada scored once in the second and late in the third, it looked like the Canadians were on their way. The Germans had one more miracle up their sleeves however, which they used when Ernst Kopf tied it at 17:38. It stayed tied through overtime, and it took to the second round of the shootout before Eric Lindros scored for Canada and Peter Draisaitl couldn't beat Sean Burke. It was almost as big an upset as the United States over the Soviets in 1980.

Canada 4, Germany 3

The United States would lose to the Unified Team 5–2 in the semi-finals, while Canada went down to them 3–1 in the final (a one-game-and-out playoff formula had been adopted).

And then there was 1994, in Lillehammer, Norway. And how Swede it was for the Tre Kroner, winners of their first gold medal in the most exciting possible way. Canada, with a much younger team than two years before, shone, while the United States, also young, struggled and wound up eighth.

It was Sweden, made up of former NHL stars like Hakan Loob and Mats Naslund, future NHL stars like Peter Forsberg, and excellent fill-ins from the domestic league, that left everyone breathless.

Canada and Sweden were tied after regulation in the gold medal game, and overtime couldn't decide it. So it went to a shootout for the big prize. And that required a second round of shooters before Forsberg beat Corey Hirsch on Sweden's seventh shot and Tommy Salo stopped young Paul Kariya on Canada's next try.

A gold medal decided on a shootout. Traditionalists fell over in a dead faint.

The Shadow of the Dominator

Hoo boy. 1998. NHLers all around as the league shut down for two weeks to send everyone to Nagano. The best of the best. Canada and the United States in a possible gold medal showdown. Wayne Gretzky vs. the World. Bring it on.

Things, however, did not go as planned—unless you happened to be living near Wenceslas Square in Prague.

The United States, with such stars as Brett Hull and Chris Chelios in the lineup, exited early. Not content to just let their humiliation lie, a small group of Americans trashed their room in the Olympic Village, nearly setting off an international incident.

Canada, meanwhile, marched into the semi-final with the Czech Republic and was stoned by goaltender Dominik Hasek of the Buffalo Sabres, who held the fort in the shootout and took the underdogs into the final with the Russians, where they pulled off the upset and set off a huge celebration in the aforementioned Wenceslas Square.

Things hadn't worked out the way the NHL had hoped, either, especially with television ratings (bad time zone problem) and with the Americans' poor sportsmanship.

Aw, I Knew That!

Q. The Unified Team won gold in the 1992 Games with a six-man defense, all of whom went on to become NHL regulars. Name them.

A. Alexei Zhitnik, Sergei Zubov, Dimitry Yushkevich, Dmitri Mironov, Igor Kravchuk, and Vladimir Malakhov.

Stars of the Era

➤ The Soviets' KLM line of Vladimir Krutov, Igor Larionov, and Sergei Makarov were arguably the best unit in the world during the 1980s. They played two Olympics together and eight in total, scoring 31 times and amassing 72 points.

➤ Terry O'Malley played defense for Canada in three Olympics—1964, 1968, and amazingly, 1980, appearing in 19 games and winning a bronze medal along the way.

➤ Jiri Holik made four Olympic appearances for Czechoslovakia, winning silver medals in 1968 and 1976, and bronzes in 1964 and 1972. The forward played 319 total games for the Czechs in Olympics and world championships, scoring 132 times.

➤ Bill Christian played in two Olympic Games for the United States, winning gold in 1960 and playing again in 1964. Scored the final two goals in the 3–2 win over the Soviet Union in 1960 to put the United States into the gold medal game.

➤ Forward Sven Tumba (formerly Sven Johansson), played in four Olympics for Sweden, winning a silver in 1964 and a bronze in 1952. Played 245 times for Tre Kronor, scoring 223 times. He also made one appearance on the national soccer team.

Men's Olympic Gold/Silver/Bronze Winners	
1920	Canada/United States/Czechoslovakia
1924	Canada/United States/Great Britain
1928	Canada/Sweden/Switzerland
1932	Canada/United States/Germany
1936	Great Britain/Canada/United States
1948	Canada/Czechoslovakia/Switzerland
1952	Canada/United States/Sweden
1956	Soviet Union/United States/Canada
1960	United States/Canada/Soviet Union
1964	Soviet Union/Sweden/Czechoslovakia
1968	Soviet Union/Czechoslovakia/Canada
1972	Soviet Union/United States/Czechoslovakia*
1976	Soviet Union/Czechoslovakia/West Germany*
1980	United States/Soviet Union/Sweden
1984	Soviet Union/Czechoslovakia/Sweden
1988	Soviet Union/Finland/Sweden
1992	Unified Team/Canada/Czechoslovakia
1994	Sweden/Canada/Finland
1998	Czech Republic/Russia/Finland

* Canada did not compete

The Least You Need to Know

➤ Canada dominated the Olympics up to 1956, winning all but one gold medal.

➤ The Soviets became the best club at the Games from 1956 on to 1992.

➤ The United States won two surprising gold medals in 1960 and 1980.

➤ Pros were finally let into the Games in the 1980s.

➤ The Czech Republic won the first Olympics at which all NHL players were available, in 1998.

Chapter 12

A Federation for the Worlds

In This Chapter

➤ Canada controls the action early

➤ One cocky Irishman

➤ The coming of the Soviet Machine

➤ Canada checks out

➤ Soviet–Czech hatred

➤ Canada comes back

➤ The loss of the talent base

The world championships would first be competed for in 1920 and be held bi-annually after that until 1930 and then every year from then to the end of the century, save for a break for World War II. In addition to good hockey, the worlds, and the politics surrounding them, also produced more bitter disputes than many of those seen in any boardroom, congress, or parliament across the globe. A lot of them revolved around a bantam-sized self-promoter from Ireland who became the bane of Canadian officials, especially. After years of Soviet domination in the 1960s, 1970s, and 1980s, professional players began to seep into the tournaments, changing the names engraved on the gold medals. At the same time, the importance of the worlds began to wane. In this chapter, we'll look at those issues.

Canada Leads Off

The first three world championships were really misnamed because the Olympic champions—that would be Canada—were automatically given the title by dint of winning the big gold medal.

It wasn't until 1930 that the world tournament was broken off from the Olympics and given status of its own (though the best European team in the world would also, quite often, wind up designated the continent's top club) when the International Ice Hockey Federation hosted 12 clubs in Chamonix, France, and, when the ice melted, in Berlin.

Canada, of course, represented each year by amateur club sides instead of a true national team, won that first title, as it did every title until 1936 (including the joined 1932 Olympic and world crowns). The exception was 1933, when the United States beat the Toronto Sea Fleas 2–1 in overtime.

Significant in that first tourney was the introduction of forward passing in the defensive zone, three 15-minute periods instead of two halves, and medals instead of certificates.

But the most significant event of this period was the introduction onto the scene of a man who would dominate world championship hockey in the boardroom for 40 years.

A Cocky Little Irish Conniver

That's what Canadian writer Jim Coleman called John Francis "Bunny" Ahearne, a former Merchant Marine radio operator, who, when he appeared on the scene in 1933, was the general secretary of the British Ice Hockey Federation. He also was the travel agent for Canadian teams tripping to Europe.

Aw, I Knew That!

Q. What team from a strong hockey country debuted in the world championships in 1939 but had to wait 56 years for its first gold medal?

A. Finland. Beat Sweden for the gold in 1995.

He was either loved (if his decisions supported your country) or hated (if his decisions went against you). But this Ahearne was no dumb bunny. He would eventually maneuver himself into position as the head of the IIHF and run it as a practical fiefdom until finally replaced by Gunther Sabetski in the 1970s.

Ahearne was "capable of acting unscrupulously in pursuit of his own advantage," wrote one observer.

In the battle of eligibility of British "Canadians" for the 1936 Olympics (see Chapter 11, "Olympic Hockey [Men's Division]"), Ahearne came out the winner, and he seemed determined to stick it to the Canadians, whom he blamed for the fight, at every opportunity.

He would convene meetings while the final stages of Olympic or world competitions were still being played, and make sure rules for determining winners and losers were changed to the disadvantage of Canada. He did it in 1936. He did it in 1948. He did it in 1964.

Ahearne also set himself up as arbiter of just what was an "amateur" and what wasn't. He fought bitterly against allowing Canadian or American pros into the worlds and Olympics in the 1960s and 1970s, precipitated the crisis that saw Canada withdraw from International Hockey for six years, starting in 1970, but seemed quite willing to turn a blind eye to the obviously professional players from the Soviet Union and Czechoslovakia.

It seemed that the thorn in Canada's side would grow endlessly through the years.

The European Fifth Column

The situation when the world championships were picked up again after the World War II was thus: Canada had won every time, except for the 1933 upset in the finals by the United States and the disputed 1936 Olympic loss to Great Britain.

In 1947, the hockey teams of the world got together in Czechoslovakia to rebuild what they once had. Some rule changes: Three 20-minute periods were brought in, the standard goal net of 4 feet by 6 feet was adopted, a goal line and center red line were introduced, and there would be no more 1- and 3-minute penalties.

Canada didn't send a team in 1947, and the fight between rival organizations over which had the right to send a team representing the United States that would keep the Americans out of the 1948 Olympics also kept it out of the worlds. The host Czechs won the tournament, and hockey was back in business on a world level.

That Czech team, by the way, would be wiped out in a tragic plane accident on November 8, 1948. The entire club died, including such stars as Zdenek Jarkovsky, Miloslav Pokorny, Vilibald Stovik, and Ladislav Trojak (see Chapter 18, "Tragedies and Triumphs—Czechoslovakia/Czech Republic/Slovakia").

Aw, I Knew That!

Q. Who was the longest-serving referee in world tournament history?

A. Jan Krasl of Czechoslovakia, who worked the games from 1933 to 1955.

The Ebb of One Red Tide, and the Rise of Another

For the next three years, it was Canada, still represented by amateur club teams rather than a national unit, that won the worlds, but the end of that country's ability to dominate proceedings with a second-rate club was on the horizon.

Not that the Canadians themselves were very happy. It cost a lot of money to send clubs, which invariably would play two dozen or more exhibition games (to full houses) before and after the world tournament, and officials felt they weren't getting any return on the investment because European promoters were keeping most of the profits.

So in 1953, Canada chose not to send a club in a sort of protest, while the United States also chose not to go, also for money reasons.

Point made, however, Canada and the United States returned in 1954 when it was expected the Canadians would get their title back.

Not this time. A new tide of red made its debut, and the world of international hockey underwent another huge change.

Tactics

When Canada flew through the 1954 qualifying round at 7–0, including an 8–0 victory over host Sweden, it looked as though the red and white, represented by the Toronto (East York) Lyndhursts, were back with a vengeance.

The Russian bear, however, had a little trick up its furry sleeve. Just as dominant in most of its games, the Soviet Union, coached by Boris Mjakinkov, tied the Swedes 1–1. Not as good as Canada, right?

Sure, but as observers at the time would realize, the Soviets held a lot back against Sweden to help lure the Canadians into a false sense of happy security. And then the bear pounced, whacking Canada 7–2 in the final.

Canadian fans were up in arms.

"Not since the Olympics of 1936 had there been a hockey defeat that cut so deeply into the Canadian psyche," wrote Jim Coleman.

Think about that. Canada sends a second-rate (by NHL standards) club to a championship it doesn't take that seriously and winds up losing when the opposition finally catches up in talent. And then they go nuts?

A little late, Canada.

Canada would win four more world titles up to 1961 (not in 1957, when the United States and Canada boycotted proceedings to protest the Soviet invasion of Hungary in 1956), and the Soviets, still sorting out the bugs of their late appearance on the hockey stage (see Chapter 16, "Teachings from the Tsar [1946–September 1972]"), but once.

The world, and the worlds, had changed, however, and the world championships were about to enter their most contentious, and potentially disastrous, decade and a half.

Aw, I Knew That!

Q. What playing-coach of Canada's 1961 world champion Trail Smoke Eaters went on to be coach of the year in both the NHL and WHA?

A. Bobby Kromm.

A Small Aside of Rules and Refs

By 1960, the differences between European hockey and North American hockey were readily apparent to anyone who watched both for a short period:

➤ The most obvious difference was the size of the rinks. An NHL rink was 200×85 feet, whereas an international one was 200×100. That changed the way the game was played—more wide open, play tended to go laterally across the ice rather than up and down, positioning was far more important, and skating and passing were at the top of the list of requirements for competitiveness. Also, the goal lines in Europe were somewhat farther out from the end boards, which gave more room behind the net in which to set up plays.

➤ Goaltenders changed ends at the 10-minute mark of the third period (that came from the need to resurface outdoor rinks more often than those indoor, and the tradition was kept even after arenas came into play), though to what advantage or disadvantage was open to argument.

➤ Starting in the 1960s, all players donned helmets, which was obviously a lot safer. That would lead to an interesting incident in 1977, when the NHLers who had missed the playoffs made their debut for Canada and the United States and were forced to wear helmets (almost none did regularly). Phil Esposito of Canada was so mad at the rule that after the last game he fired his helmet into the stands in the direction of the new IIHF president, Gunther Sabetski. The Canadian federal health minister was standing next to him, and she caught it. "Oh look," said Iona Campagnolo, "he threw me his helmet as a souvenir."

I Remember …

When the Penticton Vees won the world title in 1955, they took the tournament trophy home with them. Asked to return it 10 months later for the 1956 worlds, Grant, Bill, and Dick Warwick, members of the team, had a jeweller create a perfect copy and sent that back instead. According to Jim Coleman, for years the real trophy sat on display in an Edmonton restaurant before going into a safety-deposit vault, where it apparently still sits today. "We won that trophy from the Russians," said Bill, "and we were damned if we were going to give them another chance to hold it."

➤ Politics were a much bigger factor in international hockey, and not just in the board-rooms where Bunny Ahearne was running wild. Arguments over what country every-body from the referees to the goal judges to the scorekeepers were from were regular occurrences, especially in games involving Canada.

➤ The philosophy was so very different—Canadians, and Americans to a slightly lesser extent, finished their checks, played with physical abandon, and tended to hit every-thing that moved. Europeans tended to shy away from heavy checking (until the late 1960s, only defensive players in their own end were allowed to body check, and no one could hit someone else up against the boards), relying instead on set plays, pretty passing, and puck movement. European fans and the press would regularly hammer away at the North Americans for their "goon" tactics. They weren't dirty, said the Canadians, they were tough, and there was a big difference between the two.

➤ And then there were the referees themselves. From the time the first puck was dropped in 1920 until, say, last week, refereeing has been the most contentious issue in any international tournament involving North American teams, and espe-cially Canadians. The refs can't skate, complained the Canadians. (Too right, said the IIHF, and much work was done to improve that.) The refs don't understand the difference between tough hockey and dirty hockey. (In our hockey here, said European teams, what you do is dirty.) European teams classically slash, butt end, and even kick their opponents, and the refs don't do a thing. (What, who, us?) At major championships, there were as many arguments over who was going to referee a game (Canadians wanted an American, Americans wanted a Canadian, Europeans wanted anyone but a North American), as there were over the game itself.

Fifteen Years They'd Rather Forget

In 1962, a Canadian priest, Father David Bauer, followed up recommendations by the Canadian Amateur Hockey Association and put together the first truly national amateur program for that country. Based in British Columbia, the program kept players together for a year or two in hopes of closing the gap between Canada and the Soviet Union.

That team made its European debut in 1964 with a fourth-place finish at the Olympics.

The Soviet Union, meanwhile (which didn't go to the 1962 Worlds in Colorado Springs, Colorado, by the way, because they, the Czechs, and the other communist countries boycotted to get the North Americans back for doing the same after the Hungarian invasion), had hit its stride and, under coach Anatole Tarasov, set about dominating the world championships starting in 1963. Led by such stars as Vitaly Davydov, Alexandr Ragulin, Boris Zaitsev, and Vyacheslav Starshinov, they were next to unbeatable.

Also improving rapidly again, thanks to its own excellent development program, were the Czechs, with goaltender Vladimir Dzurilla and skaters such as Frantisek Pospisil and a big, talented center named Vaclav Nedomansky (see Chapter 18).

138

The Swedes were the other solid club, with a veteran club that also featured some excellent youngsters, including Lars-Erik Sjoberg, who would grow to be one of the best defensemen in the world.

As for the United States, relying as it was on college kids and other amateurs, the red, white, and blue basically went 0–for the 1960s.

It had become apparent by the end of the decade, however, that Soviet and Czech players were very much professionals—paid to concentrate only on hockey though technically part of the army or essential industries.

And Canada had seen enough. It was either change things, or they were packing up their skates and going home.

Good-Bye Canada, and Tough Luck Hockey Fans in the United States

This is going to get complicated, so try to follow the bouncing Bunny Ahearne:

➤ In December 1968, the Canadian government creates Hockey Canada, which would take over all national and international programs.

➤ Lawyer and NHL players' association boss Alan Eagleson goes to Europe to meet Bunny Ahearne, who at first refused, calling him, as Jim Coleman writes, "a messenger boy for a trades union." The meeting took place, but apparently left the IIHF boss unimpressed—no pros at the world championships (not officially, anyway).

➤ Canada is awarded the 1970 World Championships for Winnipeg and Montreal.

➤ At the summer 1969 IIHF meeting, delegates agreed to let Canada (and, by extension, the United States) use nine minor league professions and reinstated amateurs.

➤ Canada sends such a team to an invitation tournament at Leningrad in the fall of 1969—they finished second and were too close to the Soviets, who changed their minds and talked the Czechs, Swedes, and Ahearne into backing off the pros thing.

➤ At a convention in Geneva, the Europeans repealed the rule allowing minor league pros.

Perhaps the problem was that the Europeans had been walking all over the Canadians, and to a lesser extent the Americans, for years and didn't think they'd really do much other than whine.

Wrong. Canada would immediately announce that it was pulling out of all international tournaments, including the Olympics and world championships. And they wouldn't be back until 1977.

Father Bauer's national team, which turned out 83 players, many of whom went to the NHL and many others who graduated from university and went on to good private careers, was disbanded.

A Matter of National Pride

In 1968, democracy was beginning to take hold in Czechoslovakia. The beautiful Prague Spring had built the confidence and hopes of people in the country. The Soviets weren't about to accept a change from communism, however, and in August the tanks rolled into Prague, and democracy was crushed.

In the spring of 1969, the two teams met in the world championships at Stockholm, Sweden, for what would be the most famous pair of clashes in the history of the tournament.

Ken Dryden was one of the Canadian goaltenders at Stockholm, and his memories of the event are still sharp. He had arrived late, was very tired, and considered skipping the first Soviet-Czech game. He went, however, and never regretted it.

"It was the most emotional game I've ever witnessed," said Dryden, 31 years later. The Czechs, flying on an emotional high and determined to prove something to the Soviets, won the game 2–0 (see Chapter 18). But, as Dryden says, the repugnance the Czechs felt for the Russian team and their people was unimaginable. They players fought as though it were their last game ever.

After it was over, Dryden poured onto the rink with the rest of the fans and found himself standing next to a man wearing a cardboard sign with a tank pointing into a net. That man fell to his knees and cried to the heavens—a moment that was captured on film and shown around the world.

Dryden, sensing the moment, asked the man if he could have the sign. That sign still sits in Dryden's home in Toronto.

Great Games

March 1969

At Stockholm, the Czechs had upset the Soviets 2–0 in the preliminary round, in the most emotional game in world tournament history. The second game was nearly as emotional, as well. With Vladimir Dzurilla starring in the Czech goal and his team scoring four times to the Soviets' three, the game was won. In the stands, many people held up signs in English with the intention of having them read in North America. "In August You ... Today We" read one. After one goal, Jozef Golonka of Czechoslovakia skated by the Soviet bench, leveled his stick like a gun, and fired imaginary bullets at the players. It was an unforgettable scene.

Czechoslovakia 2, Soviet Union 0

Though they would beat the Soviets again that tournament, the Czechs could not maintain their emotion and lost to Sweden, finishing third.

Gunther Takes Charge

In July 1975, Bunny Ahearne finally stepped aside as president of the IIHF and Dr. Gunther Sabetski took over.

Dr. Sabetski, a native of Dusseldorf, Germany, was probably one of the two most important and influential men in international hockey history (along with Canada's ultimately disgraced Alan Eagleson). It was he who negotiated Canada's return to the world and Olympic tournaments, founded the European Cup in 1966, helped establish the Canada Cup tournament in 1976, and was a key figure in convincing the National Hockey League's involvement in the Olympic Games by 1998.

He retired in 1994, replaced by Rene Fasel of Switzerland, and was named honorary president. In 1996, Dr. Sabetski entered the Hockey Hall of Fame in Toronto.

Positives and Negatives

In 1977, the international hockey family was reunited when Canada brought a club made up of NHL players who had missed the playoffs. That club also included a few players from Canada's Olympic team program.

The pattern would continue through the end of the century.

Quote, Unquote

"Well done, Vladislav. You're now the main goaltender of the national team."

—Anatole Tarasov to Vladislav Tretiak after the Soviets won the gold at the 1970 worlds in Geneva. Tretiak would go on to be a legend.

Quote, Unquote

"It's a big lie. They [hockey players] are *all* professionals."

—Walter Wasservogl, IIHF Secretary, at the 1977 world championships, when NHLers were welcomed for the first time.

Hurt by early penalties caused by frustration over the refereeing, Canada walloped the Czechs 8–3 and Sweden 7–0 in the championship round but wound up fourth.

It was about here that the move by more and more European players into the NHL began to have some effect. First the Swedes and the Finns, then the Czechs, and finally, by 1990, the Soviets (about to be Russians again) were leaving in droves, which inevitably deadened the talent pool for the world championships.

And the field was evened out as a result.

Great Games

April 1994

Canada came into the championships without a world gold since 1961 but, led by the brilliant goaltending of Bill Ranford, found itself in the finals against Finland. The game was tied 3–3 after regulation and 10 minutes of overtime, which meant going to a shootout, something with which the Canadians had never had a lot of luck. It was left to Luc Robitaille of the Los Angeles Kings to net the winner on the tenth shot and finally give Canada its gold.

Canada 4, Finland 3

Significantly, while Canada had success at the worlds, even winning two titles in the 1990s, the United States, also bolstered by early exiters from NHL wars, struggled mightily. There simply weren't enough quality players to keep competitive unless all of the Americans were there.

In the 1990s, Sweden, the Czech Republic (now separated from Slovakia, which also competed), Russia, Canada, and Finland (for the first time ever) won world titles. And that would be the ultimate irony: The loss of so many good players to the NHL playoffs had finally created a situation never seen before—competitive balance.

Aw, I Knew That!

Q. Name the five members of the Soviet Union's famed Green Unit, during that country's run of world championships in the 1980s.

A. Defensemen Viacheslav Fetisov and Alexei Kasatonov and forwards Igor Larionov, Sergei Makarov, and Vladimir Krutov.

Stars of the Era

➤ Usevolod Bobrov was the best player in the Soviet Union when it debuted at the world championships of 1954 with a gold medal. He played 59 times for his country, scoring 89 times before an injury ended his career in 1957. He then coached the Soviets in the 1972 Summit Series and to world championships in 1974 and 1975. Died in 1979.

➤ Seth Martin was Canada's most accomplished international goaltender. He led the Trail Smoke Eaters to the world title in 1961 and then joined Father Bauer's national program for four more tournaments, winning bronze each time and being selected the world championships' best goalie on all those occasions.

➤ Goaltender Gerry Cosby backstopped the United States to its first world crown in 1933, earning four shutouts and allowing just one goal in five games. Went into the sporting goods business. His Gerry Cosby's store in Madison Square Garden is famous throughout the hockey world.

➤ Sven Bergqvist played both defense and forward in 30 national team games for Sweden and coached the Tre Kronor at the 1948 Olympics. A multi-sport star, he also was the goalkeeper for the national soccer team in 35 games. A tragic car accident put him in a wheelchair in 1955, and he died in 1966.

➤ Urpo Ylonen played in eight worlds and three Olympics for Finland as a goalkeeper. He was in net for Finland's first-ever win over the Czechs (1967) and over Canada (1968).

➤ Jaroslav Drobny could do it all. He played for Czechoslovakia in the 1939 worlds, survived World War II, and was on the world gold medal team in 1947. Played 31 times for his country and then switched to tennis, where he won the prestigious Wimbledon singles title in 1954, representing Egypt.

➤ Erich Kuhnhackl of Germany played forward in eight worlds and three Olympics. Took the scoring title at the 1978 worlds with 1978. Played in 211 national team games and scored 131 times.

Quote, Unquote

"You don't put financial conditions on the opportunity to play for your country, especially if you're a player who played half the season in the minors."

—Alan Eagleson on goaltender Richard Brodeur's contention he should be paid for playing in the worlds for Canada.

World Champions

1920	Canada	1936	Great Britain
1924	Canada	1937–1939	Canada
1928	Canada	1947	Czechoslovakia
1931–1932	Canada	1948	Canada
1933	United States	1949	Czechoslovakia
1934–1935	Canada	1950–1952	Canada

continues

continued

World Champions			
1953	Sweden	1985	Czechoslovakia
1954	Soviet Union	1986	Soviet Union
1955	Canada	1987	Sweden
1956	Soviet Union	1989–1990	Soviet Union
1957	Sweden	1991–1992	Sweden
1958–1959	Canada	1993	Russia
1960	United States	1994	Canada
1961	Canada	1995	Finland
1962	Sweden	1996	Czech Republic
1963–1971	Soviet Union	1997	Canada
1972	Czechoslovakia	1998	Sweden
1973–1975	Soviet Union	1999	Czech Republic
1976–1977	Czechoslovakia	2000	Czech Republic
1978–1979	Soviet Union	2001	Czech Republic
1981–1983	Soviet Union		

The Least You Need to Know

➤ As in the Olympics, Canada dominated the early years of the worlds up to World War II.

➤ The Soviets hit the scene in 1954 and won the gold their first time out.

➤ Bunny Ahearne ran the IIHF with an iron hand from the 1930s to the 1970s.

➤ Soviet hockey dominated the 1960s.

➤ Angry over the so-called "amateurs" on the Soviet and Czech teams, Canada abandoned the world championships and Olympics from 1970–1977.

➤ The growth of the European contingent in the NHL would hurt the world championships by taking so many players out of that competition in the latter part of the twentieth century.

Chapter 13

At the Summit— Canada vs. Russia, 1972

In This Chapter

➤ A showdown is arranged

➤ The Soviets leave a nation stunned

➤ Canada close to implosion

➤ An improbable comeback

➤ The blessing that was Paul

➤ What it all meant

"You can't write about Canada without writing about this series." That's what journalist Dick Beddoes said of the 1972 Summit between Canada and the Soviet Union. The most important moments in hockey history occurred over 27 days in September 1972—a time when the majority of the world was focused on Munich, Germany, and the murder of 11 Israeli athletes by Palestinian terrorists at the Olympic Games. But for the people of two countries, there was something else on their minds: For the first time, the best players from the Soviet Union and Canada were facing each other, locked in an eight-game struggle for hockey supremacy so intense, so emotional, so politically charged that it was related to by more than one as a war. A real Cold War, on ice. What happened in that series, what it meant, and why it had such a powerful effect on the future of the game will be looked at in this chapter.

Everyone Had a Reason

For Canada, denied the chance to use its own professionals when it was convinced the communist countries used them, and no longer part of the world championships or the Olympics, it was an opportunity to prove, once and for all, that Canadian hockey was still the best in the world.

For the Soviets, it was a chance to do something that, at the urging of Anatole Tarasov (the true creator of the Big Red Machine), they had been wanting to do for 10 years—play the National Hockey Leaguers.

Aw, I Knew That!

Q. Who captained the Soviet Union to their 1954 world championship gold medal and then coached the team in the 1972 Summit Series?

A. Usevolod Bobrov. He worked hand in hand with Boris Kulagin, whose dour demeanor earned him the nickname Chuckles.

For Alan Eagleson, president of the NHL players' association, it was an opportunity to pad the retirement fund of his group and cement his power as a new player on the international scene.

For the Soviet players, pride was on the line. They knew they were as good as the NHLers, and now it would be a chance to prove it.

For both countries, it was a chance to show which system—communism or capitalism—was better. Stronger. More worthy of survival.

For the Canadian players, it was, at the beginning, a chance to have a few laughs and blow the Soviets right back across the ocean.

Some of these self-interested parties would be sorely disappointed. Some would get what they wanted. But everyone would come out of the experience changed.

Credit Where It's Due

Without Alan Eagleson, there would have been no series because it was he who delivered the NHL players for Team Canada. And it was the Eagle who could bluster, threaten, and cajole right along with the most aggressive of the Soviet negotiators.

But credit for the behind-the-scenes work, the dig-in and make-it-work stuff, goes to Charles Hay, president of Hockey Canada, Joe Kryczka of the Canadian Amateur Hockey Association (whose ability to speak Polish was key), and Lou Lefaive of Sport Canada.

This is what they came up with:

Eight games, the first four in Canada and the final four in Moscow.

> ➤ Use of the two-referee system (a decision that would cause huge troubles) and no linesmen.

➤ An equitable split of the television revenues.

➤ Use of most international rules.

And so the series was set. There was excitement in both countries, but in Canada the message from the media was almost totally consistent: This would be easy.

July 12, 1972

In the Soviet Union, the Big Red Machine had been working out on and off the ice for a couple of months, while in Toronto, Team Canada was just being announced. But when Harry Sinden, the former Boston Bruins' coach who would be behind the bench for the club, gave the lineup to the press, the overwhelming feeling was: How can this team possibly lose?

What everyone meant was: How could it lose any game, not just the series.

Phil Esposito, Serge Savard, Peter Mahovlich, Yvan Cournoyer, Vic Hadfield, Rod Gilbert, Tony Esposito, Ken Dryden, Frank Mahovlich, Stan Mikita, Brad Park … this was going to be a walkover. Had to be.

Of course, there were a few bumps along the road. Gordie Howe was in his three-year retirement and wouldn't play. Bobby Orr's knees were bad, and the greatest defenseman in history wasn't available. And Bobby Hull, the superb Chicago winger, had signed with the new World Hockey Association and wasn't going to be allowed to play, despite a national outrage that included an appeal from Pierre Trudeau, the prime minister.

But it didn't matter.

The Results of a Hangover

In August, Soviet goaltender Vladislav Tretiak announced his intention to marry and was taken out for some fun by his teammates. The next day he had to tend goal for Central Red Army while in a very hungover state.

Aw, I Knew That!

Q. Seven players named to the 35 roster of Team Canada did not play in the eight games against the Soviets. Name them.

A. Richard Martin, Jocelyn Guevremont, Brian Glennie, Dale Tallon, Marcel Dionne, Bobby Orr, Ed Johnston.

Aw, I Knew That!

Q. Only three players who had been on the Soviet's gold medal–winning team in the 1964 Olympics, just eight years previously, dressed for the team in the 1972 series. Who were they?

A. Alexander Ragulin, Viktor Kuzkin, and Vyacheslav Starshinov.

It so happened that in the audience that night were Team Canada scouts Bob Davidson and John McLellan, there precisely to check out the Soviet goaltender, who had the type of horrible night one might expect. Davidson, an experienced and normally lucid scout, unaware of the reasons for Tretiak's bad showing, went right back home and told the Canadian club that Tretiak wasn't much of a 'keeper and not to worry about it.

It turned out to be one of the classic scouting boners of all time.

Setting the Stage

Canada opened its training camp on August 13 at Maple Leaf Gardens in Toronto with 35 players on hand (far too many to keep everyone happy, it would turn out). Under Sinden and an inspired assistant coach in John Ferguson (a serious physical fitness lover and former NHL tough guy), the team worked harder than it ever had in the NHL. But the Soviets were months ahead and, as we'll discuss later in the chapter, they were coming from a program that emphasized fitness 12 months a year.

Canadian players tended to emphasize the importance of getting good loft on their shots from the sand trap during the off-season.

That crucial difference would tell in the early going.

Not that the Canadian press seemed to notice. Almost without exception, they were calling for a sweep.

Quote, Unquote

"It was a nightmare coming out of the Forum after that first game. Even my brother called me a bum."

—J. P. Parise on the 7–3 loss to the Soviets in game one of the Summit Series.

Game One—a Bowl of Borscht

September 2, 1972: Montreal, Quebec

Dick Beddoes had said before the series began that if the Soviets won one game, he'd eat a bowl of borscht. Just six and a half minutes into game one, it looked as though he was safe from what he considered a culinary torture.

The Soviets were tense and tight. Canada came out flying and led 2–0 on goals by Phil Esposito in the first minute and Paul Henderson. Tretiak looked easily beatable. It was probably going to be boring.

But under coach Usevolod Bobrov, the Soviets began to settle down and, shockingly, started to take control. Evgeni Zimin and the veteran Vladimir Petrov had the game tied before the period ended. The second frame belonged to young Valeri Kharlamov, who scored twice and showed, with his strong skating, excellent puck handling, dangerous shot, and hockey sense, that he was a superstar in the making.

The Soviets were outskating the Canadians. They were controlling the play with their puck movement, discipline, and skill. Tretiak was sensational, and would stay sensational for, oh, about the next 10 years. The Soviet game was going laterally across the ice, not just up and down. And, especially, the visitors were in far better shape than the Canadians.

By the end, it was Soviet Union 7, Canada 3.

Mr. Beddoes ate his borscht and pronounced it not as bad as expected.

Game Two—Peter out of the Shadow

September 4, 1972: Toronto, Ontario

The loss in game one left the entire nation in total shock. It wasn't just that the Soviets had won, it was how. This wasn't a flukey sort of thing, they had been far better than Canada. Letters to the editor whined in frustration. The players were bombarded with fearful looks.

Time to get things under control.

At Maple Leaf Gardens, on September 4, all was redeemed. At least for a few days. With the score 2–1 for Canada in the third period, Peter Mahovlich, Frank's younger brother and a player many considered to be riding just on the Big M's coattails, scored a brilliant shorthanded goal that saw him deke a defender and Tretiak out of their Russian-version BVDs.

Final: Canada 4, Soviets 1.

Game Three—Kissing Your Soviet Sister

September 6, 1972: Winnipeg, Manitoba

"Aren't we all glad to be alive to watch that kind of hockey?"

That's what coach Harry Sinden said after the teams tied 4–4 at Winnipeg Arena (a venue chosen, in part, as a make-up for the city losing the world championships in 1970 when Canada dropped out of international hockey).

That was a pretty nice thing to say for a coach who had watched his team blow 3–1 and 4–2 advantages. Two late goals in the second by Yuri Lebedev and Aleksandr Bodonov knotted the score and when neither scored in the third despite good chances against Tretiak at one end and Tony Esposito at the other, the clubs went west to Vancouver with the series tied.

The fans were anxious, expecting game two to be the turning point where Canadian hockey would ultimately be proven better than the Soviet style. That was not happening.

Game Four—Phil Takes Charge

September 8, 1972: Vancouver, British Columbia

Four games in eight nights over three different time zones was enough to finally show the difference in conditioning between the two clubs. Boris Mikhailov scored twice in the first on Ken Dryden, and the Soviets added two more in the second on the way to a 5–3 victory.

It was here that the frustration of Canadian fans, and of the players, finally bubbled to the surface. The fans had bought into the line hugged tightly by the media that the Soviets would provide no competition worth speaking about; that Canada was number one in hockey by 10 miles if the best players were used and that this series would be the proof.

Down 4–1, the fans in Vancouver began to rain boos down on the Canadian players.

At the end of the game, Phil Esposito, one of the club's three co-captains, skated over to Johnny Esaw of the Canadian Television Network (CTV) and vented his feelings for all the team.

"To the people across Canada, we're trying our best," said Espo, while Esaw, realizing what a hot interview he had going, simply let the big center rant. "The people boo us. We're all disappointed. I can't believe people are booing us … Let's face facts. They've got a good team. We're all here because we love Canada. It's our home, and that's the only reason we came."

The feeling was that the fans had given up on the team. It was at that point that the team took on the "Us versus the world" mentality and looked within. They weren't about to give up on themselves.

Intermission

On September 12, Team Canada flew out of Toronto for a two-game series against Sweden in Stockholm. There was hardly anybody there to wish them well. As Scott Morrison wrote 17 years later, "This wasn't good-bye, it was good riddance."

When they arrived in Europe the press there jumped on them right away for dirty tactics, and it didn't help when the team played two violent exhibition games against the Swedes (who were every bit as dirty and rough, only they did it in a way the Euros were used to).

The first game in Stockholm featured a spearing of Wayne Cashman by Ulf Sterner that cut a two-inch trough in the Boston winger's tongue. The Canadians gave as good as they got, but they took all the bad publicity.

When Team Canada arrived in Moscow things got worse. Vic Hadfield, unhappy that he wasn't in the lineup for the upcoming game five, went home, as did three youngsters—Jocelyn Guevremont (his wife was very ill, though the press wasn't informed), Gilbert Perreault, and Richard Martin—none of whom were being used at all.

Game Five—Phil Slips and Canada Falls

September 22, 1972: Luzhniki Sports Palace, Moscow

Team Canada had been saying for weeks that once they got into shape they could come back on the Soviets, and for two periods in game five that looked to be true.

Events had started on a note of hilarity when Esposito fell on his butt during the pregame introductions. When he smiled, got up, and bowed low to the crowd, he instantly won the hearts of the 2,000 Canadian fans who had traveled to Moscow for the four games, and of more than a few Soviet supporters.

Led by goals from J. P. Parise, Bobby Clarke, and Paul Henderson, Canada had a 3–0 lead into the third period. After trading goals, the game was 4–1 Canada with just over 11 minutes to go.

But in just under three minutes, the game was tied as Viacheslav Anisin, Vladimir Shadrin, and Aleksandr Gusev beat Tony Esposito. With the crowd going (by Soviet standards) wild, Vladimir Vikulov put the winner in at 14:46.

A note: The tying and winning goals were set up by brilliant plays from Valeri Kharlamov, the best Soviet player on offense. John Ferguson, the Canadian assistant coach, noticed.

I Remember ...

The Soviets were playing head games with Team Canada throughout the series. They faked injuries to induce penalties, changed the rules as the series went along, "lost" the Canadians' food and beer (brought along from Canada), and tricked Canada's scouts at pretournament games. Frank Mahovlich was spooked by the whole thing. One night he found what he thought was a listening device on the floor of his hotel room. After thinking about what to do, he decided to unscrew the "bug," only to hear a loud crash from the next floor down. The Big M had unscrewed the bolt holding the chandelier for the room below.

Game Six—Paul Henderson Enters a Darkened Stage

September 24, 1972: Moscow

Years later, Esposito told an interviewer that "I would have killed someone to win that series. I mean it."

He wasn't the only one who felt that way.

Trailing 3–1–1 in games, Team Canada now saw the series as something like a war. And as in a war, some things went on that might have been considered beyond the pale in other times. They had to win three games to take the series, and that's precisely what they would do, referees and Kharlamov be damned.

Okay. First of all there was the problem of Josef Kompala and Franz Baader (nicknamed "Baader and Worse," who may have been among the worst referees in the history of hockey). Though they were West Germans, the pair seemed determined to cow to the Soviets. Some of their calls were beyond atrocious. Never has a game of importance been officiated so badly. By the end of it, Canada had received 31 minutes in penalties (split between the deserved and the totally made up), while the Soviets had just 4 minutes.

"The penalties," wrote Jim Coleman, "would have been laughable if they hadn't been so important."

Soviet and European officials, already realizing the two-man system where the refs called the lines and the penalties wasn't working with teams of this level, promised the West German pair would not be seen again.

The second problem was what to do about Kharlamov. The best Soviet on the ice was killing Canada with his talent. John Ferguson happened to mention to the players before the game that the flashy Soviet was favoring an ankle just a bit. He also mentioned something had to be done about slowing him down.

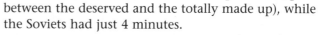

Quote, Unquote

"The Canadians battled with the ferocity and intensity of a cornered animal. We could not match them in heart and desire."

—Anatole Tarasov, father of Soviet hockey.

Bobby Clarke took it to heart, apparently, for in the second period he two-handed Kharlamov with his stick right across the ankle—injuring it so severely that he left the game and would not be a factor the rest of the series.

At the time it was considered heroic, but with the passage of time, most fans now see it as embarrassing.

Clarke would tell Scott Morrison 20 years later, "It's not something I would've done in an NHL game, at least I hope I wouldn't. But that situation, against Soviet players, at that stage in the series, with everything that was happening, it was necessary."

As for the game itself, buoyed by thousands of telegrams from fans back home, Team Canada came up with a 3–2 victory in a tightly played game that featured excellent goaltending by Dryden and Tretiak.

Up 2–1 in the second, Paul Henderson (a Toronto Maple Leaf and former Detroit Red Wing who, with his Team Canada linemates Clarke and Ron Ellis, had been among the final players chosen for the team) notched what would turn out to be the winner.

It was the first act of a performance that would cement Henderson as a Canadian legend for the ages.

Game Seven—a Real Kick in the Shin

September 26, 1972: Moscow

The Soviets earned their own piece of shame in this game when Boris Mikhailov, normally a classy player, completely lost his head. Mikhailov and Gary Bergman bumped behind the Team Canada net and started shoving each other, which was when the Soviet broke the cardinal sin of hockey by kicking at the Canadian's shin with his skate.

You can cross-check, you can slash, you can punch someone in the head and eventually be forgiven. But kicking with the sharp steel toe of the blade is way beyond the pale.

Years later, Mikhailov would apologize profusely on television for what he did, but at the time, it just served to inflame feelings even more.

It also evened the cheap and dirty score at 1–1.

Tied 3–3 in the third period, Henderson was ready for Act Two of his personal drama. A tie would have meant the best Canada could do was draw the series at the end, and that would have been a major victory for the Soviets.

With just over three minutes left, Serge Savard hit Henderson with an outlet pass that put him alone against two Soviet defenders. He promptly deked both (something Henderson said he had never done before and would never do again), and while falling forward toward the ice he somehow swiped the puck that went into the roof of the net for the winner.

That's two winners in a row for the forward. The series was now 3–3–1.

I Remember ...

Igor Kuperman, now head of communications with the Phoenix Coyotes of the NHL, grew up in Moscow. During the series, his parents saw how much it would mean to get him to a game at Luzhniki Arena. At the time, the average monthly salary in Russia was 120 rubles a month. After game five, tickets were going for 2 rubles, so Dad went out to get a ticket from a scalper. Dad found they had jumped to 25 rubles each and said no. After game six, Kuperman's parents took a deep breath and changed their minds, so Dad went out to the scalpers again and found the price was now 100 rubles. That was almost a month's salary. Poor Igor never got to the Summit Series.

Game Eight—Phil, Paul, and a Country Enthralled

September 28, 1972: Moscow

The final game, in brief:

➤ The Soviets, now feeling the pressure, attempt to switch the refereeing assignments back to Baader and Kompala. Canada wants Uve Dahlberg of Sweden and Rudy Bata of Czechoslovakia, and it's supposed to be their choice. Huge fight. Referees are set at Kompala and Bata.

➤ A Soviet official tells Alan Eagleson that if the series is tied, the hosts are claiming a win on goal differential.

➤ Kompala lives up to his reputation and calls a crappy game, so enraging Jean-Paul Parise of Canada that he does the almost unthinkable and threatens to hit the ref with his stick. He gets shown the gate.

➤ The Soviets, led by two from Aleksandr Yakushev, leads 5–3 into the third.

➤ Esposito, by now the acknowledged team leader and the best player in the series, makes it 5–4 at 2:27 of the third, and Yvan Cournoyer ties it at 12:56 on assists by Brad Park and Espo.

➤ Dryden and Tretiak are playing well.

And then ...

Aw, I Knew That!

Q. The public address announcer at Luzhniki Sports Palace was a Canadian who had defected to the Soviet Union. Who was he?

A. Carl Watts, formerly of Winnipeg.

The Most Famous Goal in History

With barely a Canadian back home anywhere but in front of a television (schools either let the kids out for the afternoon or set up televisions in the gym and brought everybody in), this is the way it set up. With a minute to play, Cournoyer heads for the bench, changes his mind, and goes back to his place on the right side. Esposito stays on. Henderson (doing something else he'd never done before) calls Pete Mahovlich off the ice, convinced he's going to do something special. Because Cournoyer got back to his wing, he intercepts a Soviet clearing attempt and tries to hit Henderson on the fly, which, as Foster Hewitt described:

"Henderson takes a wild stab for it and fell ..."

Henderson slides into the end boards.

The Soviets try to clear up the side, but it's intercepted by Esposito, who shoots it desperately at the net. Tretiak lets out a rebound. Henderson gets the puck and fires; Tretiak stops it and lets out another rebound.

"Here's another shot. Right in front. They score! Henderson scores for Canada."

As Hewitt sounded like he was falling out of the booth, Henderson whipped the puck by Tretiak with 34 seconds to go.

Pandemonium. Canada kills the last seconds.

More pandemonium.

Abandoned by their own media, booed by some disaffected fans, insulted by the European press, and left for dead by almost everyone, Canada had come back to win the greatest series in hockey history and set off the second biggest celebration the country had ever seen (right up there with the day the Second World War ended in Europe).

But what did it all mean?

Quote, Unquote

"I will always count that goal as the most maddening of all goals scored on me in hockey."

—Vladislav Tretiak on Paul Henderson's series-winning goal in game eight.

Hindsight

There have since been endless arguments about who got what out of the Summit Series. But some things are beyond argument:

➤ Hockey would never be the same. A game that had always looked to Canada for leadership, players, and coaching now looked to Europe as well.

➤ The Soviets were so much better conditioned than the Canadian NHLers and the latter only caught up when their conditioning caught up as well. After this series, proper off-season workouts, showing up for training camp already in shape, and taking care of bodies became the norm. Assistant coaches, fitness trainers, and even nutritionists and sports psychologists became part of NHL teams.

➤ The Soviet style of lateral passing and playmaking merged with the North American style of going up and down the wings to become a new multi-directional approach. Soviet/Russian players no longer always tried to force the puck into the slot for a chance. They began to shoot from the periphery as well.

➤ Europeans began to learn to hit. North Americans learned to stickhandle and pass with more proficiency. Europeans began to learn how to battle along the boards and dig in the corners. What many couldn't learn to do, especially the Soviets, was to play with the emotion that the North Americans showed.

➤ NHL officials began to look at Europe for talent, so much so that the demographics of the game began to change forever.

The biggest effect, however, was on the psyche of Canadians as a whole. They no longer assumed they were the world's top hockey nation simply because they invented the game. They now realized they would have to work to maintain that title, change the way young players were coached, and alter their approach. And most of the time, that new approach would work.

Stars of the Series

➤ Phil Esposito led the way for Canada with 7 goals, 13 points, and the type of grit and leadership needed to come back from 3–1–1 down.

➤ Vladislav Tretiak played all eight games in goal for the Soviets, astounding critics who predicted he would be his team's weak point, by posting a 3.87 goals against average and making numerous superb stops.

➤ Paul Henderson finished second in points for Canada (10) and first in the country's heart by getting three consecutive game winners, including the most famous one in game eight.

➤ Valeri Kharlamov was only healthy for five of the eight games but still came up with 7 points, 17 shots on goal, and a spirited 16 penalty minutes. Considered the best player on the Soviet team by the Canadians.

➤ Tony Esposito and Ken Dryden split the eight games in goal for Canada. Espo, the brother of Phil, gave up 13 goals for a 3.25 goals against average, while Dryden had a 4.75 mark, though he improved greatly as the series went on.

➤ Aleksandr Yakushev led the Soviets in scoring with 7 goals and 11 points and was on the ice for 5 more goals for than allowed. If the Soviets had won game eight, he would have been the hero.

The Least You Need to Know

➤ The series was supposed to determine whose hockey and political system was better.

➤ Canada was expected to dominate.

➤ The Soviets won two of the first four games and tied another.

➤ Canada was under extreme pressure from its own press and fans after the first half of the series.

➤ Refereeing was terrible in Europe, causing some of Team Canada to lose their heads in frustration.

➤ Canada won the last three games to take the series.

➤ Paul Henderson scored the winning goal in games six, seven, and eight.

A Huge Upset on Ice

Thanks to the inspired television call of Al Michaels ("Do you believe in miracles? Yes!"), the victory of the United States' Olympic hockey team in 1980 at Lake Placid has forever after been called The Miracle on Ice. But as many writers, chiefly Kevin Allen, have pointed out, the team put together of college players and minor pros by coach Herb Brooks was a highly talented group, led by a core of players who would go on to have excellent careers in the National Hockey League. Therefore, while they weren't expected to beat the big bad Red Machine, it wasn't quite like the Sisters of the Poor pulling off a miraculous finish. On the other hand, there were more than a few players who played better in Lake Placid than they ever had—or ever would again. How did the "miracle" happen? Why was the effect on the American public, many of whom had never watched a hockey game before, so strong? And what changes in American hockey came as a result? In this chapter, we'll look at those issues.

The Last Man Cut

Herb Brooks came out of East St. Paul, Minnesota, a good enough player to earn a scholarship to the University of Minnesota, from which he graduated in 1962. One of the legends that would come out of his story after coaching the 1980 Olympic winners was that being the last man cut from the 1960 "miracle" U.S. Olympic club would give him the drive and inspiration to pull off the big victory 20 years later.

Perhaps. But Brooks did play on the 1964 and 1968 Olympic clubs, which may have been as important because it allowed the cerebral future coach a chance to study European training and playing techniques, especially those of the Soviets.

From 1972, Brooks coached the University of Minnesota and won the NCAAs three times during that span. As William Martin writes, he overwhelmed organizers of the 1980 club with flow charts, proposals, and plans and got the head coaching job.

Now he had to get a team.

Aw, I Knew That!

Q. Who was the only holdover from the 1976 Olympic team to play for the 1980 U.S. gold medal winners?

A. Buzz Schneider.

The Cauldron

Armed with his young assistant, Craig Patrick (grandson of Lester), Brooks began to pare down a list that started with 400 players, cut it down to 68 a few months later, and then had it down to a 26-man group from which he would choose the final roster.

The next four months were spent touring Europe and playing exhibition games with minor-pro teams before a 20-player team emerged.

Along the way, the players all came to one conclusion—they all hated Coach Brooks.

He worked them. He cajoled them. He publicly embarrassed them in front of teammates. He turned them into the best-conditioned, best-prepared team in the world. He and Patrick also taught them something new—a perfect combination of North American physical hockey and European conditioning and puck handling.

Herbies

Brooks had many different sayings he like to pull out at important moments (Martin said they were often "pure zen"):

"You don't punt on first down."

But coach, this is hockey.

"Passes come from the heart, not from the stick."

Huh?

"We went to the well again, and the water was deeper, and the water was colder."

Okay.

The Cold War (Not the One on the Ice)

Relations between the United States and the rest of the world, including the traditional Cold War enemies in the Soviet Union, were at a low ebb in 1980. The Soviet Union had invaded Afghanistan, confirming Americans' view that it was, as Ronald Reagan would say later, the "evil empire." The Iran Hostage Crisis was past 100 days and would continue for the rest of the year as 52 American prisoners awaited their fate.

And the economy, as Kevin Allen says, was in the doldrums—inflation was high, confidence was very low.

The country needed something, anything, to boost it out.

Along came Herb and the boys, 10–3 losers to the Soviets in the last warm-up for both teams before the Olympics began. At that game, the awe his players felt for the Red Machine had been in evidence all night. Brooks would not permit that emotion to reappear again.

Who Were These Guys?

The oldest player was just 25—Buzz Schneider. He was the only holdover from the 1976 Olympic team, and he had been bouncing around from town to town in the low minors and even Europe ever since.

The best players were a large group that included forwards Neal Broten, Mark Pavelich, and Mark Johnson, and defensemen Ken Morrow (who would go on to win a Stanley Cup later that spring with the New York Islanders), Dave Christian (son of Bob, who had played on the 1960 gold medal-winning team), and Mike Ramsey, all of whom would be solid players in the big league.

Quote, Unquote

"My wife was hoping that Robert Redford or Paul Newman would get the role, so then she could play herself. Me, I just wish I had the money Malden made."

—Herb Brooks on the choice of Karl Malden (who was 20 years older and couldn't skate a lick), playing him in the TV movie *Miracle on Ice.*

Aw, I Knew That!

Q. Herb Brooks' next Olympic head coaching job was in 1998. What country did he coach?

A. France.

The emotional leader was Mike Eruzione, another former college star who had bounced around a bit. He was named captain.

And the goaltender was Jim Craig, as confident, as cocky, as competitive a goalie as you could find anywhere. The man not only believed he could beat anyone, he *knew* he could do it. Even some of his teammates found him a bit much.

First Steps to a Legend

The United States hit the ice against Sweden favored to do no better than maybe fourth. A bronze medal if they were really lucky, home ice advantage in Lake Placid being what it was.

It almost fell apart that first night. Brooks' boys trailed 2–1 late in the game, on the Games' opening evening, before defenseman Bill Baker scored from the point with just 27 seconds left to tie it.

Having escaped that bullet, the Americans then started to turn a few heads a few nights later by hammering Czechoslovakia 7–3. Now, wait a minute. This was the Czech team some thought might be the only club capable of upsetting the Soviets. The one with all three Stastny brothers, Peter, Marian, and Anton, on it.

Even better, seven different players popped goals for the United States, and Jim Craig was sensational in goal.

Wins against Norway, Romania, and the tough West Germans left the United States at 4–0–1 and starting to fly higher than a kite.

Unfortunately, the first game of the medal round would put them up against the Soviets.

Well, it was a nice dream while it lasted.

Friday, February 22, 1980

5 P.M. EST

One of the myths of the whole 1980 piece is that an enthralled nation watched the United States–Soviet game live on national television. Actually, ABC TV hadn't thought enough of hockey to schedule the Americans' game for prime time, and the audience had to see it on tape delay.

So in a media vacuum, 20 young Americans set out on a journey with endless possibilities that even they weren't completely sure *was* possible.

It would be long before the final whistle that they all, to a man, realized that Brooks had been right. It was possible. It was reachable.

The Big Red Machine came out in, well, red, and looked every bit the champions they were. This was a team that everyone realized by now was fully professional, better than most NHL clubs, and equal to the best pros Canada could put out as an all-star team.

They were coached by Viktor Tikhonov, himself a taskmaster in a system where task-mastering was an art form.

Their goaltender was Vladislav Tretiak, considered the best in the world, or one-two with anyone else.

First Period

The Soviets built a 2–1 lead in front of the 8,000 fans at the Lake Placid Arena who were loud, proud, but not that optimistic. Jim Craig stood as tall as he ever had, however, so the Red Machine was unable to pull away.

Enter Mark Johnson, son of coaching legend Badger Bob Johnson and a player all considered the most talented scorer of the bunch. Near the end of the frame he fired a hard shot from the blueline that, as Allen writes, "bounced off (Tretiak's) pads as though there were a string attached."

It bounced right back to Johnson, who buried it to knot the score at 2–2. A quick glance at the scoreboard showed but one second remaining.

Timing, in this game especially, was everything.

Second Period

Viktor Tikhonov was always known as a man who played by one set of rules—that would be his rules. What often left many of his players confused, however, was where, how, and why he came up with the gospel according to Viktor at any specific time.

Apparently, Tretiak's rebound (he almost never gave up rebounds) must have broken some sort of commandment, because when the second period started, the world's best goalie had been replaced by young Vladimir Myshkin (actually, the kid had come in with that one second to go in the first, further humiliating Tretiak).

"Tretiak," noted Mark Mulvoy, "sat on the Soviet bench with his head hidden by his gloves, experiencing, he said later, the worst moment of his hockey career."

Except what no one knew at the time was that, during the intermission, a couple of Kremlin representatives had come down from the stands and "suggested" the goaltending change was a good idea. As Lawrence Martin writes, Tikhonov took all "suggestions" from the Kremlin to heart. Myshkin was left in.

Aw, I Knew That!

Q. Which two members of the 1980 team would later win Stanley Cup rings?

A. Ken Morrow, four times with the New York Islanders, and Neal Broten, with the New Jersey Devils in 1995.

Not that Myshkin was a sieve, by the way. It was he who had shut out the NHL all-stars (that's all the all-stars, not just the Canadians) in the final game of the Challenge Cup the year before. But if you have the best in the world, why replace him?

Apparently stunned by the change, the United States gave Myshkin the kind of welcome any good host would—they took exactly two (count 'em) shots at the Soviet goal, while Craig was under fire again, finally allowing Alexandr Maltsev to put the Red Machine ahead 3–2.

All must have felt fine in the dressing room for the favorites. They were finally in control.

Second Intermission

The sound started at the top of the Lake Placid Arena. It traveled in waves down the rows of fans until it reached the glass around the rink and then bounced upward again toward the roof, where it reverbed back toward the ice: USA! USA! USA! USA!

In the dressing rooms, both teams could hear it. All American players could feel it, down to the depths of their souls. All their lives, hockey had been secondary in the American fan's mind to baseball, football, and basketball. Probably even golf and tennis in most places.

But now, hockey was on the verge of making a step none of the young men had dreamed possible.

Out of the dressing room they came, ready to do what seemed the impossible.

Third Period

The United States was down a goal. They had managed only two shots on net in the second period. Somehow, however, Brooks got them recharged, and they buzzed out of the room for the final frame.

Up and down the game went. Chances at both ends. Craig coming up big.

Into the eighth minute, Dave Silk, of Scituate, Massachusetts, by way of Boston University, took a wide leap of faith and attempted to thread a pass across the ice to Johnson that would have to go through the skates of two Soviet defensemen. But hey, it was magic time.

Johnson took the pass and blew it by Myshkin to tie the game 3–3.

USA! USA! USA! USA!

Less than two minutes later, it was time for Mike Eruzione to advance center stage and cement his name in American sports history in the way Paul Henderson had cemented his in that of Canada.

Eruzione. An in-betweener. Not quite a natural scorer. Not quite a plumber. Absolutely a heart-and-soul type. The captain found himself alone in the slot with the puck on his stick and he put it home, past Myshkin, for what would be the winner.

As the game counted down, Al Michaels got ready to toss out his now-famous line, Jim Craig shut the door, and the upset was in the history books.

A wild celebration began on the ice and in the stands that moved out to the streets of Lake Placid and spread slowly across the country (remember, this game was not live), until people who couldn't even spell hockey and who wouldn't know an Eruzione from an Italian import car were celebrating in the streets.

Hockey was, for a moment, every American's favorite sport.

A Minor Little Detail

Many people continue to believe that the Americans upset the Soviets and won the gold medal.

Uh, no.

There was the little detail of the USA's final game, two days later, against Finland. Actually, that one was every bit as important as the Soviet contest, medal wise. If Herb's boys didn't win, they not only wouldn't take home the gold, they wouldn't take home anything at all. That's how close the final standings would be.

The Finns led the game 2–1 at the end of the second period, which could have meant the big victory of Friday would have gone down as the biggest morale boost in American hockey history, and nothing more.

Brooks summed it up for his charges before the third: "Twenty minutes, gentlemen. If it's not 20, you'll never live it down. This will haunt you the rest of your lives."

I Remember ...

The 1980 Winter Olympics was the highlight for many athletes, but it was also the high point for one of sport's greatest television directors. Ron Harrison was hired by ABC Sports to direct the hockey coverage for the entire world from Lake Placid. When the U.S. team beat the Soviets, Harrison took what he thought was the finest shot of his directorial career—the Soviets in stunned silence on their blueline, a perfect shot for the world to see. Just then, the "red phone"—a direct link with Roone Arledge, the legendary sports producer for ABC—rang. "Get off that shot and get back to the United States celebrating," said Arledge. Harrison did as he was told, the needs of world viewers taking a backseat for that moment to the needs of ABC.

And out came an unstoppable machine for that final 20. Goals from Phil Verchota, Rob McClanahan, and Johnson again, sewed up the game, the gold, and a special place in American history.

It was such an important place that 20 years later, *Sports Illustrated* magazine would honor the young men by calling their achievement the greatest sporting event of the century.

Quote, Unquote

"We never thought of losing, never thought it could happen. That's why they call it a miracle because it could have happened only once in a lifetime."

—Slava Fetisov, Soviet defenseman, 1980, later a New Jersey Devils' star.

What It All Meant

These are the basic totals, as compiled by William Martin: In 1979–1980, there were 10,490 hockey teams in the United States. Two years later, there were 11,094. Ten years later there were almost 15,000. Seven years after that, almost 30,000 teams were registered, covering almost half a million players.

In more human terms, the story was the same everywhere: In St. Albans, Vermont, a 10-year-old hockey player watching the games on television knew right then what he wanted to do.

"Every kid in the United States wanted to play for the Olympic team after that game," he would say many years later.

That young man was John LeClair. In 1990–1991, he would make his NHL debut with the Montreal Canadiens. And in 1998, he would realize his other dream of playing on the Olympic team.

Forever at the Pinnacle

The members of the U.S. team went their separate ways after the Olympics, as did the coaching staff. All but one played at least one game in the NHL, and many had careers in Europe or the minor leagues before entering other careers.

Two are of real note.

Jim Craig, the goaltending hero, went straight to the NHL with the Atlanta Flames. For whatever reasons, he was never again able to rise to the same level he had displayed at the Games, lasting small parts of three seasons, finally finishing his career in the Central Hockey League in 1984.

Quote, Unquote

"Heroes? Vietnam vets are heroes. The guys who tried to rescue our hostages in Iran are heroes. Me, I'm just a hockey player."

—Mike Eruzione on being called a hero after the 1980 Olympics.

I Remember ...

The remarkable U.S. victory in 1980 made the entire team instant celebrities, especially goaltender Jim Craig. One of the biggest thrills for the club was an invitation to the White House to meet then-President Ronald Reagan. Apparently wanting everyone to feel right at home, White House staff called each player to ask what he would like to eat during the visit. "I couldn't believe they called me from the White House and asked me what I wanted to eat," said Craig, later. "I told them I wanted two lobsters. After all, we did beat the Red Tide."

Mike Eruzione, the captain, ended his career at the top. Right after the Olympics, despite pro offers, he retired. Nothing he could ever do in hockey with his relatively limited skills could ever top the gold medal, so he called it a career and went into coaching and broadcasting.

But what a way to go out.

Brightest Lights in a Blue Field of Stars

➤ Rob McClanahan and Buzz Schneider, both out of the University of Minnesota, tied with Dave Christian for second most points on the American team with eight. McClanahan played five NHL seasons, while Schneider played in Europe before retiring.

➤ Mark Johnson led the Americans in scoring with 11 points, including the two huge goals against the Soviets. He played 11 seasons in the NHL.

➤ Dave Christian and Ken Morrow were pillars of strength on the United States defense. Christian would play 14 excellent seasons in the NHL (as a forward, actually). Morrow won a Stanley Cup that year with the New York Islanders and played nine seasons before going into coaching and scouting.

➤ Jim Craig put together a paltry 2.14 goals against average in the Olympics, and beat the Soviets despite facing 39 shots. He played three NHL seasons.

➤ Mike Eruzione, a checker who could put the puck in the net when needed, scored the winning goal for the team he captained against the Soviets. He retired right after the Games.

➤ Herb Brooks coached with Minnesota, New York Rangers, New Jersey Devils, and Pittsburgh Penguins in an NHL career that was still going into the new century.

The Least You Need to Know

➤ Herb Brooks did a masterful job of preparing the United States for the Olympics in 1980.

➤ The United States almost lost its first game to Sweden before coming back to tie.

➤ Two third-period goals, the last by Mike Eruzione, led the United States to a huge upset over the Soviet Union.

➤ A win over Finland two days later gave America its second Olympic gold medal in hockey.

➤ The victory spurred the growth of hockey in the United States.

Chapter 15

Other International Seriousness

In This Chapter

➤ Soviet tours

➤ 1974 Summit Series

➤ Canada Cups

➤ Challenge and Friendship Cups

➤ The World Cup

➤ Juniors

Tours and special series between European and North American teams have actually been going on since the 1950s, when the Soviet Union first made its appearance for a Canadian exhibition series. Some of the games and tournaments have been especially memorable—the Canada Cup of 1987, for example, produced a best-of-three final that may go down as one of the tightest and most exciting short series ever played. There have been surprises, such as the United States' victory at the inaugural World Cup, and stunning events, such as that surrounding the Soviets' tour of NHL cities in 1976. It was also in the last 25 years of the twentieth century that the junior-aged players of hockey-playing nations finally began to take the stage. In this chapter, we'll look at these events.

Early Soviet Invasions

From the time the Soviet Union entered world hockey competition in 1954, officials of the Red Machine had looked across the Atlantic to North America as a place to test themselves and their theories of hockey against the best opposition they could find.

The first tour of a Soviet team to North America was in 1957. As Stan Fischler writes, the lure of money for a cash-strapped program brought the USSR over for an eight-game series against Canadian junior and senior teams. Coached by Anatole Tarasov, the Moscow Selects (the best of Central Army, Spartak, Dynamo, Wings, and Locomotif), won five and tied another, setting a pattern for years to come.

They were back again for five games in American cities in 1961.

As early as 1963 and 1964, Tarasov was lobbying to have the Soviets play NHL clubs in exhibition games, but a combination of reluctance from National Hockey League officials and the IIHF denied the opportunity.

For the rest of the 1960s, the Soviets would make regular appearances in North America (including a famous 3–2 win over a combined junior/professional Montreal team in 1964), and each time they would easily come out on the winning end.

It had become very apparent that the Soviets were far better than the clubs they were allowed to play, and a showdown with the NHL seemed inevitable.

Aw, I Knew That!

Q. The Izvestia, or Baltica Cup, is a December tournament held annually in Moscow with a variety of national teams competing. Canada was represented twice by professional teams from WHA in the 1970s. Which teams were they?

A. The Winnipeg Jets and the Quebec Nordiques.

The Second Summit

Hockey Canada approved the 1974 series between the Soviets and Canada after the upstart World Hockey Association asked for a similar series to the one the NHL had in 1972. Using a similar format (four games in Canada, four in Moscow), the series got underway in September of that year in Quebec City with a large number of aging stars in the Canadian lineup—Gordie Howe, 46, Bobby Hull, 35, Ralph Backstrom, 37, Frank Mahovlich, 36, Pat Stapleton, 34, J. C. Tremblay, 35, and Paul Henderson, 31.

The first game was tied, and, led by the goaltending of Gerry Cheevers, Canada won the second, 4–1, in Toronto.

It was then, as Jim Coleman noted, that Cheevers' father-in-law died, and he had to leave the team for a while. With veteran international goalie Smokey McLeod in goal, the Soviets hammered the home side in game three to even the series. Game four in

Vancouver had been led by Canada, 5–2, but the Soviets put on one of their patented comebacks and it finished 5–5.

After four games, Team Canada '74 had a better record than Team Canada '72: 1–1–2.

In Moscow, however, the larger ice surface did in the older Canadians, who lost the first two games, should have won the seventh but for a disputed no-goal call when Bobby Hull scored with a second to go and the Soviet officials said *nyet*. It remained a tie. Game eight went to the Soviets.

The most important result of the series, writes Coleman, was the realization by the Soviets that players could still contribute past the age of 30, something they had never believed. Suddenly, older Soviets found themselves back in the hockey picture.

The New Year's Eve Game

The first of nine tours of NHL cities by Soviet teams between 1975 and 1991 begat two of the most memorable games of them all.

The first, on New Year's Eve 1975 at the Montreal Forum, matched the Central Red Army club against the Montreal Canadiens, a team just beginning its incredible run of four straight Stanley Cups. By the time it was over, the contest had proven three things: that the Montreal Canadiens were the best team in the world, having outplayed the Army by a wide margin; that Canadian hockey, now adapting to the lessons learned since 1972, was as good as, and probably still a step better than, anybody else's; and that Vladislav Tretiak, who stopped 38 shots that night to preserve a 3–3 tie while Ken Dryden at the other end faced just 13, was, with the possible exception of Philadelphia's Bernie Parent, the best goaltender in the world.

The second memorable contest also involved the Red Army, which found itself in Philadelphia to meet the defending-cup champion Flyers. That would be the Broad Street Bullies, who were the antithesis of the Canadiens—intimidating and often brutal.

Quote, Unquote

"I thought that this would be just another game, but you put on the Canadian sweater and you realize that it's not just another game."

—Gordie Howe, after game one of the 1974 Canada-Russia series.

Quote, Unquote

"The Philadelphia fans are not a band of cutthroats. We are the best hockey team in the world. We were criticized because we are the best team. It's just that we have more guts than any other team."

—Fred Shero after the Flyers–Red Army battle of January 11, 1976, at the Spectrum.

With the crowd going nuts, the Flyers beat the tar out of the Red Army so much in the first period (Ed Van Impe, for one, elbowed Valeri Kharlamov in the head so badly the Soviet had to be carried off) that the visitors left the ice, refusing to return. It was only after lengthy negotiations between Alan Eagleson and Soviet officials, including a promise the dirty stuff would stop, that the game resumed. The Flyers, combining brawn with offensive zeal and a style that approximated the Soviets' own with its short passes and lateral play, outshot the visitors 49–13 and won 4–1.

While xenophobes were thrilled, hockey fans in general found the game disturbing. Perhaps winning that way wasn't what real hockey purists wanted.

Quote, Unquote

"If there was a cat in the building, you thought it was singing the national anthem."

—Larry Robinson on the noise and emotion during the anthems on New Year's Eve, 1975, before the Montreal Canadiens played Moscow Red Army in a famous exhibition game.

Canada Cup, 1976

When Canada agreed to re-enter world competition in the spring of 1977 by sending along pros who had missed the NHL playoffs (and into a situation where they would surely lose), it was a trade-off for what would be called the Canada Cup—a bi-annual tournament, held mostly in Canada with some games in the United States, that would match the very best players from the top five or six hockey nations of the world.

I Remember ...

Team USA entered the 1976 Canada Cup with a roster full of NHLers, but they couldn't come close to matching the talent caliber of the Canadians. After losing to Canada 11–1 in a pretournament exhibition game, the Americans were just hoping not to be embarrased. Coached by Bob Pulford and Harry Neale, Team USA found itself down 3–0 to Canada in the game before Fred Ahern and Steve Jensen made it close. Then with the goalie pulled, the Americans charged the Canadian zone in the final minute. Gary Sargent of the L.A. Kings took a shot from the point that looked like it was headed for the net and the tie, until ... "I could see the hole," remembers Neale. "The shot was going in. Rogie Vachon did not see it, but no, it hit (American forward) Alan Hanglesben right in his big, fat ass." Canada scored in the empty net to win 4–2.

The first was held in 1976, and it didn't take long for the Soviet Union to start playing games. Wanting to cover itself if they lost to Canada, the Soviets left their top line of Vladimir Petrov, Valeri Kharlamov, and Boris Mikhailov at home, plus two of its best defenders, instead sending an "experimental" team under a young coach named Viktor Tikhonov.

After a 3–3 tie against Sweden early on, the Soviets claimed to be so incensed with the Canadian referee they threatened to go home. Eagleson offered to help them pack their bags. They stayed.

After the United States, the Soviets, Sweden, and Finland fell by the wayside, the best-of-three final came down to Canada and the Czechs. Which ended in two straight as Darryl Sittler beat veteran goalie Vladimir Dzurilla, back from a four-year retirement to play in the tournament and sensational up to that point, with a famous overtime goal in the second contest.

The other interesting thing about the tournament was that it was Bobby Orr's final chance to shine. Ignoring his aching knees, he was the Canada Cup's most valuable player. His career, however, had entered its final stages. Orr, who had signed with Chicago that summer, played just 20 games with the Hawks in the coming season, skipped the next one, and then appeared in only six more in 1978–1979.

Great Games

September 1976: Montreal Forum

Canada skated out to play the Czechs in the round-robin of the Canada Cup tournament possessing what many think may be the best team ever assembled in the country. What they didn't count on was the goaltending of Vladimir Dzurilla in the Czechoslovakian goal. Dzurilla, a star in the 1960s, had been called out of a four-year retirement for the Canada Cup, and he looked anything but rusty. In the first meaningful game between the best the two countries could offer, Dzurilla won a wide-open goaltending battle against Rogie Vachon, 1–0. Milan Novy scored for the Czechs. Canada would beat the Czechs two straight in the final to win the tournament.

Czechoslovakia 1, Canada 0

First Blood for the Soviets

By now, the public's desire for top-level international hockey was at a fever pitch, and with lots of money to be made, the NHL and its player's association were willing to give it to them.

In 1979, league officials chose to ditch their regular all-star format and organize a three-game series between the best NHLers and the Soviets, held at Madison Square Garden in New York over a five-day period.

Having seen Canada win in 1972 and 1976, the NHL (which would have all of its stars, including Europeans such as defenseman Borje Salming), agreed unofficially that the winner of the 1979 series would be considered "World Professional Champions."

Oops.

With Vladimir Myshkin in goal instead of Tretiak, the Soviets, who by then were featuring the best teams they would ever have, split the first two games with the NHL, setting up a game three showdown that was completely dominated by the Red Machine, 6–0.

Coach Viktor Tikhonov, now full-time national coach, had his revenge for 1976.

Canada Cup, 1981

The changing demographics of the NHL were at the forefront in 1981 when the second version of the Canada Cup tournament began (they were going to play in 1980, but the Soviets' invasion of Afghanistan put that off). For the first time, three teams had a significant number of National League players. Canada's full roster, of course, was NHLers, but so was the United States' (including goaltender Tony Esposito, a Canadian who had been a hero in the 1972 series; he wanted to honor his adopted country by playing for the United States, something that left a number of Canadians grumbling).

Sweden would have a dozen NHLers and Finland four.

Aw, I Knew That!

Q. Grant Fuhr played every minute of every game for Canada at the 1987 Canada Cup. Who were the forgotten two goalies on the roster?

A. Kelly Hrudey and Ron Hextall.

The story in this tournament was the youngsters. Wayne Gretzky was making his top-level international debut (he had played in the world juniors), as were a number of future Soviet stars, including Igor Larionov and Viacheslav Fetisov.

Canada, which had struggled all through the preliminary round, beat the United States, and the Soviets downed the Czechs in the semi-finals.

That set up what some called "the darkest day in Canadian hockey history"—September 13, 1981, when the Soviets simply hammered the home side in the one-game final at Montreal. It was 8–1 when the slaughter ended.

Trying to take their hard-won trophy home, the Soviets put it in a duffel bag and headed for the door—only to be met by Eagleson, who grabbed it back and refused to let it out of the country.

Canada Cup, 1984

This was supposed to be the year of the United States (it certainly wasn't the year of the Finns—they had finished an embarrassing seventh at the worlds that previous spring and were replaced by West Germany for the fall tournament). For the first time, the U.S. NHL contingent contained more than mere pluggers. Brian Trottier, another ex-Canadian, Bobby Carpenter (the first American to score 50 goals in an NHL season), Joe Mullen, Rod Langway, and young goalie Tom Barrasso were all in the lineup.

Canada featured a ton of Edmonton Oilers, chosen by coach Glen Sather, who also looked after the NHL club.

Things looked good for the United States in the early going—tying Canada 4–4 and making the semi-finals—but it all came apart there with a rotten 9–2 loss to Sweden.

On the other side, Canada, struggling badly in the preliminary round, wound up against the Soviets again in what would be a beautifully played game that was decided in overtime on a deflection by Mike Bossy.

The final was anticlimactic, with Canada winning two straight over Sweden, 5–2 and 6–5.

Remember that last score, it's going to be significant.

The Quebec Hockey Carnival

In 1987, the NHL again threw out its all-star format in favor of a two-game series in Quebec City, organized by Marcel Aubut, owner of the NHL's Quebec Nordiques, and set around the city's famous annual winter carnival.

As Stan Fischler writes, the event became a cross between a hockey series and a cultural event, with concerts such as Crystal Gayle, the Bolshoi Ballet, and the Soviet Army Band, parades, a fashion show, and a few battles on the ice.

The games went 4–3 for the NHL all-stars and 5–2 for the Soviets.

And more money to the participants and the NHL pension fund.

Mario's Party

Dan Kelly was a famous play-by-play announcer who had cut his teeth with *Hockey Night in Canada* before becoming the voice of the St. Louis Blues in the expansion year of 1967.

Great Games

September 1987: Copps Coliseum, Hamilton

Game two of the best of three final at the 1987 Canada Cup found the host nations down 1–0 in games to the Soviet Union. The second contest went into overtime tied 5–5. Facing a loss if they didn't score, Canada went back and forth with the Soviets again and again before, finally, Wayne Gretzky set up Mario Lemieux for the game winner in double overtime. The two would combine again two nights later for the winning score in the deciding game.

Canada 6, Soviet Union 5

173

Though he had called many a famous goal, none would stand the test of time more than the one that ended the 1987 Canada Cup tournament:

"Here's Gretzky ... to Lemieux ... He scores!!!"

Back up a bit.

Mario Lemieux came into the NHL at a time when the future of Quebec as a province in Canada was in doubt. There was a separatist government in power (the Parti Québécois), and the idea of a separate country of Quebec was on a lot of people's minds. Though he never said one way or the other (he would actually settle in Pittsburgh after his career ended), there were some in the country who suspected Lemieux was a separatist.

But, there he was, playing for Canada, and providing, at the last moment, one of the great hockey highlights in the country's history.

Lemieux was teamed with Gretzky, and suddenly he blossomed from a huge man of immense potential into a huge man of great talent realized.

Canada and the Soviets again met in the best of three final, all games of which were settled by the same score (did you remember it?) of 6–5.

Game three, at Hamilton's Copps Coliseum, was as wide open, intense, and superbly played as the first two. But this one would go Canada's way. Lemieux broke up a Soviet rush, poke-checked the puck away from Igor Kravchuk over to Gretzky, and away to the races the two went with Larry Murphy along for the skate on the right side.

Gretzky faked out the defender and instead of shooting himself slid it over to Lemieux, who fired it past goaltender Sergei Mylnikov.

Lemieux wound up with 11 goals in the Canada Cup, and as Brian Kendall pointed out, 9 of them were on assists by The Great One.

I Remember ...

During game two of the 1987 Canada Cup final between Canada and the Soviet Union, referee Paul Stewart called back two Soviet goals, infuriating the Soviets. Coach Viktor Tikhonov sent captain Slava Fetisov over to talk to Stewart, and while that conversation was going on, the two noticed Tikhonov holding his nose in the direction of the referee. Stewart said to Fetisov: "Either he's trying to hail a cab or you guys haven't washed your uniforms in quite some time."

Friendship Far Away

In 1989 and 1990, a pair of NHL clubs went to the Soviet Union for a Friendship Tour in the fall exhibition season that taught the visitors a lot. Like the food was awful, the hotel rooms were not up to par, the planes were a little scary, and the hockey, like hockey anywhere, was hot and heavy.

What made the first tour truly fascinating was the inclusion of Sergei Makarov in the Calgary Flames' lineup. That was the year the Iron Curtain for hockey players opened somewhat and six players, including Slava Fetisov with New Jersey, came through.

The Washington Capitals also went along on the first tour.

Montreal Canadiens and the Minnesota North Stars went on tour number two.

Not surprisingly, the results were mixed, but the tours went much further than who won and who lost. It indicated the beginning of a new, open relationship between the Soviets and the NHL.

Aw, I Knew That!

Q. Name the young Czech goalie who played every minute of every game for his country in the 1987 Canada Cup?

A. Dominik Hasek.

Canada Cup, 1991

The final Canada Cup turned out to be a strange one for a number of reasons.

Czechoslovakia and the Soviet Union both struggled terribly, the former finishing last and the latter missing the playoffs. Between them they went 2–7–1.

This was the series in which a new player for the 1990s appeared—the United States. From goaltender Mike Richter out, the seeds planted in American minor hockey by the United States victory at the 1980 Olympics began to flower. Stars such as Pat LaFontaine, Brian Leetch, Brett Hull, and Mike Modano were ready to carry the flag in pro international competition like never before. The general manager of the club was Craig Patrick, who had been Herb Brooks' assistant at Lake Placid.

While Canada was beating Sweden 4–0 in one semi, the United States was hammering a very good Finnish team in the other, 7–3, setting up an all–North American final.

It was in game one, taken 4–1 by Canada, that one of the great illegal cross-checks of all time put Wayne Gretzky out of the series, courtesy of Gary Suter's questionable hit. Angered by that play, the Canadians came flying out for game two and won 4–2.

In five Canada Cups, played mostly at home on Canadian ice and on the smaller North American rinks, Canada won four times. The Soviets took the other.

That would be the end of the tournaments, however, partly because of the fall from grace of Alan Eagleson, long the tournament's chief organizer, and partly because the

NHL had a couple other ideas in mind. One was putting NHLers in the Olympics, which would happen in 1998.

The other was a proper World Cup of Hockey, set for the summer of 1996.

A Star Spangled Winner

The first World Cup of Hockey, August and September 1996, matched Canada, the United States, Russia (the Soviet Union was five years in the grave), the Czech Republic and Slovakia (now separated), Sweden, Finland, and Germany (now one country) in two groups, one of which played its preliminary round in Europe, which was the biggest change from the old Canada Cup system.

Playoff action, involving six clubs, was all in North America.

As in 1991, the United States and Canada met in the three-game final, only this time the result was different.

American coach Ron Wilson had a highly talented team, to be sure, but he also had one willing to play with the extra grit needed when under intense fire. And intense it would be.

As Kevin Allen writes, Wilson reminded his club that hockey history was like a bus ride, with the Canadians "always in the driver's seat" and the Americans relegated "to the back of the bus."

Aw, I Knew That!

Q. Which American-based professional team was the first pro club to compete in the prestigious Spengler Cup in 1996?

A. The Rochester Americans of the American Hockey League.

Something got through. What was different this time, Allen wrote, was that for the first time the Americans understood something the Canadians always had—winning meant burying your ego in favor of the team. The team was everything in this kind of tournament.

In the final, the teams split the first two games, though Canada had peppered goaltender Richter in both contests, only to be stopped in their tracks time and again. Game three was tied, 2–2, with under three minutes to play when Tony Amonte scored what would be the winner for the United States. Two empty net goals and it was 5–2 for the Americans.

The roster that featured Brett Hull, John LeClair, Doug Weight, Brian Leetch, Keith Tkachuk, and a long list of other talented individuals had come together as a team.

Juniors on the World Stage

Junior hockey, for players under 20, didn't get its first official championship until 1977, when Banske, Czechoslovakia, hosted a tournament that would be played regularly right up to today.

It was actually the Soviets and Czechs who came up with the proposal to hold an annual world tourney, approaching the IIHF in 1973. Three unofficial affairs were held over the following seasons before it became official for 1977.

At that first official tournament, Viacheslav Fetisov led the Soviets to a 7–0 record and the gold medal, while Dale McCourt took Canada to a silver, with the Czechs taking the bronze.

The following year, at Montreal, Fetisov was back, along with a new face—Wayne Gretzky, then just 16. The Soviets beat Canada 3–2 and went on to win the gold.

Future Stars on Ice

Those perusing the program at the 1979 championship in Sweden might have been impressed by the talent in the lineups, but they might not have realized exactly how many future stars they were seeing. Brian Propp and Brad McCrimmon for Canada; Mike Ramsey, Neal Broten, and Dave Christian (all to go on to a gold at the 1980 Olympics) for the United States; Alexei Kasatonov, Vladimir Krutov, and Igor Larionov for the Soviets; Jari Kurri for Finland; Mats Naslund and Hakan Loob for Sweden; Anton Stastny for the Czechs. The list was endless.

And that's how it would continue, year after year.

Sweden finally stopped the onslaught of the Soviets in 1981, winning gold.

Coached by Dave King, Canada found its way to the front of the bus in 1982, with defenseman Gord Kluzak its best player, but the Soviets were back for the following two seasons.

The Lights Went Out, and the Party Continued

The darkest, and most famous, incident in junior world history began in the final game of the 1987 tournament at Piestany, Czechoslovakia.

With the Soviets already eliminated from a medal following a rotten tournament, they met Canada in a game that would sew up top spot for the latter if they won—which they were on their way to doing when, suddenly, a small brawl broke out on the ice. Strange as this was, since the Soviets absolutely never brawled, before you knew it there were fights all over the place, and both benches, led by the junior Red Machine, emptied.

It was wild. Players grappled with each other. Goaltenders wrestled in full equipment. Punches were everywhere. The Cold War had turned hot.

With the referees refusing to intervene, arena officials tried turning out the lights to quell the violence. But it just kept going in the dark until the combatants were exhausted.

The result: Both teams were kicked out of the tournament, and Finland backed into the gold.

There were many who were sure the Soviets started the brawl on purpose to deny Canada a gold when it would be meaningless either way for the Red Machine. Others thought all those years of not being able to fight each other had both sides willing and able to answer the bell when it went off.

Whatever the cause, it was a black eye for the sport.

Either Way, It Was Red and White

Back and forth the Canadians and Soviets, and later Russia, went with gold medals at the world juniors until 1993, when a club led by Paul Kariya and Chris Pronger started Canada on a string of five-straight world titles. This was despite Peter Forsberg's unbelievable 31 points for Sweden that year. Whether the tournament was held in Europe, the United States, or Canada, the North American version of the red and white prevailed.

That wouldn't change until 1998, when the host Finns won the championship—their first-ever world title at any level of the sport (winning by default in 1987 doesn't count).

The final years of the century went the Russian's way, but in 2001 the Czech Republic took the junior title, giving it domination of the major world championships, the Olympics, World and World Junior (Under 20).

The Least You Need to Know

➤ The first tour of North America by the Soviets was in 1958, during which they lost just one game.

➤ The Canada Cup, starting in 1976, became the unofficial professional world championship until the early 1990s.

➤ Soviet clubs dominated tours of NHL cities.

➤ The United States won its first major international crown outside the Olympics in many decades when it took the 1996 World Cup.

➤ The junior world championships, starting in 1977, were dominated by the Soviets/Russians and the Canadians.

Part 4

Beyond the Iron Curtain

Outside of Canada, the most important influence on the development of hockey has been that from the Soviet Union (now Russia). Determined to make a mark in the sport, the Soviets studied the game, broke it down scientifically in the post-war period, and created a world-class program within a decade. Over a 50-year period, Soviet advances would help change the way hockey was played. Having built a tremendous program, however, weaknesses within their own system, and the autocratic dictates of one coach specifically would seriously damage the Soviet/Russian ability to sustain quality. In Czechoslovakia (Czech and Slovak Republics), a similar system would take an already solid program and turn it into one of the world's best. Though beset by defection, dissension, and money woes, hockey people in the Czech Republic, especially, would find a way to continue to produce winners on the world stage.

Chapter 16

Teachings from the Tsar (1946–September 1972)

In This Chapter

➤ Ball hockey to puck hockey

➤ Quick success

➤ Tarasov

➤ The fabulous sixties

➤ The end of Anatole

How did the Soviet Union rise so quickly in the world of hockey? How could a system that was only able to produce third-class hockey equipment, had hardly any indoor artificial ice rinks as compared with Canada (and none at the beginning), and was so determined to produce its own coaches and style of play come to dominate the hockey world for so long? The answer lies in many places, but the chief source of understanding comes in an introduction to a bulbous-nosed, surprisingly independent player and coach who found a way around all these difficulties, forged a new approach to the game, and triumphed in the process. In this chapter, we'll look at Soviet hockey from the post-war years to the Summit Series of 1972.

From Bandy, with Love

When sports and government officials (the two were always intertwined) decided at the end of the Great Patriotic War against Adolf Hitler to turn away from "ball hockey" to "puck hockey," it was for one reason—puck hockey, or ice hockey, was a world and Olympic sport, and ball hockey, or bandy, wasn't.

It was the stated goal of the Great Soviet, spoken through Josef Stalin and his son Vasili, for communism to show the world it was the strongest system of government, and one of the ways it would do that would be by dominating international sports. Hockey was just one of those sports (soccer was considered at the time more important politically), but it would turn out to be the one that would come closest to realizing that goal.

As Lawrence Martin writes in *The Red Machine,* his brilliant work on Soviet hockey, there were two key factors already in place when the first Soviet national hockey league was formed in 1946: The first was the game of Bandy (see Chapter 1, "Whose Game Is This, Anyway?"), which provided the basic skills needed, especially skating and handling of the stick. The second was the sports-club system begun in 1923 with the founding of the Dynamo Sports Society, run by the Cheka (the Soviet Secret Police that would eventually become the KGB), and of the Central Army Sports Club, run by the army.

That system, which identified young athletes at an early age, funnelled them to sports the government felt they would be best at, and then put them into sports schools around the USSR, and would pay huge dividends in all sports, none more so than hockey.

Aw, I Knew That!

Q. The captain and leading play-off scorer for the 1937–1938 Chicago Blackhawks was actually born in Russia. Who was he?

A. Johnny Gottselig, born in Odessa, Russia.

Quote, Unquote

"Our players did not know how to raise the puck. To raise it was considered a fantastic achievement."

—Yuri Korolev on early Soviet attempts at hockey in the 1940s.

From Zero to Sixty in Nine Years

December 1946 found large numbers of talented bandy players in Russia proper apprised of a change in sport—they were to drop ball hockey right away and take up the Canadian game of puck hockey. A league was starting and they were playing in it—like, tomorrow. They didn't know the rules. They didn't know how to hold the stick. They hardly had any sticks, for that matter. But the government had spoken, so off they went.

From that inauspicious start did grow the Soviet hockey legacy.

Teams in that first season included Moscow Dynamo (the KGB club), Air Force (Vasili Stalin's outfit, which he ran with an iron fist and filled simply by grabbing anyone he wanted off other outfits), Central Army, Moscow Spartak, two from Leningrad, and six others spread across the central Soviet Union. Four of the clubs were KGB-sponsored.

Early stars would include many of the men who would be key players in the 1950s and 1960s, including the first superstar, Usevolod Bobrov (a brilliant soccer and bandy player), Yuri Korolev, Boris Kulagin, Vladimir Yurzinov, and a pudgy, enthusiastic, dynamic man named Anatole (also Anatoli, and Anatoly—depending on which Western translation of the Russian alphabet you prefer) Tarasov.

Equipment was basically made up as they went along—helmets were from cycling, sticks often came from straight from carpenters, and the skates were a nineteenth-century design.

The Russians knew that they would have to get outside help to move up quickly in the sport, but they wouldn't go to the west. Actually, they didn't have to. Czechoslovakia, the new Soviet puppet state, had been playing the sport for 50 years, and that's where the help would be found in the form of LTC Prague, a club team that came in 1948 to show off its prowess and teach skills.

The Russians actually went 1–1–1 against the Czechs and realized three things: Their own skating and passing were excellent, their teamwork was strong, but their stick-handling and shooting skills were lousy.

They knew what to work on.

I Remember ...

On January 7, 1950, an SI-47 aircraft took off from Moscow, carrying 11 members of the VVS Air Force team, plus coaches and officials, to a league game in Sverdlovsk, far to the east in the Soviet Union. Some hours later the plane would crash in a blinding blizzard at Koltsovo airdrome near its destination, killing all aboard. Run by Vasili Stalin, the son of the Soviet dictator, VVS Air Force had contained some of the best players in the country, including Yuri Tarasov, younger brother of Anatole. Stalin went right to work rebuilding the club the way he had done it in the first place—by taking the best players from other teams. Ironically, one of the athletes who was supposed to be on the plane was Usevolod Bobrov, who, for reasons never confirmed (too drunk, slept in, mad at the coach, afraid of airplanes), missed the flight. He went on to be the most famous Russian player of the 1950s and later coached the national team.

Father

Anatole Tarasov. The Father of Soviet Hockey. One of the greatest hockey teachers and thinkers in history. Big-nosed guy. Could drink anyone under the table. Independent in a country that didn't handle independent thought very well. Co-coached the national team to three Olympic wins and nine world championships. Elected to the Hockey Hall of Fame in 1974.

Tarasov had been a fine bandy player who switched to puck hockey when everyone else did, playing and soon player-coaching Central Army to three of the first five Soviet championships. He was a brilliant tactical thinker, planner, and organizer. And what he came to realize, as he looked up over the North Pole to Canada, was that to do well—and quickly—in the sport, his athletes (he became the national coach in the early 1950s) would have to take advantage of their natural skills—skating and passing—to develop a style of their own.

Great Games

March 1957

The Soviets and Sweden played the final game of the world championships that year in front of 50,000 fans at an outdoor arena in Moscow. Needing only a tie for the gold, the Swedes led 2–0 after the first period before watching the hosts pump in four in the second frame for a 4–2 lead. With the crowd going wild, Sweden scored twice in the third to get their tie. The Moscow crowd, enamored of the play of Swedish star Sven Tumba Johansson, rushed the ice, lifted the opposition star to their shoulders, and carried him off in a show of incredible sportsmanship.

Sweden 4, Soviet Union 4

Tarasov's effect on Soviet hockey, and the sport in general, was immense:

➤ It was Tarasov who realized that intense training and teamwork were the only ways the Russians could compete against the Canadians—a country with vast numbers of indoor ice rinks and all the best equipment.

➤ It was Tarasov who instituted the system of almost year-round training schools in which players would spend 11 months working out two or three times a day, living in dormitory conditions, getting out once a week, if lucky, and living and breathing the game constantly. Realizing how short ice was (there wasn't a single artificial rink in the early years), he concentrated on dry-land training.

➤ It was Tarasov who brought in the lateral (cross-ice) style of play, hanging back to set up the best play rather than simply dumping the puck in and using strong forechecking as the Canadians favored.

➤ It was Tarasov who emphasized team play over individualism, giving the Soviets their greatest strength in hockey, and perhaps their greatest weakness.

➤ It was Tarasov, and co-national coach Arkady Chernyshev, who created the unit system wherein the same three forwards and two defensemen would be on the ice together as often as possible, thus creating as much unity as they could.

➤ It was Tarasov who was always thinking of ways to make his players better. He made a young Vladislav Tretiak carry a tennis ball with him at all times (even when swimming), had players drag tires around behind them on the ice, and used soccer and basketball to keep them in shape. His list of ideas was endless.

Great Lines—Part One

As Martin points out, each decade in Soviet hockey would produce one especially brilliant forward line. The line for the 1950s featured wingers Usevolod "Seve" Bobrov and Yevgeny Babich, centered by Viktor Shuvalov.

Bobrov, previously a national soccer player star, was himself an independent thinker (which often put him at loggerheads with Tarasov, who liked his own independence but didn't like it in his players) who liked the offensive so much that he often hung around the center line looking for the quick outlet pass, at the expense of team defense.

Children of a certain vintage might have referred to him as a "goal suck."

With his Air Force teammates Babich and Shuvalov, however, Bobrov became part of a superior line, one that complemented each other's talents and would take the Soviet Union through most of the 1950s.

The System

For over four decades, the training of hockey players in the Soviet Union followed a similar pattern. Youngsters would play at a local hockey school tied to a sports club and, if considered talented, would join that sports organization(say, the Dynamo Club in Leningrad), where they would often stay with the same coach for as many as five years until they reached junior age where they would play on the national junior team or with the junior team at the club, and then move to the big time—the Soviet national league.

That system expanded hugely in the 1960s with the introduction of the Golden Puck Tournament, an annual affair whose playdowns started in the regions and then worked their way to Moscow for the finals.

Growing up far from Moscow didn't mean you were stuck there if your talents could take you to one of the bigger organizations, especially one of the four in the capital. If they wanted you, they usually got you.

Aw, I Knew That!

Q. Name the Russian player who debuted in the Central Red Army sports school at age 9, after lying to officials that he was 11?

A. Viacheslav Fetisov.

From that training ground came the stars that would lead the Soviets to victory time and again.

The Stunner

The Soviet Union had planned on making its true international debut in 1953, but when Bobrov was injured at the last minute, officials withdrew the team, despite protests from Tarasov, who for once didn't get what he wanted.

So it was 1954 when the USSR graced hockey's world stage for the first time, and what an opening performance that club gave.

The coach at that worlds was Tarasov's main, and often heated, rival, Arkady Chernyshov. He had taken over for Tarasov when it was thought the latter's training regimen had exhausted the team—they performed poorly on a tour of Czechoslovakia.

Led by the Bobrov, Shuvalov, and Babich line, the Soviets went to Sweden as an unknown entity. That didn't last long.

As Jim Coleman writes, Canada, represented by the Toronto (East York) Lyndhursts, "bumped into a hornet's nest in Sweden." Both teams went undefeated in the preliminary round (the Soviets had one tie, while Canada was unblemished), until they met each other. The Russians, led by Bobrov, bombed the shocked Canadians, 7–2.

It was an utter humiliation for the Canadians, who felt they would never be in this position if they could send their best NHLers to the world championships. That was probably true for about another 10 years, but within that decade, the Soviets had practically caught up to the pros.

I Remember ...

Just before the Toronto (East York) Lyndhursts took on the Soviets for the world championship in 1954, a Swedish newspaper ran a cartoon showing a little student labeled "Bobrov" cowering at his school desk with a giant teacher, wearing a Canadian sweater, standing over him. After the Soviets humbled Canada to win the gold medal 7–2, the same newspaper re-ran the cartoon, this time with the Canadian sitting at the desk and "Bobrov" towering over him. Canada's assumed supremacy had disappeared forever.

Tuning the Big Red Machine

The rest of the 1950s, under Chernyshov (though most of the players were Tarasov's from Central Army), then Tarasov, then by 1962, under both of them, was a time of building and fine-tuning for the team that would dominate the following two decades.

After losing the 1955 worlds thanks to a 5–0 defeat by Canada, the Soviets went to their first Olympics in 1956 and took the gold. In 1957, the largest crowd in hockey history, 50,000 fans, came to the outdoor final in Moscow only to see Sweden win gold over the hosts. Canada and the United States had chosen not to come in protest of the Soviet invasion of Hungary the previous year.

The next two years also failed to produce world gold, and then came the United States' "miracle" win at Squaw Valley in the 1960 Olympics. After a loss in 1961, officials decided to put Tarasov and Chernyshov together. They also decided to skip the 1962 worlds as a payback for the Canadians and Americans skipping in 1957.

That pairing, despite their differences with each other, was golden. Especially since the players (who, remember, had just been introduced to the game 16 years previously) were ready to take over the international hockey scene.

Quote, Unquote

"Their slowest skater was faster than our fastest skater."

—Canadian opponent Eric Unger, on the 1954 Soviet world championship team.

Quote, Unquote

"The defensemen, Ragulin and Ivanov, would certainly be welcome on any of our best professional teams."

—Jackie McLeod, Canadian forward and future national team coach.

Great Lines—Part Two

From 1963 to 1972, the Soviets went on an unprecedented run that saw the club to seven-straight world championships and three Olympic gold medals. The Czechs finally stopped the run with the 1972 world title.

The win in 1963 (4–2 over Canada) in the final was special, because, as Martin writes, the games were on television in the USSR and the players went from mere heroes to hockey gods in the eyes of the people.

Though Anatole Firsov was probably the best Soviet player of the 1960s, the best unit was the A-Line of Veniamin Alexandrov, Konstantin Loktev, and Alexander Almetov—the Academicians.

Alexandrov, blond hair flying in the wind, scored 351 goals in 400 league games. Almetov (who had terrible drinking problems that would constantly plague him), seven years on the national team, scored 212 times in 220 games. And Loktev potted 213 goals in 340 games. All were members of Tarasov's Central Army club (he thought they perfectly represented the Soviet hockey mentality of skate, pass, think), which was important because they played together for years—they knew each other's moves and could read each other's thoughts in their sleep.

This was a key for the Soviets—unity. Units stayed together. Individual players were not often taken for the national team without their linemates or defensemate.

Overseas Odysseys

Despite early international success, Tarasov believed strongly that in order for the Soviets to truly test their progress, they would have to test their mettle against professional players, especially the NHLers.

It would take 15 years from the Soviet's first trip to North America, in 1957, before that dream would come true, and Tarasov, ironically, wouldn't be part of it.

The Soviets came all the way west in 1957, when they played the Whitby Dunlops at Maple Leaf Gardens and then went on to win five of the next seven.

Trips such as these were repeated throughout the 1960s, but always against junior or senior clubs, amateur all-star teams, the national team (also amateur), and, in one case, a Montreal junior team that had been augmented by a number of former pros from the Quebec Senior League. They were always successful for the Soviets.

But during those trips, and off in the board rooms of the International Ice Hockey Federation, two themes were now being regularly heard—if Canada could use their pros, the Soviets wouldn't stand a chance, and all the Soviet players are pros anyway.

It was those two themes that would lead to the famous Summit Series in 1972.

Aw, I Knew That!

Q. Only two players have been selected the top forward at the world championships on three different occasions. Who are they?

A. Anatoli Firsov and Alexander Maltsev.

Professionals

Is this a professional? Take an athlete. Put him in the army or an essential industry. Send him to a hockey camp for 11 months a year and fill 6 of 7 days with hockey and dry-land training each of those days. Pay for his meals, travel, and equipment. Make sure his family has an apartment and enough money to live. Don't require him to show up for any army assignments or days of work at the factory.

That was a Soviet hockey player in the 1950s to 1980s. That was a professional.

Canadian and American officials knew the Soviets and the Czechs were pros because a Czech journalist had tipped them off. A little more digging and *voilà*. But pressured by the Soviets and Czechs, the IIHF never admitted it until 1977, and that frustrated the Canadians especially to no end. They would finally pull out of international hockey in protest in 1970.

It was right then that the Soviets and Canadians began to cook up an eight-game series between both countries' best players that would settle the question of who was best, once and for all.

Goaltenders

Tarasov considered goaltending to be his greatest worry. At least, until he discovered a skinny teenager with a goose neck in the late 1960s on whom he lavished constant and strict attention—Vladislav Tretiak.

Harry Mellups, a native of Latvia, was the best of the early goaltenders, but he had the misfortune to be on the doomed Air Force plane that went down in 1950.

The acrobatic Nikolai Puchkov would take over and lead the team through most of the 1950s before handing off to Viktor Konovalenko for the 1960s. Though others were brought in and out, Puchkov and Konovalenko were the main goalies in the first 20 years. They played well, but Tarasov, especially, thought the system could produce something better: the best goalie in the world.

And that was where Tretiak came in (see Chapter 17, "High and Low Tides [September 1972–2001]").

Aw, I Knew That!

Q. Whom did Vladislav Tretiak replace as number-one goaltender of the national team?

A. Viktor Konovalenko.

Quote, Unquote

"Don't listen to the compliments. When they praise you, they steal from you."

—Anatole Tarasov, to a very young Vladislav Tretiak.

Good-Bye Anatole

Tarasov had always been in and out of favor with his bosses at the sports ministry and in the Kremlin. Once he took his team off the ice in a game against Spartak to protest the officiating and was removed from the national team for a while. But in 1972, he was still there, still co-coach of the national team at Sapporo for the Olympics.

He got in trouble with the Kremlin again when he allowed his players to take $200 each for an exhibition series in Japan. Despite going on to win the Olympic gold medal, the bosses, as Martin writes, decided to give him and Chernyshov a break from coaching—permanently.

The father of Russian hockey had his family taken away from him at its most crucial moment, just prior to the Summit Series in September 1972 with the best of the Canadian pros.

There were many afterward who felt if the change hand not been made, the Soviets might have won it.

Great Games

Spring 1969

Moscow Spartak and Central Red Army found themselves in a one-game showdown for the league title that year, but hockey would take a backseat to the dramatics caused by Anatole Tarasov. With Spartak leading 2–1, Army forward Vladimir Petrov scored the tying goal with one second left on the clock before the standard switch of ends at the halfway mark of the third. But the officials ruled it no goal, causing Tarasov to blow his stack and take his team to the dressing room, where he stayed put despite pleas from all and sundry. Suddenly, a messenger from General Secretary Brezhnev, who was at the game, showed up with the suggestion Tarasov should get his butt back out there. Which he did. Spartak scored again and won the championship.

Moscow Spartak 3, Central Red Army 1

Stars of the Era

➤ Usevolod "Seve" Bobrov is considered by many observers to be the best player the Soviets produced. The first captain of the national team, he played in four world championships and the 1956 Olympics. Was head coach of the nationals for three years, 1972–1974.

➤ Veniamin Alexandrov played in 3 Olympics and 11 world championships in addition to 14 seasons with Central Red Army. Played with Konstantin Loktev and Alexander Almetov as a winger on the best Soviet line of the 1960s.

➤ Anatoli Firsov, also among the best Soviets ever, was a forward at three Olympics from 1964 to 1972 and won eight straight world titles from 1963. Scored 344 goals in 474 league games with Spartak and Central Red Army. Firsov died of a heart attack at age 59 in 2000. He had become a deputy in the Russian parliament in 1989. It was on his death that word got out the reason he had missed the 1972 Summit Series with Canada was because officials had feared he would defect to North America.

➤ Defenseman Alexander "Rags" Ragulin was on three Olympic-winning and nine world championship clubs. Four times a world all-star, he capped his career with the 1972 Summit Series against Canada, playing one more league season after that. Played 427 league games before he went into junior coaching.

➤ Vyacheslav Starshinov was another talented forward on the teams of the 1960s. Had 405 goals in 540 league games over a career that ran from 1957 to 1979. Played most of his league career with Spartak Moscow.

The Least You Need to Know

➤ The Soviets switched from bandy (ball hockey) to hockey (puck hockey) in 1946.

➤ Anatole Tarasov is the father of Russian hockey.

➤ The Soviets won the first world championship they entered, in 1954.

➤ From 1963 to 1972, the Soviets dominated international hockey.

➤ Soviet hockey was built on passing, skating, and intense physical training.

High and Low Tides (September 1972–2001)

Soviet hockey from the end of the Summit Series until the turn of the millennium fell into four periods: the struggle of the mid-1970s; the happy era when Viktor Tikhonov took over the club and made it the best in the world; the Glasnost era that saw a trickle of Soviet stars to the NHL become a flood; and the 1990s, when the domestic league began to fall apart and the real cost of Tikhonov's policies began to be realized. In this chapter, we'll look at those four periods.

The Real Winners

Who really won the Summit Series in 1972? Was it the Canadians, thanks to Paul Henderson's late game eight heroics? Was it the Soviets, by proving they not only belonged on the same ice as the Canadian pros, but were pretty much equal to the best the NHL could offer?

The Soviets were told by their superiors upon leaving for Canada to open the eight-game affair not to get embarrassed. But as the series went on and success came the Soviets' way, demands were raised so that by the end, nothing short of a victory was the requirement.

That, however, was the official view.

As Vladislav Tretiak writes, the people on the street—the regular people of Moscow and beyond—were thrilled beyond belief with the team's success against Canada and not the least bit down by the loss. That opinion was actually more important to the players than anything the guys in the black suits had to say.

"Boris and Irena," however, would also soon enough alter their opinions and begin to expect more and more of their national side.

As for the Soviet players themselves, they were upset by what they felt was an opportunity for the upset of a lifetime that was lost. Many, including Tretiak, blamed Usevolod Bobrov, the co-coach, for being too soft with the players, especially when they got back to Moscow for games five through eight.

They felt it would not have happened under Tarasov.

And there was another worry. Could the Soviet players, forced to come from behind or cling to a close game in the final minutes, pull it out? Did they have what it took to win the big ones?

Time would provide the answer.

So who won? As discussed in Part 3, "International Incidents," the real winner was the game of hockey, changed forever by the series of the century.

Tretiak

Vladislav Tretiak, the answer to Anatole Tarasov's dream, grew up in Dmitrovo, just outside Moscow, with a father who was not too interested in sports and a mother who was a gym teacher and former field hockey player. One day, as he writes in his autobiography, young Vladislav announced to his mother, "I am definitely going to be a champion."

And he was. Tretiak first became a goaltender because he was desperate to get one of his local sports club's hockey uniforms, and the only position available was goal. From there, he went to the Red Army sports school, through the youth and junior ranks, and then on to Central Red Army's senior team as a 17-year-old.

He owed everything to Anatole Tarasov, who saw in the youngster the makings of greatness and set out to ensure that greatness would happen. Tarasov turned all of his creative genius on Tretiak, creating dozens of unusual drills such as tossing a tennis ball to a wall with his right hand and catching it with his left—first alone, then with someone in his face, then with two others right in his space, trying to throw him off.

The variations were endless.

Tretiak joined the senior national team while still a teenager and made his debut as its number-one goaltender in 1971. By 1972, he was ready to stun the hockey world with his talents by playing superbly in the Summit Series.

He would go on to a long career, winning the respect and admiration of North American fans. After retiring in 1984, he went into coaching goaltenders and was still doing so, in the NHL, at the end of the century. He was elected to the Hockey Hall of Fame.

Aw, I Knew That!

Q. Who was Vladislav Tretiak's direct successor in goal for the Soviet team?

A. Yevgeny Belosheikin. He was between the pipes for the Soviets at Rendezvous '87.

Great Lines—Part Three

Valeri Kharlamov, Boris Mikhailov, Vladimir Petrov. Teammates with Central Red Army. The Soviet line of the 1970s.

Mikhailov captained the national team throughout the entire era, including its happiest time when the club was the best in the world. He was also the top scorer in Soviet history, notching 427 goals in 572 games. Where most of the team was impassive on the ice, Mikhailov was a bundle of energy, yelling, exhorting, pushing.

Vladimir Petrov had 370 goals and was an outstanding forward internationally.

Two great players.

But the one most fans remember, the one that left even the most ardent capitalists thrilled, was Kharlamov.

Aw, I Knew That!

Q. This player set the all-time record for most games played on a Soviet national team. Who was he?

A. Alexander Maltsev. He appeared 319 times in a Soviet uniform.

Valeri Kharlamov was born of a Russian father and Spanish mother and came to Central Red Army in 1967 as a revelation, even among swift-skating, beautifully stickhandling Soviets. He was the real deal: a beautiful scorer, skater, thinker. And struck with a hockey life out of a Greek tragedy.

In 1972, Bobby Clarke purposely slashed his ankle so badly he was effectively eliminated from a Summit Series he had dominated. In 1974, Rick Ley cut him in the face for a number of stitches. In 1976, Ed Van Impe of Philadelphia elbowed him with such force Kharlamov was throwing up in the dressing room.

That same year, he was in a terrible car accident with his wife that, doctors said, would end his career. But he battled back and almost made the Soviet lineup for the 1981 Canada Cup. While that team was in Edmonton preparing for a game on August 27, 1981, Kharlamov and his wife were in a car outside Moscow (Irina driving) that crossed the lane into an oncoming truck. Both were killed instantly.

"Soviet hockey still looks for a player who can replace him," wrote Lawrence Martin. "Many greats followed, none with the quixotic flair, the Spanish dash, and charisma of the successor to Bobrov."

Down in the Dumper

Tretiak credited it to a belief in victory that was so well developed by 1976 that he and his teammates thought they would win no matter how they played.

Whatever the cause, for a two-year period—1976–1977—the Soviet Union's Big Red Machine went right in the tank.

In April 1976, after winning the Olympic gold two months earlier, the club went to Poland for the world championships and met the hosts in the first game. And lost 6–4. To Poland, for gosh sakes. As humiliating a loss as anything Canada took in its long international history.

I Remember ...

Rather than get in trouble for taking his Red Army team off the ice at Philadelphia in 1976 (as Tarasov had in a 1969 league game), just before the end of a first period in which the Flyers had gooned the Soviet club at every turn, coach Konstantin Loktev actually got in dutch from his Kremlin masters for going back on again. Loktev had returned after NHL president Clarence Campbell and Alan Eagleson went to the dressing room and assured the coach the dirty play would not continue. When he got back to Moscow, writes Lawrence Martin, Leonid Brezhnev got on his case for continuing the game. Loktev, drawing up his courage, suggested to the General Secretary that if the Kremlin didn't want him to go back on, they could have called him in Philadelphia.

Though the Soviets finished with the silver, losses to Sweden and the Czechs at the same worlds were terribly embarrassing.

Then, fall of 1976, a Soviet "experimental" team (which Canadian writers say was sent because the Soviets were afraid of losing they set themselves up to lose, while Soviet writers say there were so many injuries to key players they just had to send a lot of youngsters), not only lost the first Canada Cup tournament, it didn't even make the final round.

Then Kharlamov's accident. And in 1977 a loss to the Czechs at the world championship and a bronze medal. Bronze. It was too much to bear.

It was also too much for the hockey bosses, who turned to a young coach they had sent to the Canada Cup for experience, as the new savior of the program.

A coach named Viktor Tikhonov.

Viktor Rules

Two views of Viktor:

"It's no secret that we were cautious at first about our new coach, but once we got to know Viktor Tikhonov, we knew that we could follow him through fire and water."

That would be Vladislav Tretiak.

"The coach pretends to take care for his athletes, but he cares only for himself."

That would be Slava Fetisov.

Love him or hate him, Viktor Tikhonov would have, after Tarasov, the most important positive effects on Soviet hockey since the Patriotic War. He would also be the man responsible for killing the domestic Soviet program by the late 1980s.

He was a man who started working at the age of just 12, in 1942. A middle-talent player, he found a place on the famous Air Force team because Usevolod Bobrov recommended him, and then went to Dynamo.

As a coach, Tikhonov made his name in Latvia, with Dynamo Riga (remember, Dynamo was

Aw, I Knew That!

Q. In the 1973 worlds, this Soviet forward set a tournament record by scoring 18 times in just 10 games. Name him.

A. Vladimir Petrov. He added 16 assists for 34 points.

Aw, I Knew That!

Q. Who was the first Soviet player selected in the NHL amateur draft?

A. Viktor Khatulev, Dynamo Riga, selected by Washington in the 1975 draft, 116th overall.

supported by the KGB), which he dragged all the way from the second division to the Elite League by 1973. His star there was Helmut Balderis, with whom he had a rotten relationship, once even punching the forward after an altercation on the ice.

Tikhonov took the Soviet team for the 1976 Canada Cup overseas and picked up the full national team in 1977.

Emotional, patriotic, a confirmed Stalinist, cursed with a bad temper, he was also a brilliant coach and tactician. And he was sure what to do about the Soviet's bad run in the middle 1970s—steal all the best players off the other teams in the league, concentrate them at Central Red Army, and basically keep the national team together 11 months of the year.

And for a long while, it worked. Casting aside the upset to the United States at the 1980 Games, they won two Olympics, numerous world championships, crushed the NHL in the Challenge Cup series of 1979, and took the Canada Cup tournament of 1981.

However, Tikhonov also kept his players trapped at the training camp outside Moscow for 11 months a year, usually 7 days a week (not that Tarasov didn't do that as well, but that was a more patriotic time), kept them from their families, yelled and screamed at them regularly, lied to them to keep them under control, and often caved in to pressure from the Kremlin.

It was Kremlin officials who talked Tikhonov into removing Tretiak from the net after the first period of the 1980 game with the United States, something his players credited for the famous loss.

And he upset his stars (especially Slava Fetisov) to the point that they were desperate to get out of the Soviet Union, and to the NHL, just to get away from him.

The most revealing incident between Fetisov and Tikhonov came in the 1987 Prague worlds, when the coach started to scream in the face of his captain, only to have Fetisov stand up, put his hands on the coach's chest, and shove him backward so hard he almost fell over.

That battle for power and respect would spill over one final time.

Great Lines (Plus Two)—Part Four

Viktor Tikhonov was able to take Tarasov's idea of keeping lines, and even fivesomes, together to its ultimate point with the 1980s unit of Vladimir Krutov between Igor Larionov and Sergei Makarov (the KLM Line), with the defense pairing of Slava Fetisov and Alexei Kasatonov (who despised each other) along to complete the "Green Unit" (for the sweater color they wore in practice).

The trio, or fivesome, dominated play during the decade and was the first of the great four units not to finish its career solely in the Soviet Union. All five would go to the National Hockey League.

I Remember ...

At the 1985 tournament, the Soviets did something they almost never did—precipitating a brawl with the United States in a meaningless game they would win 11–1. Late in the game, all heck broke loose after Slava Fetisov pounded Jim Johnson and then decked another American with one punch; Tim Thomas and Irek Gimaev slugged each other to a standstill; coach Viktor Tikhonov got into a screaming match with a bunch of American officials; and U.S. coach Dave Peterson raced onto the ice to argue with the officials. 14,000 fans in Prague put the capper on the scene by screaming USA! USA!

What made the KLM line go was Krutov, the Tank, who would stand in the slot taking abuse while the other two flitted around the outskirts, setting up plays and looking for good scoring chances that were often developed by the rushes of Fetisov and Kasatonov.

Take Your Job and Shove It

Gorbachev's Glasnost/Perestroika movement, which slowly brought greater freedom to the Soviet Union in the late 1980s, and would eventually lead to its breakup, could not help but have an effect on the hockey program.

That effect was simple. The players, led by Fetisov, basically told Tikhonov to shove his dictatorial regime because they were sick of it. Sick of not seeing their families. Sick of having every day of their lives regimented from before sun-up to well after sundown.

Sick and tired.

Fetisov's and Tikhonov's hatred for each other had gotten past the point of reconciliation, and for the defenseman, who was exhibiting incredible courage by standing up to the coach, it was a turning point.

The team itself was playing badly (for them) and the top line was slumping. Larionov was upset because Tikhonov was messing with his mind, keeping him from certain tournaments for weak reasons. Pressure was mounting to keep winning at the rate the club had done in the early 1980s.

Quote, Unquote

"With Sergei Makarov, we have the Gretzky of the east."

—Viktor Tikhonov, 1986.

And questions about the Soviets' ability to win in the crunch (they lost the Canada Cup in 1987 on a late goal in game three of the final by Mario Lemieux) still remained.

Hockey's greatest long-running show was ready to crack to pieces.

Aw, I Knew That!

Q. What three players had been expected to comprise the Line of the 1990s for the Soviet Union before the doors to the west opened?

A. Pavel Bure, Sergei Fedorov, and Alexander Mogilny.

Quote, Unquote

"This is kind of stealing."

—Georgi Oganov, Soviet Embassy, Washington, after Sergei Fedorov defected from the Soviet team at the 1990 Goodwill Games in Seattle and signed with the Detroit Red Wings.

Large Cracks in the Foundation

In 1988, the smallest of cracks in the Iron Curtain appeared, and Sergei Priakin, a long-time member of the Soviet Wings and three-time member of the national team as a third and fourth liner, was allowed to leave and sign with the Calgary Flames.

Priakin, a right winger, would prove that every member of the Soviet team actually couldn't make a go of it in the NHL—in 46 games he would amass just 3 goals and 11 points. His importance was far greater as a symbol, however. He was free (okay, much of his salary was going back to the hockey authorities in Moscow, but we're talking in relative terms here).

More were about to come.

Rumors had been rampant for a long time that older Soviet players might be allowed out to finish their careers in the NHL. But something, even in the summer and fall of 1988, was holding up the process. That something was Viktor Tikhonov, who wasn't about to let his meal ticket disappear without a fight.

Ultimately, Fetisov's courage at standing up to the dictatorial coach went the longest way to opening the doors through which five players would pass for the 1989–1990 season (see Chapter 19, "Breaking Down the Iron Curtain"). But what really hurt the program was the defection of Sergei Fedorov in the same year—costing the Soviets its best young player.

Tikhonov held on as coach of the national team right through the breakup of the Soviet Union in 1991 and on to the 1992 Olympics, when Russia and the former puppet states would stick together one more time as the Commonwealth of Independent States (CIS). Tikhonov would take them to the gold medal.

But for 1994, with so many players refusing to play for him, Tikhonov would be gone. Not forever, however.

The Palace Crumbles

What Tikhonov sowed in the early 1980s by raping other clubs in the Soviet league of their best players, ruining competitive balance, turning away the fans in droves, and basically turning the whole operation into a house league for his own club's benefit, grew into a bitter harvest by the 1990s.

Realizing they had no chance to win, other players in the domestic league simply mailed in their games with Central Red Army, which further turned off the fans and cooled the forge within which the national team had always been able to temper its steel to a fine edge.

Even an attempt to inject some excitement into the league by introducing playoffs for the first time was cut down by Tikhonov, because he thought it would tire out his national team players too much.

The number of applications for sports schools had dropped to almost nothing, the number of teams in the Golden Puck youth tournament had fallen away, and fans' attention was on other things—like eating.

When Tod Hartje, former captain at Harvard, went to the Soviet Union in 1990–1991 to play for Sokol Kiev as an experiment set up by Mike Smith, then general manager of the Winnipeg Jets, he found the system for training players—long days, total immersion, etc.—still in place. But rinks were falling apart, equipment was still lousy (after all these years they still couldn't make decent hockey gear in Russia), players were often drunk, and many teams were unable to draw flies.

Worst of all, with communism dead, most of the teams in the domestic league were no longer being supported by the government (the army continued to fund Central Red Army), and because they had never been forced to develop marketing plans and the like to raise their own funds, many clubs were left high and dry.

And it continued to get worse before it got better.

After the Soviet Union won the world championship in 1990, it would win just once more in the decade, take third once, and be out of the medals the rest of the time, culminating in the humiliation of losing to Switzerland (!) and finishing eleventh as hosts at St. Petersburg in 2000.

On the other hand, the Russian NHLers came together in 1998 and almost pulled off the gold medal at the Olympics in Nagano.

And the first act of the new century after the disaster of the 2000 worlds? Rumors began to spread that the Russians were looking to the past to find a coach who could turn the fortunes around once again.

A coach named Viktor Tikhonov.

Quote, Unquote

"I tried to imagine the Great Gretzky, doing his own hockey laundry, tailoring his shin pads with a hacksaw, and taping nickels and quarters to his hockey jersey to make it fit."

—American Tod Hartje, who played for Sokol Kiev for one season in the early 1990s.

Stars of the Era

➤ Helmut Balderis, "the Electric Train," was one of the fastest players in hockey history. A native of Latvia, he played for Dynamo Riga under Viktor Tikhonov for eight years, until 1977, then switched to Central Red Army before his rotten relationship with the national coach sent him back to Riga. Scored 333 times in 462 league games and spent 5 seasons on the national team.

➤ Viacheslav Fetisov, arguably the greatest player ever produced in the Soviet system, was a junior star who made his national team debut in 1980 at the Winter Olympics in Lake Placid, and eventually became the captain of the club. Five times best defenseman at the world championships and on the all-star team at the 1987 Canada Cup. Became one of the first Russians to join the National Hockey League. Would win two Stanley Cups with the Detroit Red Wings.

➤ Vladislav Tretiak is a Hall of Fame goaltender who made his big-time debut at the 1972 Summit Series. Played in 4 Olympics and 13 world championships. Four times top goaltender at the worlds, tournament most valuable player in the 1981 Canada Cup.

➤ Valeri Kharlamov is considered one of the greatest talents in hockey history, but like Bobby Orr, he was often hurt. Scored 293 goals in 438 league games and, with Boris Mikhailov and Vladimir Petrov, was a member of the Line of the 1970s. Killed in a car accident in 1981.

➤ Vladimir Krutov, Igor Larionov, and Sergei Makarov were the KLM Line of the 1980s for the Soviet Union, dominating international play in that era. All three went to the NHL in 1989.

The Least You Need to Know

➤ The Soviets changed perceptions of hockey with their play in the 1972 Summit Series.

➤ The program went through a bleak time in the mid-1970s.

➤ Viktor Tikhonov took over the club in 1977 and got it back on the winning track.

➤ Tikhonov's methods stripped the Soviet league of its competitiveness and upset the national team's players.

➤ The Soviet Union allowed its best older players to head for the NHL in 1989.

➤ Domestic troubles with the hockey program and player losses to the NHL left Russia an uncompetitive national club in the 1990s.

Chapter 18

Tragedies and Triumphs— Czechoslovakia/ Czech Republic/ Slovakia

---

In This Chapter

➤ Two tragedies greet the second half-century

➤ Baby booms

➤ Battles with the Soviets

➤ Triumph in the 1970s

➤ Forcing open the gates

➤ First overall

As we learned in Chapter 5, "Over the Big Frozen Pond," Czechoslovakia had been among the first group of countries (as Bohemia) to join the International Ice Hockey Federation in 1910, and one of the first to taste success in the European championships. In the two decades before World War II, they were one of the few clubs that could regularly give the Canadians a decent game. So by 1947, when the world championships began again, they were an established club with a long history with the game. Since then, tragedy and triumph have been the order of the day. Politics, either internal or external, have never been far from the script, especially in dealings with the Soviet Union. Despite its peaks and valleys, by the end of the century, the Czech Republic (split from Slovakia in the early 1990s) was on top of the world. In this chapter, we'll look at those issues.

Sadness and Injustice

In 1947, Czechoslovakia hosted the first world tournament following the war and, without Canada (another in the ongoing arguments with the IIHF over power and money) and the United States (arguments over just who in that country could officially send a team) involved, won the title.

Aw, I Knew That!

Q. What famous NHLer had parents who took the family out of Czechoslovakia to escape the communist rule following World War II and came to Canada, where their son would grow to stardom?

A. Stan Mikita.

It seemed, after a silver medal at the 1948 Winter Olympics, that it was the Czechs who would give Canada the willies during the 1950s and not, as it turned out, the Soviets.

But on November 8, 1948—two years before the VVS Air Force crash killed that team—the entire Czech national club died in a plane crash, including stars Ladislav Trojak, Vilibald Stovik, Miloslav Pokorny, Karel Stibor, and Zdenek Jarkovsky.

Imagine the joy that replaced the sorrow in Prague, then, when a very young Czech team came to the 1949 worlds in Sweden, upset the Canadians 3–2 (Stanislav Konopasek with the winner), and won the gold for the second straight time.

Another tragedy was on the way, however.

It's said that the only thing more ruthless than the oppressor is the student of the oppressor. In 1950, the Czech national team learned that lesson the hard way.

As Igor Kuperman writes, on March 13, 1950, the entire national club was arrested by Czech secret police and charged with treason and espionage—the police claimed that everyone on the team was going to defect when it got to London for the worlds. They spent seven months in jail before even being informed of the charges.

Actually, two years previously, many had been approached about defecting but had turned the offer down. All except two, who did run. The rest had stayed loyal.

The court found all guilty. Goaltender Bohumil Modry (actually no longer playing for the national team and the greatest European goalie of his time) got 15 years; Gustav Bunik, 14; Stanislav Konopasek, 12; Vaclav Rozinak and Vladimir Kobranov, 10; and seven others terms ranging from 8 months to 6 years.

Most, Kuperman writes, served five years.

They were used as an example for all athletes.

Starting Over

Well, there was the best club in Europe, beginning again with no veterans to help. Hardly surprising then that the best they could do in the 1950s was four bronzes in the worlds and no medals in the Olympics.

In the 1960s, however, with a serious rivalry with the Soviet Union now in full swing, the Czechs were ready to re-emerge as a top player with the Russians and Canadians on the world scene.

The Men of 1944

Vaclav Nedomansky was born on March 14, 1944. Four days later, Jiri Holecek made his debut, followed two weeks later by Frantisek Pospisil and, two weeks after that, Oldrich Machac Oldrich. Late to the party being held in war-torn Czechoslovakia was Jiri Holik, who came by on July 7.

Within less than four months, the basis of the Czech national hockey team from the mid-1960s to the mid-1970s had been born.

Coached by the legendary Vladimir Kostka, who had taken the job in 1957 and would hold it, with a couple of years off for rest, until 1973, and his assistant Jaroslav Pitner, those five players and their teammates would earn silvers at the worlds four times up to 1975, win it once, take a pair of Olympic medals, and give the Soviets fits.

The old guard, such as Vlastimil Bubnik and Vladimir Zabrodsky, had left the scene by 1965, when the Czechs went to Finland and finished second behind the powerful Soviets.

Aw, I Knew That!

Q. Name the Canadian-born coach who took Czechoslovakia to the 1947 and 1949 world championship gold medals?

A. Matej "Mike" Buckna.

Aw, I Knew That!

Q. One Czech player was named to the world championship all-star team more than any other. Who was he?

A. Goaltender Jiri Holecek.

Training

The Czech system after World War II was similar to the Soviets', but not quite as regimented.

Young players joined sports clubs, which led to junior teams and then—for the best—on to the Czech domestic senior league (the Extraleague). Leading teams in the top loop

Aw, I Knew That!

Q. Name the Czech hockey star who won a gold medal for his country in 1947 and 1949, moved to Egypt, and won the Wimbledon singles tennis title for that country in 1954?

A. Jaroslav Drobny.

have included ZKL Brno and Krlovo Pole, Dukla Jihlava, Kosice, Poldi Kladno, and Slovan Bratislava.

Bratislavla was one of three teams from Slovakia in the Czech senior league, along with VSZ Kosice and Dukla Trencin—teams that produced a plethora of stars including the famous goaltender Vladimir Dzurilla, Nedomansky, the three Stastny brothers (Peter, Marian, and Anton), Igor Liba, Peter Bondra, and Zigmund Palffy.

What truly set the Czech system apart starting in the 1970s, was the way permission was given for older players to continue their careers in western European leagues, especially Germany and Austria. The Soviets did it, but much more rarely.

Great Games

March 1973

The Soviets had come to the world championships for the first time without their long-time mentor Anatole Tarasov, but still expected to win the thing, even in Prague. After all, they had won 11 times in a row. In the final game, however, the Czechs came out roaring and, spurred on by their crowd, earned the victory, 3–2, thanks to a pair of goals by Vaclav Nedomansky and one from Richard Farda. The pair were elevated to all-time heroes. Ironic-ally, just one year later, both heroes would be in Toronto, having defected to the World Hockey Association Toros.

Czechoslovakia 3, Soviets 2

Hatred

According to Vladislav Tretiak, the Russian players could never understand why they were so hated by the Czech fans.

Might have had something to do with the tight control the Soviets kept on the Czechs as a puppet state. Or the invasion in August 1968. Or the ruthless version of communism the Czech leaders themselves perpetrated on the populace, which many blamed on the Soviets.

Whatever the reason, you can forget the Toronto Maple Leafs and the Montreal Canadiens, or the Habs and the Detroit Red Wings, or even Canada and the Soviets. None of those rivalries could hold a Hallmark candle to the Soviets and the Czechs—ironic, since it was the Czechs who had gone to Moscow in 1947 to help teach puck hockey to the hosts there.

As we saw in Chapter 12, "A Federation for the Worlds," the most famous games between the two sides were in the 1969 world championships, six months after the Soviets sent tanks into Prague to ruthlessly stamp out the small flame of democracy that had grown there. Inspired, the Czechs beat the Soviets twice in Stockholm the following spring but still lost the gold because they couldn't keep their emotions up for a key game with Sweden.

The true revenge would come in the 1970s, when the Czechs would finally break through to win their first worlds since 1949. Actually, they'd do it three times.

First, Finally

Under coaches Kostka and Pitner, the Czechs of 1972 had finished third in the Sapporo Olympics, thanks to a key loss to the Soviets in a game that basically decided the gold.

But in the year that the Soviets would prove their worth against the Canadians in the Summit Series, Team Czechoslovakia finally struck, setting off a run of excellence that would run the rest of the decade.

Hosting the tourney, the Czechs greeted the Soviets, who had won 10 straight worlds, by beating them and taking the gold—first time in 25 years.

That was just the start.

I Remember ...

After the Czechs had won the 1971 European title over the Soviets, the two teams were at the championship banquet when the band began playing the song "Kalinka." Without introduction, Anatole Tarasov went to the middle of the floor and danced a Russian folk dance, soon to be joined by a number of his stars including Valeri Kharlamov. Suddenly, a young man tossed his jacket aside and carried away with his emotions began to show he could compete with the Russian players and coaches even on the dance floor. He was Ivan Hlinka, a supreme Czech star, and soon the entire Czech team joined him. The rivalry continued even off the ice.

The coaches retired and Dr. Jan Starsi, a Slovak who had played 73 times for the national team in his youth, took over the club (with co-coach Karel Gut), a position he would hold until 1979, and then again from 1984–1988.

After a third in 1973, the Czechs pushed the Big Red Machine to the wall in a 3–1 loss in 1974 (silver medal), took another silver in 1975, and went into 1976 brimming with confidence.

Starsi was absolutely convinced they had what it took to win the gold medal at the Olympic Games in Innsbruck, Austria.

In Sickness and in Health

There was a rotten flu going around the Olympic Village in 1976, and wouldn't you know it—practically the entire Czech team came down with it just before the tournament began.

Desperate to feel better, Frantisek Pospisil, the brilliant defenseman, took an over-the-counter medication that contained codeine (on the list of banned substances). He was tested. He was caught. A win against Poland was overturned.

But the Czechs fought their way to the final game for the gold with the Soviets anyway, and actually led the thing, 2–0, halfway through the second period. Granted a two-man advantage for a full two minutes, they couldn't come up with another one and the Big Red Machine came roaring back to win it 3–2.

Exit gold. On to Poland for the worlds.

Who could have known that the mighty Soviets were ready to go falling over their feet with an embarrassing loss to the Poles, which they followed up with a 3–2 loss and 3–3 tie against the Czechs.

Aw, I Knew That!

Q. Who is the only player to have played in a major international tournament for three different countries?

A. Peter Stastny. Czechoslovakia, Canada, and Slovakia.

Enter gold. Second of the decade.

Off to North America for the first Canada Cup tournament, August 1976, in which the Czechs were thought to be, at best, third-place finishers. Led by the goal-tending of Vlad Dzurilla (out of a long retirement to play), they surprised by making the finals, where they lost in two straight to the hosts. But everyone was paying attention now.

And then Vienna, in the spring of 1977, with the Canadians back for the first time since 1969, and a gold medal to defend. In their first meeting of the tournament, the Soviets destroyed Dr. Starsi's team 6–1. So much for the new reputation.

However, the Soviets were dumped themselves, 5–1 by Sweden, setting up another opportunity for gold.

With Dzurilla practically turning cartwheels in the net and the shooters hotter than they had ever been, the Czechs built up a 3–0 first-period lead over the Red Machine that they made stand up. Thanks to a second win by Sweden over the Soviets, the gold medal went to Czechoslovakia for the second straight year.

By the end of the decade, the Czechs had earned three world championships, four silver and a bronze, plus a silver and bronze in the Olympics.

They might not have been the Russians, but they were a proud and reasonable facsimile.

Exit Big Ned

Vaclav Nedomansky. Big Ned. Czech captain. Three-time world all-star. Wasn't there to see most of the heroics of the 1970s.

In 1974, Big Ned defected. Snuck out of town with teammate Richard Farda. Bid the communist world and the Iron Curtain good-bye and headed for North America to join the Toronto Toros of the World Hockey Association.

Czech officials, who had always been paranoid about defection (remember they had thrown the entire national team in jail in 1950 because of that fear), were furious. They broadcast nasties about Big Ned. About his manhood. About his love of country. And they crossed their fingers and hoped he would be the only Czech to check out.

Nedomansky, 6'2", 205 pounds, was a big (for his time) centerman who could handle both the puck and the rough play. His defection was a revelation in the west, precisely because he was the first big-name player from a communist country to do so. And not only that, he was the Czech captain, for gosh sakes.

In the WHA, Nedomansky had seasons of 41, 56, and 36 goals before leaving for the Detroit Red Wings partway through the 1977–1978 season after forcing his release from the Birmingham Bulls. He would have two sparkling seasons with the Wings, notching 38 in 1978–1979 and 35 the following season, but hobbled by injuries and starting to grow old, his totals began to drop off. He retired from the New York Rangers after 1983.

Though he was a great player, perhaps Big Ned's biggest contribution was that his defection gave other athletes an idea.

The Badly Built Barn Door

Little did Czech officials realize they were on the way to providing the NHL with its third source of great players, behind the Swedes and the Finns.

Quote, Unquote

"My parents still talk about the great 1969 games. Beating the Russians is still a big thing for that generation."

—Petr Svoboda, who scored the winning goal in the gold medal final, 1998 Olympics.

The border closed up tight for five years as the secret police and hockey honchos kept a very close watch on the players heading to the west for tournaments and vacations. As soon as they let up for a minute, however, a couple of Stastnys snuck through.

In the summer of 1980, Peter Stastny, his pregnant wife, and brother Anton, helped by Quebec Nordiques' general manager Marcel Aubut, snuck out of Innsbruck, Austria, for Canada, by way of Amsterdam. One year later, they literally bought brother Marian's way out of the country.

That was the beginning of a flood—a deluge that Czech authorities tried to stop right away by making agreements with their oldest players to let them out, in hopes of keeping the kids.

Jiri Bubla and Ivan Hlinka came, with blessing, to the Vancouver Canucks in 1981, for example, and others would follow.

But keeping the kids, talented, run of the mill, or otherwise, would not be easy. Through-out the 1980s they lost a number—Peter Ihnacek to Toronto, Miroslav Frycer to Quebec. Michal Pivonka took off. In 1989, Petr Nedved, one of the best youngsters ever produced, jumped ship at just 15 years old from the Mac's Midget Tournament in Calgary.

With the fall of the Iron Curtain in 1991, of course, entrance to the west and the NHL was wide open for anyone, as long as the pro team paid a fee to the Czech club for the privilege.

Great Games

February 1998

No one expected the Czech Republic to even make the gold medal final at Nagano, what with all the NHLers on the Canadian and American rosters. But thanks to goaltender Dominik Hasek, there they were, up against the hated Russians with everything on the line. The game went along scoreless for the longest time before Petr Svoboda, whose name means "freedom," hammered one in from the left point for the winner in a 1–0 game. That gold was a prize the former Czechoslovakia had never been able to grasp.

Czech Republic 1, Russia 0

Which should have made it difficult for the Czechs (now split from Slovakia) to compete strongly in internationals.

Should have, but didn't.

Heroes of the Late Century

With all of the men it lost from the domestic league to the NHL, including the best Czech player ever, Jaromir Jagr, who was drafted in the first round by Pittsburgh in 1990 and left immediately to join the Penguins, it looked as though the country would struggle regularly, which it did for a while.

But the world was about to learn something about the spirit of Czech players, and about a young goaltender named Dominik Hasek, who as the starter at the 1991 Canada Cup had struggled along with everyone else to a sixth-place finish.

Eighth at the first World Cup in 1996 was also bad, but there was lots of hockey left in the country, as it had already shown by winning the worlds the previous spring over Canada in a year that had also seen Slovakia return to the A pool following consecutive wins in the C and B levels over the previous two seasons.

Quote, Unquote

"This is the greatest day ever in Czech hockey. Nothing else comes even close to it."

—Martin Straka, on the 1998 gold medal victory.

Still, nothing could have prepared the hockey world, or the fans stuffed into bars around Wenceslas Square in Prague, for the 1998 Olympics. With Hasek incredible the whole way, the Czechs won their first Olympic gold. And they would follow that up with wins at the worlds in both 1999, 2000, and 2001.

At the international level, despite the fact the domestic league was no longer subsidized by the government and was seriously short of cash, the Czech Republic was number one.

Stars of the Era

➤ Ludec "Ludie" Bukac coached the Czech national team to world championships in 1985 and 1996. He also coached the German and Austrian national clubs. As a player, he suited up 30 times for the national team. First Czech to coach in the North American pro ranks as an assistant with the Oklahoma City Blazers in 1965.

➤ Vladimir Dzurilla came to prominence in North America with his spectacular goal-tending in the 1976 Canada Cup tournament—near the end of his career. Prior to that he had played in 3 Olympics, 10 world champions, and over his time won 3 world gold medals. Started in 1959 with Slovan Bratislava. Retired from the German League in 1982.

211

➤ Forward Ivan Hlinka played 16 years in the Czech league and wore the national jersey 11 times in the world championships before he went to the NHL in 1981. Played two seasons with Vancouver, scoring an impressive 123 points in 137 games in his late 30s. Went on to coach the national club for a number of years and was the head coach of the 1998 Olympic gold medal victory. In 2000, he became the second European-born head coach in the NHL, with the Pittsburgh Penguins, just behind Alpo Suhonen of Finland, hired the same summer to coach the Chicago Blackhawks.

➤ Goaltender Jiri Holecek made his debut at the world level in 1966 and stayed with the national club until 1978. Played with Dukla Kosice, VSZ Kosice, and Sparta Praha in the Czech League, totaling 488 games. Finished his career in Germany in 1981.

➤ Jiri Bubla and Frantisek Pospisil were considered the best defensemen the Czechs ever produced. Pospisil played in 3 Olympics and 11 world championships, was elected to the IIHF Hall of Fame, captained the national team during its brilliant run in the 1970s, and played 622 games in the Czech league. Bubla, who began internationally in 1971, helped anchor the defense in the 1970s, and went to the Vancouver Canucks in 1981, where he played five more seasons.

The Least You Need to Know

➤ An aircrash and sweeping arrests put the program behind in the 1950s.

➤ Success began to come in the 1960s.

➤ After catching the Soviets in the 1970s, the Czechs won three world championships.

➤ Vaclav Nedomansky's defection in 1974 eventually opened the door for more exits.

➤ The fall of the Iron Curtain sent many Czechs to the NHL.

➤ New Czech Republic won the Olympics in 1998 followed by two-straight world titles.

Chapter 19

Breaking Down the Iron Curtain

In This Chapter

➤ Czech players, old and young, hit the NHL

➤ Czech government opens the doors just before they are pushed open

➤ Soviet officials allow old players out, but young ones defect as well

➤ Eastern European influence becomes a force in the NHL

➤ Czech, Slovak, and former Soviet players survive and thrive

---

As each European hockey power began to send (willingly or not so) players to the NHL, they each influenced the pro game in North America in either subtle or very noticeable ways. Whatever the overall effect of Europeans in the big league, as opposed to the big leaguers playing and learning from the Europeans in the international arena, there's no denying the impact of Czech and Soviet/Russian players, and those from former states of the dying or dead communist regimes. In this chapter, we'll look at the stars that came to North America and some of their stories.

The First Wave

It would be unfair to say the Soviet/Russian and Czech influences on pro hockey in North America began with Vaclav Nedomansky's defection to the Toronto Toros of the World Hockey Association in 1974. Though extremely talented, Big Ned was more of a novelty than an influence, simply because there was only one of him. The defection of the Stastny brothers in 1980 and 1981 had more of an effect, but it was still just a beginning—a foreshadowing of what was to come. They brought the same kind of skills on the open ice and abilities with the puck that Wayne Gretzky and his teammates would at the same time in Edmonton.

After Nedomansky's defection with teammate Richard Farda, five years lapsed before the door was kicked open again with the Stastny brothers' exit to Quebec and young Petr Nedved's defection at the age of just 15 from the Mac's Midget tournament in Calgary (he would actually play for his new country, Canada, in the 1994 Olympics). Faced with more possible "illegal" exits, Czech officials began to open the door for older players, allowing Jiri Bubla and Ivan Hlinka out in 1981 to join the Vancouver Canucks at the same time that youngsters like Miroslav Frycer (1981) and Peter Ihnacak (1982) were stealing away.

Bubla, a defenseman, was 31, and his skills impressed everyone. Though already up there in age, he put in five seasons with the Canucks, playing 256 games. Hlinka, also 31, had been playing international for the Czechs since way back in 1969. He would last but two seasons in the NHL, though he had at least 60 points each time.

Jiri Hrdina, who arrived after playing for Czechoslovakia in the 1988 Olympics, went right into the Calgary lineup for the regular season and playoffs. The following year, by then a 31-year-old center, he would help the Flames win the Stanley Cup with 54 regular season points, but none in four playoff games.

Aw, I Knew That!

Q. Only one member of the famous Stastny brothers was actually chosen in the NHL amateur/entry draft. Which one, what team, and what year?

A. Anton Stastny, Philadelphia, 1978. Chosen 198th overall.

Catching a Draft

In the early 1980s, NHL clubs began to think about drafting Czech players (they had tried with Bubla and Hlinka by holding a special draft, but Vancouver got them on a legal technicality). A few of the players would pay dividends relatively soon, while others were long-term projects.

Vladimir Ruzicka, twice the Czech player of the year, was drafted in 1982 by Toronto, even though that club knew it would be years before they could get their hands on the center unless he defected—which he didn't. He would eventually debut with Edmonton in early 1990. Ruzicka would last five seasons before returning to finish his career in the Czech Republic.

Goaltender Dominik Hasek, who would eventually become one of the greatest ever, was taken by Chicago in 1983, but would stay with his country until debuting in 1990 with the Hawks. A little-used backup for two seasons, Hasek would be traded to Buffalo in the summer of 1992—a deal Chicago would like back.

Defender Frantisek Kucera was taken in 1986, also by Chicago, and would arrive in 1990.

Center Michael Pivonka, taken in 1984 by Washington, would defect and appear by 1986.

As the breakup of Czechoslovakia in 1991 neared, some creativity came into play. Bobby Holik was drafted by the Hartford Whalers in the first round of the 1989 draft, and they wanted him badly. It happened that tennis star Ivan Lendl was a member of the Whalers' board of directors, and he went to Prague and negotiated Holik's immediate release. He would score 20 or better 3 years in a row (traded to New Jersey in 1992), and would be a key member of the club for 2 Stanley Cup wins.

One Line for the Ages

The early 1990s may have been the time when the flood from the former Soviet Union really opened up, but it was also when the very best Czech and Slovak players would hit the big time. Slovaks such as Peter Bondra (Washington, 1990, drafted 156th overall and over 300 goals in the decade), Ziggy Palffy (Islanders, 1994), and Robert Svehla (Florida, 1995) would all make an impact on the NHL.

But it was one line, from the Czech junior teams of the late 1980s, that would contribute the most.

The center was Robert Reichel, who would join Calgary for 1990, and within two seasons post back-to-back 40-goal years (1992–1993 and 1993–1994). He would eventually be traded to the New York Islanders and Phoenix Coyotes.

At left wing was Holik.

And on the right side was a formerly skinny kid with long, flowing hair, a rock 'n' roll attitude, and extraordinary natural gifts. Taken fifth overall by Pittsburgh in 1990 (behind Owen Nolan, Petr Nedved, who went second to Vancouver, Keith Primeau, and Mike Ricci—it was an amazing draft crop), by the end of the decade he would be considered by many the greatest active player on earth.

A Jaguar at Full Speed

Simplistic though it is, a quick look at the standings shows something interesting under the title Pittsburgh Penguins. In the eight seasons before Jaromir Jagr joined the club as a rookie in the fall of 1990, the Pens missed the playoffs seven times. Five of those were with Mario Lemieux.

In the first two years after Jagr made his debut, Pittsburgh won back-to-back Stanley Cups. It wasn't that the tall, skinny Czech from Kladno made a huge impression of the scoring standings with his 57 and 69 points (as compared to his 100-plus years later in the 1990s)—it was that he was able to take some pressure off Lemieux by being another threat.

Quote, Unquote

"I'd have to be on another solar system to be able to get on their wavelength."

—Kevin Stevens, Pittsburgh Penguins, on what it was like trying to emulate the brilliant combination of Mario Lemieux and Jaromir Jagr.

And that's what Jagr has been all through his NHL career—a threat. And the players know it. In 2000, for example, St. Louis defenseman Chris Pronger was chosen as league most valuable player by hockey writers. Jagr, however, was chosen the best player for the second year running by the members of the NHL Players' Association.

His colleagues knew who was best, no doubt. By then the captain of the Penguins, Jagr was thought by many to be the best player in the world in 2000—despite a chronic groin injury.

I Remember ...

Jaromir Jagr has always been considered a shy, almost unapproachable athlete who has declined the chance to let fans get to know him better. But there's another side to him. Early in the 1990s, Chris Span, team receptionist, took a brief break from her duties while Jagr was in the office. Fascinated, the burgeoning star took her place behind the desk and started answering calls from fans asking for information. He even briefed a fan on details of a trade earlier that day involving teammates Mark Recchi and Paul Coffey. When things got too complicated, Jagr asked a fan to try again later, because there was nobody here "except a guy from Czecho."

The Dominator

He flopped. He dove. He "lost" his stick and played without it. He lay on his back flapping his legs and arms around so much that goaltending the Dominik Hasek way became known as "making snow angels."

And he was the best goaltender on earth during the last years of the century, twice winning the NHL's most valuable player award—the first goalie to win even won since Jacques Plante did it in 1962.

In 1993–1994, Hasek's goals against average of 1.95 was the first sub-2.00 mark in 20 years since Bernie Parent did it. He would also have years of 2.09 and 2.11.

In 1998, he took a Czech Republic team that generally couldn't put a puck into a soccer net without a lucky deflection all the way to a gold medal at the Olympic Games, beating Canada 2–1 in a shootout and then Russia in the finals.

In the spring of 1999, despite missing tons of time with a bad groin, Hasek came back in the playoffs to drag the Buffalo Sabres to a place in the Stanley Cup final, which they would lose in six games to the Dallas Stars.

Before the 1999–2000 season, Hasek, tired of battling his sore groin, announced he would retire by the end of the year. But, the Dominator had changed his mind.

The Old Age Home Invasion

The season of 1989–1990 may have been one of the loudest, strangest, and most important in the NHL's history.

Quote, Unquote

"A slinky for a spine? ... Priceless!"

—Credit card commercial on Dominik Hasek, referring to his style in net.

Suddenly, after years of speculation, the Soviet government announced that it was opening the doors and allowing older veterans on the national team to come to the National Hockey League. Of course, with the effects of Glasnost sweeping the nation and the effects of Slava Fetisov's one-man insurrection against Viktor Tikhonov sweeping the national hockey program, the Kremlin didn't have much choice.

I Remember ...

In 1989, Sergei Makarov joined the Calgary Flames carrying a very limited knowledge of English with him. Wanting to pair him with a good role model on the road, they assigned him as a roommate with Jim Peplinski, who was both a tremendous leader and the team's practical joker. On the first trip, Peplinski raced up to the hotel room first. When Makarov got there, Peplinski had pushed the two beds together and was lying across them, stark naked. "This is how we do things here in the NHL. Come over and lie down," said Peplinski. Instead, Makarov took his pillow and went into the bathroom. Peplinski said later Makarov spent the entire night sleeping in the bathtub.

So over to North America went the first wave—Igor Larionov (slow starter, would hit his stride eventually and still be playing in 2001 with two Stanley Cups to his credit) to Vancouver with Vladimir Krutov (too fat, too uninterested, bombed out quickly), Sergei Makarov (rookie of the year, two 30-goal seasons, too many injuries on too old a body) to Calgary, and Sergei Starikov (just 16 games overall) to New Jersey with Fetisov (solid for 9 years, with three Stanley Cup rings—two with Detroit and the last as an assistant coach in Jersey).

The press went wild. Some of the other players, fearing for their future if the Iron Curtain were to be lifted, went quietly wild. Don Cherry went loudly wild (suggesting the Russians should just go home).

Quote, Unquote

"If someone gave the Russians a football, they'd win the Super Bowl in two years."

—Former star Frank Mahovlich, on his admiration for the learning abilities of Russian players.

Quote, Unquote

"I think the Russians who play in the NHL should donate a small percentage of their salaries to help the veterans who paved the way for them."

—Evgeny Mishakov, five-time world champion and twice Olympic gold medallist. He lives on a $100 a month pension from the Russian army.

Fetisov would go wild himself when the Devils signed his former defensemate Alexei Kasatonov in January of 1990. Slava thought Alexei was a good little communist who was Tikhonov's fair-haired boy. There were times when Fetisov wouldn't even look at Kasatonov, even on the ice.

The Soviet players, most of whom didn't speak any English at the beginning, had all sorts of troubles adapting to a new league, a new country, to endless food in the grocery stores (keeping their wives from racing back to the store early each morning to buy everything they could, remembering the long lines for bread in the Soviet Union, became one of the first jobs for those helping the new families adjust). And to the number of games on the schedule, plus the killing travel.

But the Soviets survived to set the stage for others to come. Much to the Soviet's surprise, of course, some of those others arrived a little quicker than they might have thought.

A Fear of Flying, Not a Fear of Flight

While the NHL and the Soviets were happily arranging for the older players to jump to North America (with half their salaries going back to the Motherland), the Buffalo Sabres were happily helping 20-year-old Alexander Mogilny defect to the land of the 10-cent chicken wing.

The Soviets were furious. The NHL was actually upset, fearing the move would ruin the new relationship with Ronald Reagan's "evil empire" (fat chance, with all those American greenbacks available to Moscow). The Sabres were merely ecstatic.

At least for a while.

As Stan and Shirley Fischler write in *Red Line,* Mogilny was an unusual character, a young man who danced to his own tune, which was usually playing quietly in the back of his mind.

It was February 10, 1990, when Mogilny first refused to board a jet taking the club to St. Louis. His intense fear of flying (possibly mixed with his realization that Buffalo wasn't New York City) had finally grounded the winger.

He came back. He missed a later trip. He came back again. Some in the press hammered him and some were sympathetic. Same with his teammates, coach, and general manager. Psychologists chipped in with their opinion. Everyone had an idea. The club even let him take a limo from one spot to another if it was close enough.

As with Wayne Gretzky (possibly the worst flyer in league history), Mogilny would eventually find a way to handle it. And over the following decade, he would come up with some superb years, including 76 goals in 1982–1983 and 55 with Vancouver (after forcing a trade from Buffalo) in 1995–1996.

His output was dropping through 1999, and some thought he was about done. But Mogilny surprised with a strong second half in 2000 and an excellent (43 goals) 2000–2001. In the summer of 2001, he would sign a huge free-agent contract with the Toronto Maple Leafs.

Aw, I Knew That!

Q. What rookie of the year's win caused a change in the eligibility rules for the Calder Trophy?

A. Sergei Makarov, 1989–1990. He was 31. After that, no player older than 26 could be eligible for the top rookie award.

When a Defection Isn't a Defection

Alexander Mogilny takes off and the Soviets said he'd never be allowed home again—at least not without being arrested.

Sergei Fedorov, 21, defects in the summer of 1990, and the Soviets say, well, maybe we'll let him come home.

Pavel Bure comes to Vancouver in November of 1991, and everything is okay.

In two years, the Iron Curtain fell, the Soviet Union died, and the world changed forever. Even for hockey players.

From there on, each year would bring an excellent Russian, or for that matter Latvian (goaltender Arturs Irbe and defenseman Sandis Ozolinsh), Belorussian (defenseman Ruslan Salei), or

Aw, I Knew That!

Q. Only 7 have ever totaled over 70 goals in an NHL season. One of them is a Russian. Name him.

A. Alexander Mogilny, Buffalo Sabres. Scored 76 goals in 1992–1993.

Lithuanian (defenders Darius Zubrus and Darius Kasparaitis) to the NHL.

Some would play well and be important cogs in the wheel, such as Valeri Kamensky, Sergei Nemchinov, Dimitry Yushkevich, Alexei Zhamnov, Alexei Zhitnik, or Sergei Zubov. And a few would be superstars.

The Red, White, and Green Unit

Scotty Bowman always knew a good idea when he saw one. Even if he had seen it a number of years before.

The Soviet plan of keeping three forwards and two defenders together as a single unit (remember the famous Green Unit) had always fascinated Bowman, and in the fall of 1996 he was handed a perfect chance to try it. On his club he had center Sergei Fedorov, wingers Viacheslav Kozlov and Igor Larionov, and defensemen Slava Fetisov and Vladimir Konstantinov.

Why not throw them together and see what happens?

Aw, I Knew That!

Q. In 1992, a Czech was chosen first overall in the NHL draft, and a Russian was taken second—the only time that has happened. Who were the players?

A. Roman Hamrlik, first overall by Tampa Bay, and Alexei Yashin, second overall by the Ottawa Senators.

Great Games

June 1992

Game one of the Stanley Cup finals found Pittsburgh at home to Chicago with the Penguins out for their second straight cup. Chicago led 4–1 at one point, but the Penguins came roaring back with four consecutive goals. The key one may have been the best ever by Jaromir Jagr, who picked up the puck along the boards, decked four Blackhawks on his way to the net and then slid the puck behind goalie Ed Belfour. Chicago never recovered, and the Pens swept the series in four straight.

Pittsburgh 5, Chicago 4

Now Bowman was too much of a tinkerer to let them stay together all the time in the regular season (the forwards combined for 162 points overall), but in the playoffs he let them fly. With Fetisov and Konstantinov taking care of the back end and the classic

Russian thinking on the fly, across ice, creative approach taking over, the fivesome became killers. In the playoffs, they would combine for 53 points in 20 games (212 projected over an 80-game season), including an amazing 14 goals on the powerplay.

They could have stayed together the following season and done it again. Fate, however, had other plans.

Friday the Thirteenth

On Saturday, June 7, 1997, the Detroit Red Wings won their first Stanley Cup since 1955. Six days later, Friday, June 13, 1997, they gathered for a team golf tournament in Bloomington, Michigan, partied until late, and then split up to take limos home. Slava Fetisov, Vladimir Konstantinov and team conditioning coach Sergei Manatsakonov were riding in a car driven by Richard Gnida. The driver later claimed he was trying to avoid something, but whatever the reason the car left the road and hit a tree. Fetisov, sitting backward, was seriously shaken up. Konstantinov and Manatsokanov, sitting facing forward without seatbelts on, were thrown head first through the glass partition behind Fetisov, suffering severe head injuries from which both would only partially recover.

One year later, the Wings, wearing a patch honoring both men on their uniforms, won their second straight cup, after which they brought Konstantinov onto the ice to celebrate the victory with them. It was an emotional exclamation mark on a career that might have left the Russian star ranked among the greatest defensemen of all time.

He was Fetisov the younger. He was tough, could take hits all night and not care, could dish out thunderous blows, was excellent with the puck, and was a natural leader. Nobody messed with him. A runner-up for top defenseman more than once, he was obviously a future award winner.

He had, remembered one man who knew him while a player, "a hockey face." He looked like a hockey player. He thought like a player. He fought like a player. He changed people's views of what Russian players were all about.

Great Games

December 1996

On the day after Christmas, the Detroit Red Wings hosted the Washington Capitals at the Joe Louis Arena. Jim Carey, then a star goaltender for the visitors, gave up five goals in a 5–4 loss to the Wings. What made the game special was the performance of Detroit center Sergei Fedorov, who scored all of his team's goals that night.

Sergei Fedorov 5, Washington 4

Aw, I Knew That!

Q. Name the only Russian to lead the Stanley Cup playoffs in scoring.

A. Sergei Fedorov, Detroit, 1995. He had 24 points in 17 games.

The Riddler

In the last years of the century, Russia's contribution to the superstar class of the NHL was a youngster with Hollywood leading-man good looks, a quiet, almost distant demeanor, and scorer's hands that had been blessed by the hockey gods.

Pavel Bure.

Sixty goals in only his second season, 1992–1993 with Vancouver. And 60 again the following year. After struggling with injuries for a few seasons, 51 in 1997–1998. Then a long holdout and a forced trade to the Florida Panthers on January 17, 1999.

Bure was born in Moscow in 1971 as the son of swimmer Vladimir Bure—who competed in three Olympics, winning silver and bronze—and as a member of a family that had once been famous as the tsar's watchmakers. Along with his brother Valeri, born three years later (ineffective in his first years with Montreal, traded to Calgary where he hit his stride, scoring 35 times in 1999–2000), Pavel would make the NHL. He would be a revelation for his play and a mystery for his attitude and—some claimed—his choice of friends.

As Kerry Banks would write in a biography of the star, *The Riddle of the Russian Rocket,* "unconfirmed stories linking him with one controversy or another repeatedly surfaced in the media."

Among them:

➤ That he had paid thousands of dollars to Russian extortionists back home where the rule of law was being overrun by organized crime. Never proven.

➤ That he held up the Canucks for a new contract in 1994, refusing to play in the playoffs unless he got it. Never proven.

➤ That when he tried to get the family watchmaking business restarted in Europe, and Russian mafia money was part of it. Never proven.

➤ That his falling out with his father (they weren't talking at this writing) had something to do with restarting the watchmaking business. The fallout was true (Valeri wasn't speaking with dad, either), but the rest was pure conjecture.

As Banks writes, controversy just seemed to follow him. And yet, the goals would keep coming. And, as with so many other Russians and others from the former Soviet Union, he had made his mark on the world's best pro league.

Stars of the Era

➤ Petr Nedved defected as a midget-aged player and made his debut in 1990 with the Vancouver Canucks. In a career that included Vancouver, St. Louis, New York Rangers, and Pittsburgh, he would have years of 45, 38, and 33 goals, but he also struggled at times and would sit through two long holdouts. Played for Canada in the 1994 Olympics.

➤ Jaromir Jagr, considered the best player in the world at the turn of the twenty-first century, began his NHL career with Pittsburgh in 1990, and would win two straight Stanley Cups. Team captain by the end of the decade while suffering off and on with a bad groin. Helped Czech Republic to the gold medal at the 1998 Olympics.

➤ Pavel Bure debuted in 1991. Had two-straight 60-goal seasons with Vancouver and one of 51. Forced a trade to Florida in 1999. Helped Russia to the silver medal at the 1998 Olympics. Traveled with a cloud of unproven innuendo over his head.

➤ Igor Larionov, the ageless one, began his pro career with Khimik in 1977 and was still playing in 2001 at the age of 40. A steady, if not spectacular, center, his assist total was always double that of his goals, and his playoff totals were excellent. Won two Stanley Cups with Detroit.

➤ Sergei Fedorov came to Detroit in 1990 at age 20 and made an immediate impact, scoring 31, 32, 34, and 56 goals. A two-time Stanley Cup winner, he was still one of the top centers in the league 10 seasons later.

The Least You Need to Know

➤ The first wave of Czechs to arrive legally came in 1988.

➤ After numerous defections and a new regime in Eastern Europe, the doors opened for all Czech and Slovak players in 1991.

➤ The Russian Invasion began in 1989, both legally and by defection.

➤ Most of the early players allowed out of both countries were older and near the end of their careers.

➤ By 2001, the Czech, Slovak, and Russian influences in the NHL were strong and permanent.

Part 5

Scandinavia

Sweden and Finland had remarkably different hockey stories for 50 years. One country, which had fallen hard for the game at the turn of the century, developed its skills and abilities right up to World War II, while the other, which was introduced to the fastest game on earth before the turn of the twentieth century, lost it again for 30 years. Both, however, would find themselves trailing Canada, the Soviet Union, and Czechoslovakia decade after decade, until, in the last 20 years, they would begin to take their rightful places among the true powers. And Scandinavia would become the largest producer of talent for the National Hockey League outside of North America by the turn of the twenty-first century.

The Three Crowns— Sweden

Like the Czechs, the Swedes have spent most of the last 50 years as bridesmaids to the Soviet Union. Until, that is, the Red Machine finally was broken up, leaving the stage open for whomever could grab the spotlight. And Sweden was ready, coming up with three world championships in the 1990s and the country's first Olympic victory. None of that could have been possible without the groundwork set by generations of Swedish stars and years of work setting up the internal system needed to succeed. In this chapter, we'll look at these issues.

The Welcome La Mat

When American movie distributor Roul La Mat came to Sweden in 1919, bringing Canadian hockey with him, he found a nation mad for bandy. Which, of course, gave them a step up in the same way bandy experience would help the Soviets 30 years later.

His enthusiasm was so catching that just a year later he convinced officials to send a team to the unofficial 1920 Olympic hockey tournament. The only player with any experience was Nils Molander, who had been competing in Germany, but with Nils and 10 bandy players, the Swedes would finish second to Canada and, as the story goes, would so impress the gold medallists that they actually let them score a goal.

Patronizing, but nice enough.

That was enough to give the sport a major boost in the country, which led to the formation of the domestic championships in 1922. Most teams at that time would center around Stockholm. There wouldn't be an artificial rink in the country until 1931 (built in an airplane hangar).

Internationally, Sweden wouldn't win a European crown that had more than two teams in the tournament (they won in 1921 with only the Czechs as an opponent). The first official Winter Games produced a fourth for the club, which came roaring back with a second in 1928.

Despite losing 11–0 to Canada in the medal round, the club beat Switzerland and Great Britain for the silver.

The Depression would hit Sweden as hard as anywhere else, and it would fail five times to send a team to the world championships in the 1930s. There also was no money for Lake Placid and the Olympics in 1932, though a fifth came along in 1936 when Tre Kronor returned for the Games. Its best player in the 1930s was Sven Bergqvist, the first Swedish superstar, who would go on to coach the Olympic team in 1948.

While they were struggling in the 1930s, however, the youngsters who would take them through the 1950s were beginning to learn the game.

Sven and the Boys

The 1950s would see the Soviet Union enter the world stage and immediately make an impact. But it would also see Sweden establish itself as one of the Big Four, which included the Canadians, Czechs, and Soviets.

After a silver in 1947 (Canada hadn't come back to the worlds as of yet), and a fourth in the 1948 Olympics, the country would, for the most part, find itself within the top four for the rest of the century.

As the 1950s went on, the parts for a competitive team began to come together.

Sven "Tumba" Johansson joined the national team in 1951 and he would stay until 1966. The flashy forward would rise to a new level of popularity outside of Sweden in 1957, when Moscow hosted the world championships for the first time. Playing in front of 50,000 fans at an outdoor venue, Johansson would lead Tre Kronor to a key 4–4 tie with the hosts and take the gold medal. He played so well the Russian fans poured onto the ice and carried him off on their shoulders.

Lars Bjorn started his career in 1950 and played 11 years, establishing himself as one of the best defensemen of his time. Other stars of the period included Lars-Erik Lundvall, Nils Nilsson, Ronald Petterson, and Roland Stoltz (who would play well into the 1960s on the Swedish defense), with his partner Lasse Bjorn.

And then there was Ulf.

A Sterner Demeanor

Ulf Sterner was born in Deje in 1941 and was growing up to be what one thought a young Swede interested in hockey might be: a strong national and international player. The hockey gods had something just a little more interesting in mind, however.

Beginning with Forshaga IF in the Swedish League in 1956, then transferring to Vastra Frolunda in 1961, the 6'2" left winger played in nine world championships and two Olympics. He would go on to help win the gold at the 1962 world championships.

Aw, I Knew That!

Q. What future WHA all-star was caught using a banned substance at the 1974 worlds in Helsinki?

A. Ulf Nilsson. He used Ephedrine to combat a common cold. Sweden lost the points from a 2–0 win over Poland.

Aw, I Knew That!

Q. Name the great Swedish forward who joined the Boston Bruins in 1957 but never played a game?

A. Sven "Tumba" Johannson.

Pretty straightforward stuff, until a New York Ranger scout stepped into the picture after the 1964 Olympic tournament, offering Sterner the chance to be the first Swedish-born and -developed player in the NHL.

He would only last 4 games with the Rangers (no points), sandwiched between 16 games with the St. Paul Rangers of the Central League (21 points) and 52 with Baltimore of the American League (44 points), all in 1964–1965.

Sterner, who had to put up with endless shots at his nationality (he was the first to hear the Chicken Swede slur), decided to head back to Europe the following season, where he regained his amateur status for world play. He would not be eligible for the Olympics, however.

Always the Bridesmaid (or the Maid of Honor)

From the time Sweden won the world championships in 1962 under legendary coach Arne Stromberg to their next gold in 1987 under Curt Lindstrom, a quarter-century would pass.

It wasn't as though they couldn't put out a competitive team (seven silvers and seven bronze at the worlds during that time); it was that they couldn't quite put out the players needed to overcome the Soviets.

Hard workers like Lennart Haggroth, Inge Hammarstrom, Leif Holmqvist, goaltender Goran Hogosta, Tord Lundstrom, and Lennart Svedberg provided the basis for solid clubs.

And there were the stars like Sterner, Anders Hedberg (who hit the national team at just 18 years old in 1969), Ulf Nilsson (who came along in 1973), and brilliant defensemen Lars-Erik Sjoberg and Borje Salming (see Chapter 22, "Courage Under Fire—Swedes and Finns in the NHL," for all of these).

The problem would become keeping them in Sweden to play for the national program.

Look at the losses: In 1973, Salming and Hammarstrom went to the Toronto Maple Leafs of the NHL. One year later, Nilsson, Hedberg, and Sjoberg were gone to the Winnipeg Jets of the World Hockey Association.

How do you replace five stars like that?

This would continue onward for the rest of the century, each year finding more and more players heading to North America, making them unavailable for the world championships and not eligible (until the 1990s) for the Olympics.

And yet, the Swedish development system had become so strong by this time that they could, and did, replace those cogs well enough to keep more than competitive. From Salming's exit in 1973 until 1987, Sweden would finish worse than fourth at the worlds just once.

And when they came together as a full club for Canada Cup tournaments, they could surprise people, as was the case in 1984 when the Soviets and Czechs were awful and Sweden went to the finals against Canada and lost.

Vertical Attachments

If you take away the army uniforms, the barbed wire, and the rotten food, there are many similarities between the Swedish system and that of the former Soviet Union.

Quote, Unquote

"In my country, players receive money *under* the table."

—A very honest Rudolf Eklow, Sweden's representative to the IIHF in 1969, when the issue of professionals was being discussed.

Aw, I Knew That!

Q. Name the Canadian who took over the head coaching duties of the Swedish national team in 1971 from legend Arne Stromberg.

A. Billy Harris.

First, it's a vertical system—if you are born in a paper-mill town owned by MoDo, chances are you'll wind up in a sports club run by that company that eventually leads all the way up to their senior elite team in the Swedish league. Or if not into a sports-club system, you may follow the district system where you play for your home area until 14 or 15, when one of the top clubs will draft your behind and send it on into its own system. Time to leave home is about 16, unless you're lucky enough to have grown up in the shadow of one of the elite clubs.

The Swedes, like the Russians, believe in practice, preferring a ratio of two teaching sessions to each game.

At the adult, elite level, the Swedish league's most famous club is Leksands IF (four national titles), founded in 1919, and considered to carry the same tradition in Scandinavia as the Montreal Canadiens do in the NHL. The most accomplished, however, is Brynas IF Gavle, 11 times national champions since being founded in 1955, and the breeding ground of Salming, Hammarstrom, and Mats Naslund.

Aw, I Knew That!

Q. This head coach of the Swedish national team competed in 13 world championships as a player and won 2 gold medals before taking over the nationals for 1974–1976. Name him.

A. Ronald Petterson.

I Remember ...

Lars-Erik Sjoberg was a superb defender for Sweden and in the World Hockey Association with the Winnipeg Jets. His reputation was that of a talented, great thinker, whose observations were worth hearing. When he returned home from his first year in North America, everyone had lots of questions about how it was and what he thought. When asked for the biggest difference between North American hockey and Swedish hockey, he answered, "Oh yeah, for one thing, all Swedish players have their own teeth."

Other top clubs include Djurgardens IF Stockholm (14 titles stretching back to 1926; Hedberg and Mats Sundin its greatest products), AIK Solna (7 national titles, and whose most famous sons are Nilsson and goalie Pelle Lindbergh), and Sodertalie SK (7 titles, 11 times second place).

Quote, Unquote

"Deep down, I'm still a Swede, despite the Finnish, Canadian, and American influences I've had in my life."

—Juha Widing, born in Sweden, spent his teen years in Canada, and played nine years in the NHL from 1969.

The league draws well, which means money has always been there to continue the upkeep of the development programs.

As Good as a Tie

Curt Lidstrom took a strong club to the 1987 world championships that combined excellent talent playing at home in the elite league with players whose clubs missed the NHL playoffs or who went out in the first round.

This was the darkest year for Soviet hockey—they were on a downswing that Lidstrom was ready to use to his advantage. Actually, the Soviets went through the tournament undefeated. But a key tie with Sweden set up an interesting situation—all Tre Kronor had to do was beat the Canadians in the final game and the gold, the first in 25 years, was theirs.

Canada was doing exceptionally well under coach Dave King, having tied the Soviets 0–0 in the first game of the medal round, so the task looked difficult, but not nearly impossible. Forget that. Tre Kronor put one of the worst whippings on the Canadians that country had ever suffered, 9–0, and the gold went to the blue and yellow.

Great Games

August 1976

The Soviet Union came into the 1976 Canada Cup with an "experimental" team, while the Swedes showed up with a solid group that still wasn't expected to do better than fourth. But on a warm afternoon at the Montreal Forum, the two teams put on the best show of the tournament and one of the most memorable international games ever. With the Soviets leading 3–1, Borje Salming scored on an end-to-end rush to close the gap. In the final minutes, with the Swedes all around the net and the crowd clearly on their side, Anders Hedberg popped in the tying goal.

Sweden 3, Soviet Union 3

A Swedish Tide

Consider again that most of Sweden's best players were in the NHL by the beginning of the 1990s, and the country's accomplishments over the first four years of the decade take on an even brighter light.

Conny Evansson, the former Farjestads BK Karlstad star, took over the national team in 1990 and would find immediate success by mixing a few NHLers with a few future NHL stars, a smidgen of NHL stars who had returned home to play, and a large number of workers who played exclusively in the Swedish league.

Left winger Mats Naslund, who played superbly for Montreal in the 1980s (two 40-plus goal years in 8 seasons), brought his family home in 1990 at the height of his career. That was one year after Hakan Loob, a right winger just two seasons removed from scoring 50 for Calgary, had done the same. At center was young Peter Forsberg, a future NHL superstar, who would go straight from the world junior championships to the senior version in 1991 and stay through the 1994 Olympics.

The defense included youngsters Kenny Jonsson and Andreas Dackell (who doubled as an occasional fourth line winger), also on their eventual way to the NHL.

In Finland for 1991 (the last time the Soviets would appear before breaking up), Sweden finished ahead of Canada for the gold. In 1992, with Russia appearing for the first time since the breakup of the USSR, Sweden became the first team other than the Soviets to win back to back in 15 years.

Sweden would win one more worlds in the decade, that in 1998.

Quote, Unquote

"When Ulf Sterner couldn't make it, they thought all Canadians were supermen. They were dejected, rather than try again they accepted second rate status."

—Swedish national coach Billy Harris on why more Swedes were not trying for NHL careers in the early 1970s.

Putting Their Stamp on It

As Tom Ratschunas writes, new coach Curt Lundmark built his 1984 Olympic gold medal team around what he called "dads"—veteran players such as Loob (who had been having an awful year), Naslund, Tomas Jonsson, and more—who could lend their experience to a lot of fuzzy-cheeked youngsters.

Quote, Unquote

"It's a myth. Every time we play against the USA or Canada it's 'Chicken Swede.' Every time. Even our jerseys are yellow."

—Tommy Sandlin, former Swedish national coach.

Quote, Unquote

"The attitude here is different. Hockey isn't life. In Canada, it's life. They've been so long in hockey, they've been away from life."

—Thomas Gradin on the difference between hockey in Canada and Sweden.

Great Games

Winter 1931

Canada came to the world hockey championships that year riding a streak that had seen them undefeated and untied in every game they had played internationally going back to 1920. On this occasion, the Canadians would go undefeated again to win the gold medal. But they wouldn't be untouched. Sweden surprised the champs with the tightest defensive effort yet seen by a European club and came up with a tie. A scoreless tie.

Sweden 0, Canada 0

He also had an experienced goalie in Hakan Algotsson (always great to find a good goaltender in Sweden, since that was the one position they had never been able to produce copious numbers of talented youngsters in) and a 23-year-old named Tommy Salo. That final plan would go awry about halfway through the tournament in Lillehammer, Norway, when Algotsson's wife delivered their baby and he went home to be with her, leaving Salo the starter.

Sweden was third in the opening round, a set of games that included a 3–2 loss to Canada. Playoff round wins over Germany (3–0) and Russia (a tight 4–3 victory) put them into the gold medal final against Canada.

Two teams desperate for the gold. Canada hadn't won since 1952. The Swedes had never won the Olympics and, in fact, it had been 46 years since any Swedish group (in that case, the soccer team—ironically it had been that soccer win over the Soviet Union that had convinced the Kremlin to concentrate much harder on hockey) had won a team gold medal, summer or winter.

Regulation time ended 2–2 (Tomas Jonsson and Magnus Svensson for Sweden, Paul Kariya and Derek Mayer for Canada), and the 10-minute sudden death overtime was scoreless, setting up a shootout that would produce the most dramatic ending to a gold medal game in Olympic history.

Each team would choose five players to take penalty shots on the opposing goalie, and whichever team led after that would win. If no winner appeared, the teams would go to sudden death shootout, a highly controversial idea taken from soccer.

Canada went up 2–0 (Petr Nedved and Kariya scoring on Salo) before Svensson found the net behind Corey Hirsch on Sweden's second shot. With Salo holding the fort, Forsberg scored on shot four to tie it up, where it remained into sudden death.

On the thirteenth shot, Forsberg beat Hirsch and Paul Kariya missed the net behind Salo to give Sweden its first-ever Olympic gold.

Reaction in Canada was bitter.

"The showdown concept was entertaining, nail-biting, and quick, but it was no way to determine which was the better team on a particular day or over a period of four years," wrote Andrew Podnieks, in his Olympic hockey history. "A coin toss would have been as relevant."

In the Swedish room, Mats Naslund agreed: "It's not fair," he said.

No one back across the border in Sweden, however, could have cared less. A national celebration was in full swing.

And to commemorate the event, a special postal stamp was issued showing Forsberg beating Hirsch.

Curt Lundmark's team had put its stamp on hockey history.

Stars of the Era

➤ Sven "Tumba" Johansson was a national team member 245 times from 1951 to 1966, winning two Olympic medals, three world golds, and nine world medals overall. Nicknamed Tumba, he changed his name later in life to "Sven Tumba."

➤ Lars Bjorn played 11 seasons on the national team and is one of only a handful of men who have more than 200 games with Tre Kronor. Played in 3 Olympics and 10 worlds. Considered one of the best defensemen Sweden has turned out.

➤ Hakan Loob went to the Calgary Flames, where he had 429 points in 450 games and won a Stanley Cup before coming home in the prime of his career to raise his family in Sweden. Played on the 1991 and 1992 world gold medalists and the 1994 Olympic champions.

➤ Leif "Honken" Holmqvist played 202 games in goal for the Three Crowns from 1962 to 1975, including at two Olympics and nine worlds. Named best goalie at the worlds in 1969. Played one season with Indianapolis in the World Hockey Association.

➤ Tomas Jonsson was the perfect cross-over player for Sweden—a star defenseman in the National Hockey League, almost entirely with the New York Islanders (two Stanley Cups in eight years), and also played a pivotal role in Sweden's 1991 world championship and the 1994 Olympic victory.

The Least You Need to Know

➤ Sweden entered world competition in 1920.

➤ They won the worlds three times from 1953–1962, then waited 25 years for another victory.

➤ Although Sweden sent dozens of players to the NHL in the 1970s and 1980s, they were able to keep a strong national program.

➤ Sweden won three world titles in the 1990s and finally broke the Olympic gold jinx in 1994.

Chapter 21

The Outsiders— Finland

> ### In This Chapter
>
> ➤ A strange beginning
>
> ➤ Everybody's favorite opponent
>
> ➤ Equipping a growing system
>
> ➤ New life in later years
>
> ➤ Slaying the proverbial monkey

Let's start this chapter at the end. The small country of Finland had, by 2001, sent well over 100 players to the North American pro ranks. This was despite the fact that they had a relatively late introduction to the game of hockey, didn't get their first artificial ice rink until 1955, and basically had to play second fiddle to the Swedes in Scandinavia and fifth violin to the Big Four in world competitions. How did this happen? And how did the Finns build on their steady improvement as a national team to finally take the world championship in 1995? And what did one of the world's most famous equipment manufacturers have to do with any of this? In this chapter, we'll look at those stories.

Forgetting the Professor's Lessons

The year 1900 was still just over the horizon when Professor Leonard Borgstrom walked out onto the North Harbour ice in Helsinki and started teaching the game of Canadian hockey to a group of young men from the local university.

This story should continue from here to show Finland's rapid rise in European hockey ranks and their entry as a founding nation of the IIHF. Something happened, however. The game didn't take off right away, and it wasn't until the 1920s when a group of angry speed skaters would band together to make sure ice hockey became popular.

Hey, Hee, Get Off of Our Ice!

Strangest story. By 1927, the Finnish speed-skating team had had just about enough of those bandy players. See, bandy needed so much space (a frozen soccer field, you remember) that they were always interfering with the speed skaters going around the outside. I mean, there was an Olympics coming up the following February, how were they supposed to get ready if that ball kept rolling onto the oval, followed by a couple of bandy players?

So the speed skaters cooked up a plan. Having seen the game of Canadian hockey played in the 1924 Olympics, they realized a couple of important things—it took up very little space in comparison with bandy, it was played inside of boards, which would keep the players out of their hair, and they could get it started relatively cheaply.

Thus was hockey in Finland truly launched.

The first game in the new Finnish league was played in 1928, the same year that Finland entered the IIHF. It would be another 11 years before the Finns made their debut in the world championships (fourteenth out of 14), but by the time World War II came along to interrupt things, the seeds had been sown.

Aw, I Knew That!

Q. Name the Canadian and former NHL all-star who coached Finland at the 1976 Canada Cup.

A. Carl Brewer.

Aw, I Knew That!

Q. Name the first member of the Finnish national team to make a world championship all-star team.

A. Ilpo Koskela, defenseman, 1971 tournament in Bern, Switzerland.

Everybody's Favorite Whipping Boy

From 1949 through to the end of the 1960s, the boys with Suomi on their sweaters were basically cannon fodder for the Big Four of the Soviet Union, Canada, Sweden, and Czechoslovakia.

During that time, Finland never finished higher than fifth at four Olympic Games. The country pulled off a couple of surprising fourths in world play (1957 and 1962), but the rest of the time it was fifth, sixth, even five sevenths, and a ninth.

Dismal.

There was some talent around: Aarne Honkavaara was a strong forward who played in the 1952 Olympics and went on to coach the national team; Lasse Oksanen came along in 1960 and was an excellent player who hung around through 13 seasons; Urpo Ylonen debuted in 1963 and would have a long career to 1978.

But there was absolutely no depth.

There was, however, that artificial ice rink in Tampere by 1955, and if you do a little math, any four-year-old who started hockey on that rink, which in itself inspired the building of dozens more, would be coming of age right around 1970, when the Finnish program itself began to come of age.

Koho, Koho, It's Off to Work We Go

One of the problems that plagued the Soviet hockey system right from the start was the lack of decent equipment for its players. As mentioned in Part 4, "Beyond the Iron Curtain," a collection of republics that could produce such fine athletes couldn't even make third-class hockey gear.

The opposite was true in Finland. In the 1950s, a number of hockey equipment manufacturers started up, led by Koho, which would (along with Tackla, another Finnish firm) become one of the world's top makers of skates, sticks, and pads. Having excellent equipment to match with the sudden interest in hockey in that decade worked wonders on bringing new people into the sport. There was no need to gaze longingly at a pair of Canadian-made skates and wonder what difference they would make to your game. The good skates were right down the street in the store window.

Four Is a Lonely Number

By 1970, the Finns were starting to compete. Their system was producing players, their coaches were getting experience, their athletes were improving all the time.

Goaltending was ably handled by Jorma Valtonen, who debuted in 1970 and would play in 10 worlds, 3 Olympics, and a Canada Cup, and Urpo Ylonen, who had two big wins to his credit already—1967,

Quote, Unquote

"I guess this is my line of work. This is what I want to go on doing."

—Alpo Suhonen in 1978, 22 years before he would be named the first European head coach in NHL history.

Quote, Unquote

"We will be able to compete for a second- or third-place finish, but a world championship is out of the question."

—Goran Stubb, manager of the Finnish Ice Hockey Federation, April 1977. Beaten before he started.

when Finland beat the Czechs for the first time, and 1968, when they beat Canada for the first time ever.

Oksanen was now a team leader. Pekka Marjamaki was considered one of the better defenders in Europe. Center Veli-Pekka Ketola had come into his own up front, as had Esa Peltonen. And Ylonen was in his prime.

Remember now, we're talking in relative terms here. But from 1970 to 1975, the Finns did very well, finishing no worse than fourth in the worlds. And no better than fourth, for that matter. After a fifth in the 1972 Olympics, they even took fourth in the 1976 Games.

Fourth wasn't a medal, but Finland was no longer just a whipping boy, either.

And the system was turning out more and better players, most of whom, of course, were finding their way to the pro ranks in North America.

This meant that from 1976 to 1991, Finland would fail to rise any higher than fourth (and do that just once) in the worlds, would suffer the embarrassment of missing the 1984 Canada Cup tournament when the West Germans finished ahead of them at the 1983 worlds, and would actually finish seventh twice.

Just like the old days.

Great Games

Winter 1978

At the European under 18 hockey championship, the Finns were having an unusually strong tournament for a team representing a country that had never won a major hockey tournament of any kind. Coached by Alpo Suhonen, the club had shocked observers by advancing all the way to the final game against the Soviet Union still with a chance to win it all. But beating the Soviets was impossible. Or was it? Trailing 2–0 at one point, the Finns battled back in front of the home crowd at Helsinki and sent the game into a 20-minute overtime at 3–3. It was 5–5 after that and on to sudden death. And at 1:42, young Jari Kurri scored to win it. Finland went wild.

Finland 6, Soviet Union 5

The System

Finland's hockey development system is vertical like the rest of Europe, but players are somewhat older before they get into clubs (or gymnasiums, which are a combination of educational and coaching schools).

I Remember ...

In 1980, Finland fought to an upset win over the hosts at the Swedish Cup in Goteborg and lined up to collect their medals and listen to the anthem. To their horror, however, when the button was pushed to play the music, the Cuban national anthem began. The crowd yelled, laughed, and booed. The Finns, however, stormed off the ice, absolutely convinced that the hosts had done it on purpose after the shocking loss at home.

Where it's different is in younger age groups, 8 to 11 years old. Those players aren't separated by skill; they play together in house leagues where winning is totally de-emphasized. At 12, the club system comes solidly into play with kids divided then by talent and age. By 16 and 17, the best are put in with older players.

Finland has total free agency with its younger players, who can choose to play wherever they want, which in turn leads to a lot of recruiting. Practice is emphasized, but top players wind up with a lot of game action.

In the Finnish senior league, the top teams include HIFK Helsinki (6 titles and such stars as Christian Ruuttu and Esa Tikkanen), Ilves Tampere (16 titles, goalie Jarmo Myllys, defenseman Jyrki Lumme), Tappara Tampere (14 championships, Teppo Numminen), and TPS Turku (7 first place finishes, Hannu Virta).

The Glorious 1990s

Finland's wonderful trip through the final decade of the century actually began at the Olympic Games in 1988 at Calgary.

Playing in Group A with Sweden, Canada, and three never-rans, the Finns wound up in a three-way tie for first with seven points, but officially took the top spot on goal differential, having given up just eight goals in five games. They beat the host Canadians 3–1 (Erkki Laine with two goals), despite a plea that Jarmo Myllys' mask was illegally wide, which caused a late power play.

Aw, I Knew That!

Q. Only one Finn has ever been named top forward at the world championships. Who is he?

A. Saku Koivu, 1995.

Sure there were future NHLers on the team in Myllys, Teppo Numminen, and Reijo Ruotsalainen, but the majority of the players for Suomi came from the senior league—guys who wouldn't move on to the pros.

While the Soviets were on their way to another gold (which would be the last as the USSR), the Finns were making a statement. Like by beating the Soviets for the first time, 2–1, on the last day. Unfortunately, they had lost 5–2 to the Czechs two days previously, so the gold still went to the Red Machine.

Something good was brewing here, however. And not even a return to form with two fifths and a sixth in the following three worlds could stop it.

There was the 1991 Canada Cup, which saw the Finns finish third behind Canada and the United States, while the Soviets and the Czechs finished second last and last.

There was the 1992 worlds, which produced a second-place finish in which the Finns went 7–1 but still lost to Sweden in the medal round after that club went a measly 4–2–2.

And there was another silver in 1994 (added to one in 1998, that would be three silvers in the decade).

And then there was the beautiful, wonderful, 1995 worlds.

After All of That ... Victory

What a strange year 1995 was for the world championships. A long lockout in the NHL had delayed the end of the season, which meant that no team would be relying on big league call-ups when the worlds got underway.

This also meant that the winning team would be the one who could call on the strongest forces from its own domestic league.

Aw, I Knew That!

Q. This goaltender won three world championship medals and three Olympic medals for Finland. Name him.

A. Jarmo Myllys.

Enter the Finns, led by a dynamic front line of Jere Lehtinen, Saku Koivu, and Ville Peltonen (future NHLers all; in fact, Koivu would go on to become the first European captain of the Montreal Canadiens). Sensing the opportunity, Finland would not be denied, even when they came up against arch-rival Sweden for the gold medal. The game was won on a goal by Peltonen, the monkey was off the back, and the country's place as a leading hockey nation was finally secured.

Stars of the Era

➤ Matti Hagman made his senior league debut at just 17 years old, playing in one Olympics (1976), four world championships, and three Canada

Cups. Had 63 points in 104 international games. Played in the NHL. Finished his career back in Finland in 1991. Amassed 750 points in 513 Finnish league games.

➤ Jorma Valtonen was one of the best goaltenders produced in Finland, playing on the national club from 1970 to 1984, retiring at 38. Was named best goaltender over Vladislav Tretiak and Jiri Holecek in the 1972 worlds.

➤ Lasse Oksanen played the most games for the national team in history, 282 over 13 seasons that included 3 Olympics, 13 world championships, and the 1976 Canada Cup. A forward, he scored 101 goals internationally.

➤ Pekka Marjamaki had a long career of his own, appearing in 251 national team games on the blueline. Had 64 points over that span. With 2 Olympics and 10 worlds, and best defenseman in the 1975 worlds, he lasted 18 seasons in the Finnish league, playing 476 games.

➤ Jere Lehtinen was one of Finland's best young players of the 1990s. A member of the 1995 world championship team, he was a tournament all-star. Went on to the NHL with the Dallas Stars, where he won a Stanley Cup in 1999.

The Least You Need to Know

➤ Finland was a late starter in hockey.

➤ Excellent equipment helped push hockey to the forefront in the country.

➤ For years, the Finns were on the outside looking in at top-flight competition.

➤ Finland finally won the worlds in 1995.

➤ Finland has sent the second-most European players to the NHL, behind Sweden.

Courage Under Fire—Swedes and Finns in the NHL

They all heard it: Chicken Swede. They all knew what it meant: You're not brave enough, strong enough, or man enough to play in the National Hockey League. Eventually, that epitaph would disappear for the most part (anyone who used it on a player in the 1990s would simply have had that player laugh back in their face), but the Swedish players who cleared the way for those that followed had to put up with incredible pressures from opponents and even teammates. Finnish players had it a little easier, perhaps because there weren't quite as many of them, or because most came a little later, but the challenge was still there—prove yourself, because you're over here stealing our jobs, so you'd better be twice as good as someone you displace. In this chapter, we'll look at Swedes and Finns in the NHL.

The Trailblazers

Perhaps it was what happened in 1972 when Team Canada played those two dirty, violent games in Sweden before going on to Russia. The Europeans remembered the "gangland" tactics of the Canadians. The Canadians remembered that huge furrow carved in Wayne Cashman's tongue by Ulf Sterner.

Perhaps it was the legitimate fear of losing jobs to the Europeans.

Perhaps it was simple xenophobia.

Whatever the cause, the first Swedes to hit the pro hockey ranks in any number went through hell most nights, trying to prove they deserved to wear the uniform.

Quote, Unquote

"We don't like losing our players, but with compensation from professional leagues we can at least rebuild our program."

—Stig Nilsson, Swedish hockey administrator, 1974.

Aw, I Knew That!

Q. This Swedish athlete actually played his hockey in Finland and was the first international player selected in the NHL draft in 1969. Name him.

A. Tommi Salmelainen, St. Louis, 66th overall.

As we discussed in Chapter 9, "Keeping Your Head Up [1968–1980]," Borje Salming and Inge Hammarstrom led the way for Swedish players into the NHL in 1973. But it was actually Thommie Bergman who was the first of the 1970s, signing with Detroit in the summer of 1972. A big defenseman, Bergman would play eight pro seasons, split between the NHL and WHA.

While those athletes were breaking down the door in one league, it was actually a larger group of Swedish men, playing in the rival loop, who would provide the biggest group of athletes to the cause.

Jets

When Bobby Hull left the Chicago Blackhawks for the Winnipeg Jets in 1972, officials in Canada's windiest city knew their biggest problem would be finding linemates who could keep up with his speed and play into his strength—that booming shot.

For two seasons things went fairly well—103 and 95 points from the big blond machine. But there still seemed to be something more that Hull could come up with, even in his advancing years, if they could get the right tools.

Enter the right tools, in the person of center Ulf Nilsson and right winger Anders Hedberg, the former from Solna and the latter from Djurgarden.

Put together, the line turned in the most dominating one-year performance by a threesome in a major pro league ever up to that time: 77 goals and 142 points for Hull, 53 goals and 100 points for Hedberg, and 94 assists and 120 points for Nilsson.

That's 362 points.

Eventually, Hull would begin to slow down considerably and his Swedish linemates would sign with the New York Rangers for 1978, where they would have varying luck.

Those two Swedes weren't the only Europeans that came to the Jets that year. Lars-Erik Sjoberg, a defenseman who was so respected by his peers he would soon become the first European captain in the NHL (with Winnipeg in 1979–1980), and Finnish center Veli-Pekka Ketola also came on board, giving the Jets an amazing (for that time) four non–North Americans.

The Jets would always be a popular locale for Europeans, including Kent Nilsson, who began there in 1977.

Drafting

By the middle of the 1970s, general managers around the NHL were beginning to get the idea that the Swedes and Finns were around to stay. They started drafting players for both the present and the future.

Thomas Gradin, a young but experienced international center, was chosen by Chicago in 1976 and would be dealt to Vancouver before he arrived and make his debut in 1978 (209 goals in 9 years). Finland's Matti Hagman was picked by Boston in 1975 (and would play 5 seasons). And in 1978, right winger Bengt Gustafsson would be drafted by Washington (he would play nine seasons), and Finn Risto Siltanen went to St. Louis, but would play eight years on defense for three teams, starting with Edmonton.

The point was that Scandinavian players were now considered eminently draftable.

The quietest and perhaps most effective draft choice was Tomas Jonsson, who already had played in an Olympics, two world championships, and a Canada Cup by the time he joined the New York Islanders in 1981. He would play eight seasons, winning two Stanley Cups on Long Island.

Aw, I Knew That!

Q. Who were the first Swedish- and Finnish-born players in the NHL?

A. Gus Forslund, played for the Ottawa Senators in 1932. He was raised from a youngster in Canada after being born in Sweden. Pentti Lund, born in Finland and brought up in Canada, played seven years with the New York Rangers and Boston from 1946 to 1953.

Great Games

April 1976

On April 15, Borje Salming had been badly beaten up by Mel Bridgman of the Philadelphia Flyers in game three of a quarterfinal series. By the end of the game, he was completely exhausted. Two days later, Salming would take a pass from Darryl Sittler, go in alone, and score the decisive goal in a game-four win over Philadelphia. The crowd went wild at Maple Leaf Gardens, and Salming's NHL legend was cemented that night.

Anders Kallur was drafted at the same time as Jonsson in 1979 but went to the Islanders immediately. Good choice—he was there for all four of the Stanley Cups.

Quote, Unquote

"What's his name ... Pekka? It's good he didn't play his hockey in Boston."

—Don Cherry on Calgary defenseman Pekka Rautakallio.

Great Games

May 1985

In game six of the Western Conference final against Chicago, Edmonton's Jari Kurri would tie a playoff record with 19 goals in 18 games. In game six, however, he went completely wild, scoring four times against the Blackhawks, ending the series, and sending the Oilers on to the Stanley Cup finals. He also would set a record for most three or better goal games in one playoff year. The performance would cement him as the NHL's top sniper.

Wayne's Winger and a Tough Little Tikker

Wayne Gretzky had a way of making his wingers better—in some cases far better than they could ever be with anyone else. In 1980, the Edmonton Oilers drafted a right winger from Finland who would go on to be the best player Scandinavia has turned out for the NHL.

He would also turn out to be a winger who could actually make Gretzky even better. His name was Jari Kurri.

Developed in the Jokerit Helsinki system, Kurri made an immediate impact on the Oilers, scoring 32 goals each of his first 2 years. And then, with Gretzky working alongside, he would explode over the next 5 seasons, scoring 45, 52, 71, 68, and 54 goals as Edmonton won 3 of its 5 Stanley Cups of the decade (all of which would include Kurri).

Kurri was the scorer, accumulating over 600 goals in his career.

In 1983, Glen Sather, the Oilers' general manager, would draft a type of player from Finland that many critics didn't think possible to find. They were wrong. Esa Tikkanen was the prototypical "North American" hockey player—tough, a tremendous checker (actually, most opponents found him a total pain in the rear, perhaps the best little pest in league history), a man who could score some when needed (30 or better goals in 3 of his first 5 years).

Tikkanen, whose Yogi Berra–type trips of the language became known as "Tikkanese," would win 4 cups with Edmonton (his career actually began in the 1985 playoffs), 1 with the New York Rangers, go to the finals with Washington, and play on 9 teams in 14 seasons. The Rangers thought so much of him they would reacquire Tikannen twice.

Talent to Burn

In the 1980s, with Finnish players coming to the league regularly and the Swedish pipeline running at full swing, literally dozens and dozens of Scandinavian players would make it to the NHL. A few would stay a short time. Most would have decent careers and a couple of those dozens would make strong impacts.

Swedish notables included center Thomas Steen (Winnipeg, 1981, 14 years as one of the most beloved players ever in that city), winger Mats Naslund (Montreal, 1982, 8 seasons, and a Lady Byng award as most gentlemanly player), defenseman Ulf Samuelsson, another hard-head who would get the reputation for hunting opponents' knees (Hartford, debuted in 1984), and right winger Hakan Loob (Calgary 1983, 6 seasons, 50 goals in 1987–1988).

Among others were Calle Johansson, Tommy Albelin, and Tomas Sandstrom.

Quality Finns in the 1980s included defenseman Reijo Ruotsalainen (Rangers, 1981, 8 seasons), center Christian Ruuttu (Buffalo, 1986, 9 seasons), defenseman Jyrki Lumme (Montreal, 1988, 12 seasons), and defenseman Teppo Numminen (Winnipeg, 1988, 12 seasons).

One player, who should have dominated the 1980s at an unusual position for a Scandinavian star, was denied his place in the hockey sun by tragedy. His name was Pelle Lindbergh.

Quote, Unquote

"About 4,000 miles."

—Barry Fraser, Edmonton's scouting director, on how far Esa Tikkanen was away from playing in the NHL when chosen by the Oilers in the 1983 draft.

Aw, I Knew That!

Q. This Finn holds the record for most goals in an NHL season by a defenseman from his country. Who is he?

A. Reijo Ruotsalainen, 28, for the New York Rangers in 1984–1985.

Pelle

One of the reasons suggested by a veteran hockey writer for why the Swedes had never been able to produce star goaltenders in any numbers is that youngsters there have never had heroes in the position to admire.

So it might come as no surprise that when Pelle Lindbergh was growing up in Stockholm, his hero was Bernie Parent of the Philadelphia Flyers. When Lindbergh made his debut with the Swedish national team in 1979, he was just 19 years old. One year later, he was a 20-year-old Olympian.

249

Ironically, given his childhood hero, Lindbergh was drafted in 1979 by the Flyers, who were still looking for Parent's replacement in the nets. His minor league career lasted one year before he made his debut for eight games with the big club in 1981.

By 1984–1985, Lindbergh was the best goalie in the league—stunning for many observers who were convinced Sweden just could not turn out a decent goaltender. He would win the Vezina Trophy that season with a goals against average of 3.02, 40 wins in the regular season, and 12 more in the playoffs.

Lindbergh was on track to become a goaltending legend, and his 6–2 start the following year showed the track was the right one.

But late one night after a Flyers' game, Lindbergh, driving alone, wrapped his sports car around a tree in a Philadelphia suburb. He was killed instantly.

Swedish children lost the one young man that could have been the inspiration for them to become a goalie.

Shedding the Image

Revenge may be a dish best served cold, but the proper way for Scandinavian players to get their own back for the Chicken Swede tag was to prove themselves in the heat of action. And by the end of the 1980s, they had done just that.

From that point, it was a case of adding to the total of excellent players.

Into the mix would come such men as Mikael Renberg, fresh out of Lulea HF in Sweden to the Philadelphia Flyers in 1993 and a place on the Legion of Doom line with Eric Lindros and John LeClair. He would score 38 goals as a rookie.

Defenseman Mattias Ohlund would join the Vancouver Canucks as that club's first choice overall (1984) in 1987 at 20 years of age and immediately show his worth on the blueline. Ohlund would be forced to battle a bad eye injury picked up in a preseason game in Ottawa in 1999 when he was hit by a puck—the same city, by the way, in which Toronto defenseman Bryan Berard would almost lose his eye later that same season.

Aw, I Knew That!

Q. Which Swedish forward took a famous slash from goaltender Ron Hextall in game four of the 1987 Stanley Cup final, causing the Flyer to be suspended for the first eight contests of the following season?

A. Kent Nilsson, Edmonton Oilers.

Aw, I Knew That!

Q. Who were the twin brothers taken in the first round by the Vancouver Canucks in the 1999 Entry Draft?

A. Daniel and Henrik Sedin.

Daniel Alfredsson, a winger, went to Ottawa in 1995 and would eventually become that club's captain.

Closing the Circle

Borje Salming was the best Scandinavian player of his era in the NHL, and by some accounts, the best ever.

The circle begun by that defenseman was completed in many ways when Nicklas Lidstrom came into the league with the Detroit Red Wings in 1991. That year he was runner-up for rookie of the year, and led first-year players in plus-minus and assists.

Over the next seasons, he would grow into one of the best playoff defensemen in the game (and win two cups with Detroit), and would be runner-up for the Norris Trophy as the NHL's best defender twice in a row.

Always a high plus-minus player, in 1993–1994, Lidstrom would be an incredible plus-43.

There were many, by the end of the decade, who felt that Salming and Lidstrom were the best players the Swedes ever sent to the NHL.

Mats and Saku, Peter and Teemu

The 1990s would produce many stars, but few outside of Gretzky and Lemieux would be any better than the ones that came out of Scandinavia.

Center Mats Sundin became the first Scandinavian to be selected first overall in the NHL entry draft when taken by Quebec in 1989. Over four seasons with the Nordiques, he would score 135 goals before being traded to Toronto in 1994 for the beloved Wendel Clark. By 1997, Sundin would be named captain of the storied franchise, adding another first—the first non-Canadian to wear the C for the blue and white.

One province to the east, Saku Koivu, also a center, went to the Montreal Canadiens in 1996, three years after he was drafted out of Finland's TPS Turku. A two-way center, his work at both ends of the ice and developing leadership in the dressing room led to his being named captain of the blue, blanc, et rouge in 1999.

There is no team in any sport whose captaincy is as honored.

Quote, Unquote

"None of the new players gets tested the way we were in the 1970s. You had to be pretty determined to stay."

—Anders Hedberg.

I Remember ...

Not all Swedish players in the NHL were seen to turn the other cheek. A few were actually seen to be as downright offensive as selected players from any other country. Take defenseman Ulf Samuelsson of Hartford, Pittsburgh, and the New York Rangers. He was accused of dirty hits that put many players out with serious injuries, including Brian Skrudland, Cam Neely, and Pierre Mondou. On a Saturday night in 1994, Samuelsson was in front of his net when Toronto tough guy Tie Domi sucker-punched the surprised defenseman, sending him to the ice unconscious. In Vancouver, where the later game on *Hockey Night in Canada* was on deck, players on both teams getting ready in their dressing room are said to have stood up and cheered when they saw Domi's attack on television. Such was the level of enmity among Samuelsson's fellow players.

Teemu Selanne exploded out of Jokerit Helsinki and onto the Winnipeg Jets in 1992, scoring a whopping 76 goals as a rookie and earning the Calder Trophy in the process. Dogged by injuries over the next four seasons, he was traded to the Anaheim Mighty Ducks in 1996 and teamed with the terrific Paul Kariya. He proceeded to turn in two straight 50-goal seasons.

And finally, Peter Forsberg, son of Swedish national coach Kent, hit the NHL from MoDo of the Swedish League in 1994 and would total over 116 points in his second season on 86 assists. One of the best two-way players in the NHL by the end of the century, he became known for his tenacity, his ability to play at both ends of the rink, and his tendency to turn up the scoring totals in the playoffs (one goal in every three regular season games, one in two in playoff games).

Stars of the Era

➤ Borje Salming led the way for Swedes and Finns in the NHL. He played 17 seasons, all but one with the Toronto Maple Leafs, and despite playing on some horrible clubs in that city, only four times out of 16 years did he have a negative plus-minus. Six times a league all-star and once a Canada Cup all-star. Elected to the Hockey Hall of Fame.

➤ Jari Kurri played 18 seasons in the NHL (most by any European), scored over 600 goals (most by a European), had over 1,400 points (same again), and won five Stanley Cups. For years he was Wayne Gretzky's right winger on the superb Edmonton clubs of the 1980s. Scored better than 30 goals a year 9 times.

➤ Nicklas Lidstrom finished his ninth season in the NHL in 2000. Already considered among the top three defensemen in the league. Has played his entire career for Detroit, winning two Stanley Cups, and was runner-up for top defenseman in the NHL twice.

➤ Esa Tikkanen played 15 seasons in the NHL, starting with Edmonton in 1985 and finishing with Washington in 1998. A two-way winger and total pest, he had 627 points in 845 games, amassed over 1,000 minutes in penalties, and won 5 Stanley Cups.

The Least You Need to Know

➤ Swedes began to come into the NHL in the early 1970s.

➤ The WHA was the first true home to Europeans at that time.

➤ Jari Kurri and Esa Tikkanen were key members of the Edmonton Oilers' Stanley Cup runs.

➤ By the beginning of the 1990s, Scandinavian players had earned their stripes in the league.

➤ Mats Sundin and Saku Koivu would take over as captains of the most famous teams in hockey in the late 1990s.

Part 6

Other Voices

For those just initiated into women's hockey in North America, the game might seem to reach back to, oh, somewhere in the 1980s, apparently when young girls discovered the game and then quickly grew up to be Cammie Granato and Cassie Campbell at the 1998 Olympics in Nagano. The truth is that women were playing hockey as far back as the late 1880s and had significant leagues and collections of teams right up until World War II, when the women's game almost died out for a while before a rebirth in the 1970s.

On the subject of significant, blacks and other minorities have played hockey for over a century, but no black player made it to the NHL until the late 1950s, a decade after Jackie Robinson broke the color barrier in baseball.

In this section, we'll look at the development of women's hockey up to and beyond the 1998 Olympics, and at the changing faces of men's hockey over the years. We'll also take a look at junior hockey leagues and at the game as it's played at the Canadian and American college level.

The Good Old Women's Game (1890–1990)

It's symbolically significant that the history of women's hockey in this chapter runs from around 1890, when the women of Lord Stanley's family had a great time messing around with hockey in Ottawa, to 1990, when the hockey women of the world gathered for the first official tournament in Ottawa. During that time, the women's game had wonderful highs and dipped to tragic lows. But through it all there were always those determined to keep the opportunities for female players open, one way or another. The story would have a happy ending, and like all fairy tales, there would be a lot of sacrifice that went into blazing the trail to the promised land—or the current version of that promised land that women's hockey occupies. In this chapter, we'll look at those 100 years of women in the game.

Lord Stanley's Girls

There is a photo in the National Archives of Canada that shows a group of women playing hockey at Rideau Hall in Ottawa, home of the Governor-General, around 1890.

In the center of the shot, a lone figure in white is reaching for the puck, one-handed, while carving a turn to her right into the ice. From her body language you can tell two things—she loves the game, and she knows what she's doing.

The figure is Isobel Stanley, the Governor-General's daughter, and she was every bit as hockey-crazy as her brothers. In fact, she helped her brothers hound the GeeGee into spending $48 on a silver cup for the Dominion's hockey champions.

Lord Stanley encouraged his daughter, her friends, his wife, and her friends, out onto the ice at Rideau Hall to try the new game of hockey. They were the forerunners of three generations of women who would take up the game before World War II and seemingly establish the opposite sex as a player in hockey.

They Didn't Need Suffragettes

It's strange, really, that in a society that seemed to go so far out of its way to keep women down at the turn of the twentieth century, hockey for women was not only accepted, but in many places encouraged.

"The history of women's hockey," writes Shirley Fischler, "both in Canada and the United States, parallels the status of women overall."

And that's true, to the extent that as women gained more political and social freedom through the 1920s and 1930s, hockey as a sport for them gained along with it. But at the turn of the century, women in hockey seemed to run in front of women's achievements in society.

Aw, I Knew That!

Q. What future NHL executive was mothered by Margaret Topp, a former showgirl and model, who was a star player on the Winnipeg Olympics in the 1930s?

A. Neil Smith, general manager of the New York Rangers in the 1990s.

As Brian McFarlane writes, in the early 1900s women's teams were popping up all over the country—even as far north as Dawson City in the Yukon, where a new arena was built in 1904 and men and women were invited to play on it. Men seemed to enjoy coming to the rink to cheer for their daughters, wives, or friends.

Women were playing in western Canada as early as 1896, though always just with themselves (playing organized games with men and boys was unthinkable, and in some places, still is).

Not all was wonderful, however. Out in the Maritimes, where the game was invented, the men "tried hard to keep the game to themselves," writes McFarlane. But then, they also tried to keep the game just for the upper classes—no riff-raff, blacks, or women allowed.

But this didn't stop women's teams from forming.

Things were not nearly as easy for women in the United States in the early century, however.

"In the early 1900s, most women limited their physical activity in an American society which dictated that, in order for a woman to fulfill her destiny as a mother, it was her duty to monitor all activities which might endanger her ability to reproduce," say writers Joanna Avery and Julie Stevens.

Women's society developed much more slowly south of the border, though there were teams before 1900 in Alaska that played friendly matches with Canadian clubs. It would not be until the women's movement of the 1920s came along, however, that American women's hockey would begin to find a toehold.

Oh, Those Skirts

When women first began playing hockey, the question of the uniform immediately came up. Women in short hockey pants and woollen stockings? Never.

So it was in long linen skirts and pretty sweaters with high collars and long sleeves that women first took to the ice. Photos from the period are startling. A Montreal ladies' team from the turn of the century is seen wearing long skirts, white blouses with high collars, and dark sweaters. They could have gone straight from the ice to a cotillion.

The truly silly thing, of course, is that in many places men weren't allowed to enter arenas to watch women play, so what did their clothes have to do with anything? They could have played naked and the men wouldn't have known.

I Remember ...

Fran Crooks-Westman was a star at the University of Toronto in the 1930s. In 1933, her Toronto Vagabonds were to play in Port Dover and posters put up in that town billed her as the best player in Ontario. Admission was set for 25 cents for adults and 15 cents for children. The place was packed. Unfortunately, Ms. Westman didn't make the game. Injury? Illness? Nope, in an interview she gave to Brian McFarlane 60 years later, Ms. Westman admitted her husband wouldn't let her go. Seemed she had two games in two nights booked, and her husband thought that was too much athletics for a woman. "We tended to listen to our husbands," she said. "I'm sure I'd react differently if I was a young woman today."

Another photo, taken just before World War I, shows women at the University of Toronto playing a spirited game outdoors, still in long skirts. But at least the hem had come up a bit and they were less restrictive.

Thankfully, the war brought many changes to society—and women's hockey wasn't left out. By 1917, the bloomer had replaced the long skirt, and female players could finally look down and find the puck between their skates.

Bloomers would stay in general use until the early 1930s, when proper hockey pants became the norm.

Now women could both see the puck and avoid bruises on the upper legs from hard shots.

Our Auld Alma Mater

Colleges and universities were hugely important to the development of women's hockey before the middle of the century. McGill University in Montreal and the University of Toronto had especially strong programs, and a three-team league was formed that ran for more than a decade during the 1920s and 1930s (the third was Queen's University in Kingston, Ontario).

The University of Minnesota had an intramural program as far back as 1916, which lasted into the 1930s, and other colleges in the state also got involved. But the onset of the Depression killed much of the opportunity for American women to play sports.

Early Heroes

Marian Hilliard was the best all-around woman athlete at the University of Toronto in the 1920s, and she found some of her greatest moments on the ice. She "amazed the onlookers with her speed and clever playmaking," writes McFarlane, this during a three-game series with the Ottawa Alerts in 1924 that was to decide the women's champions of Ontario.

Aw, I Knew That!

Q. The first goaltender to regularly wear a mask during play was actually a woman. Who was she?

A. Elizabeth Graham, 1927, Queen's University, Kingston, Ontario.

But she wasn't the only star of the era. On her own club, Shirley Moulds was considered a superb performer, and Marion Giles of Ottawa was right in their class.

Outside of university hockey, another name was making the sports pages—Bobbie Rosenfeld. Also an all-around athlete (she would win a gold medal in the 400-meter relay for Canada at the 1928 Summer Olympics—the first in which women competed officially), Rosenfeld played for the North Toronto women's club, a strong collection of talents, and was probably the best player of the era.

Another star was Phyllis Griffiths, important for another reason. She and Rosenfeld would go on to be influential sports columnists—the former with the *Toronto Telegram,* and the latter with the *Toronto Globe*—at a time when all major newspapers had women sports reporters and columnists (that can't be said of all large newspapers today).

Griffiths would be an influential voice in forming an official Eastern Canadian women's championship in 1931.

While these women were the individual stars of the time, only one club would lay claim to the title of best team.

The Preston Rivulettes

"Canadian women are not just knocking at the door of the world of sport, they have crashed the gate, swarmed the field and, in some games, driven mere man to the sidelines," wrote Henry Roxborough, of *Maclean's* magazine, in the early 1930s.

In track and field, basketball, and hockey, Canadian women were making their mark.

But only the incredible Edmonton Grads in women's basketball (502–20, 17-straight world championships between 1914 and 1939) were more powerful in their sport than the Preston Rivulettes were in hockey during the 1930s.

The Rivulettes came to prominence in the early 1930s as the Ladies' Ontario Hockey Association intermediate champs, a level they quickly outgrew. In two years they went 21–0–1, outscoring the opposition 151–9. In 1932, they upset the University of Toronto, 1–0, and did it again, by the same score, in the 1933 playoffs, this time when Marm Schmuck scored from the center line.

Preston was invited to Edmonton to play for a Dominion title against the Rustlers, where the Eastern visitors lost both rough games, 3–2. The games drew over 2,000 spectators each night.

The Rivs won the next two Eastern titles and got revenge on the west by beating the Winnipeg Eatons, 7–1 (in a wild, brawl-filled game in front of 2,000 fans in Galt, Ontario), and 3–1 in a slightly more controlled contest in front of 3,000. They took the new Lady Bessborough Trophy.

Quote, Unquote

"The girls could beat the blisters off the boys 9 times out of 10."

—Bill Bentley, father of NHL stars Doug and Max Bentley, on how good their seven sisters (Bill's daughters) were at hockey.

Quote, Unquote

"I wouldn't care to see them in the [boxing] ring either. I may be funny about my women that way, but there it is."

—Andy Lytle, *Chatelaine* magazine, 1933. He was deluged with hate mail.

Preston would continue to dominate eastern Canada, and the semi-regular Dominion title games, for the rest of the 1930s, and finished the decade 348–2—the only losses being those two in Edmonton.

Rosie the Riveter Is Shown the Dressing Room Door

During World War II, women contributed to the effort like never before—filling the factories as replacements for the men who had gone overseas to fight. There was little time for serious hockey during those years, but the war would end and everyone could get back to their sports once again.

Or so they thought.

The war ended and the troops came home and society sent women back to the kitchen, took off their shoes, and told them to get busy making babies and putting dinner on the stove. The gains for women in the 1920s and 1930s took a serious knock.

As Brian McFarlane writes, arenas that had, reluctantly, given ice time for women's games, now kept all of it for boys and men. Sponsors couldn't be found. Newspapers switched their focus to pro sports and left little space for women's sports.

Some kept playing. A three-team league in Quebec kept going for a while, as well as a few in the Maritimes. It also didn't help that universities cut back their programs in the 1940s and 1950s, leaving women without local leagues to fall back on.

But there were some young women who found a way.

Ab

In 1955, the Toronto Hockey League received an application from eight-year-old Ab Hoffman to play house league hockey. Glancing quickly at the application, they processed it and put young Ab on a team, where the youngster, as a bruising performer, played defense and made the all-star selections.

Except, young Ab was actually Abby—Abigail—a girl.

The league phoned Ab's mom to wonder if he had accidently brought in his sister's birth certificate and found out the truth. When word got out, Ab was a media darling all across the country, so what was the THL to do?

They gave her a dressing room to herself and let her keep playing.

The following year, young Hoffman tried to switch to girls' hockey, but it was barely organized and games tough to find, so Abby quit and tried other sports—such as track, where she would win two Olympic medals in the 800 meters.

Some Sort of Explanation

During the 1960s and 1970s, women's hockey began to grow once more—slowly, it must be pointed out. There were still too many girls playing the game in white figure skates and incomplete equipment. But determined organizers, especially in Ontario and Quebec, were making improvements every year.

Too slowly for some girls, who were quite happy to play with the boys. If someone would let them.

Okay, let's stop and try to set a scene here.

Many men thought girls should never play with the boys—not strong enough, dressing room issues, basic chauvinism.

Some men didn't see a problem.

Many women thought if girls could play with the boys, that was cool.

Some women thought if they did, it would make their own hockey look second rate. Or they had dressing room issues, or they, too, suffered from a basic sexism ("I'm not having *my* boy play with a girl!").

Gail Cummings et al vs. the Establishment

Into this atmosphere came Gail Cummings, an 11-year-old goaltender in Huntsville, Ontario, who was good enough to play on the boys' team. Huntsville didn't have high-level hockey for girls.

The league said no, and the issue went to an investigative commission. Gail won. Lots of money spent by both sides.

It went to the Ontario Court of Appeals in 1978. The league won. More money spent.

It went to the Ontario Supreme Court. Gail lost. More money spent.

Meanwhile, the Ontario Women's Hockey Association was officially incorporated, and it set about making girls' hockey a viable option.

An interesting out-cropping of the Cummings battle was that many leagues, faced with the same question of whether to allow girls to play, decided spending a ton of money to fight the thing in court wasn't worth it. So they found a way to let the girls in, especially in the prepuberty divisions.

Quote, Unquote

"Girls have to take the leftovers; from bantams to seniors, the boys get the preference in rinks through the province of Ontario."

—Alexandre Gibb, frustrated *Toronto Daily Star* columnist, 1938.

On the other hand, there were many teams, citing the Canadian Amateur Hockey Association rule against girls playing with boys, that simply refused to play any team with a girl on it.

It was a mess.

Go ahead again. As Avery and Stevens write, while Ontario leagues were running around preventing girls from playing co-ed, the CAHA (which had started the mess by having the no-girls rule on its books in the first place) decided to pass a rule saying girls 12 and under could play on boys' teams in areas where girls' teams weren't available.

Now things were really confused.

In the United States, girls had begun to play on boys' teams, many as a result of Barbara Broidy's fight to be allowed to play on her high school team in Oyster Bay, Long Island, New York. Now, by the time it was all sorted out, she was actually already heading for college, as Shirley Fischler writes, but it set precedents all over the United States.

Back in Canada, another huge brawl was about to start that would ultimately clear the air, somewhat.

Justine

Justine Blainey, a 12-year-old resident of north Toronto, wanted to play with the boys in 1985. Not because there weren't girls' teams. Not because she wanted to prove a point. Simply because she was good enough to play top-level boys' hockey—the highest level she could achieve—and because it had bodychecking and girls' hockey didn't.

Quote, Unquote

"Sure, I may not have a job when I get back home, but this was too important to pass up."

—Shirley Cameron, a letter carrier in Edmonton, skips out on her job to play in the Canadian women's championship, 1992.

It took four years. Tons of money. A trip to the Supreme Court of Canada. Blainey was officially allowed to play.

The Metropolitan Toronto Hockey League had fought all the way against Blainey. And the Ontario Women's Hockey Association had fought all the way as well. Also against Blainey.

"Allowing girls to leave girls' hockey simply because they want to only stigmatizes the female game as second-rate," said Fran Rider, the OWHA president. "The best way to advance female hockey opportunities is through unified efforts to develop a parallel stream for girls and women of all ages."

You can understand Rider's point to a certain degree. After all the work she and others had put in to finally establishing women's hockey, they were afraid opening the gates to co-ed games would ruin it all.

Nah. It turned out that while lots of girls had fun playing with the boys until they were about 12, very few continued after that. Most went to the ever-stronger programs open to them in all-girls' leagues.

The point was, however, that they could play with the boys if they wished.

Now what about the boys playing in the girls' league?

Kidding.

Numbers

In 1989, USA Hockey formed a girls' and women's section that put control of the sport for females in the hands of those actually running it. Similar moves were made by Hockey Canada and the CAHA north of the border.

The only real change needed now was in ice time. Arenas had been filled with boys' and men's teams, especially those in Canada. Finding time for anyone was often difficult, unless you wanted to play at midnight. Finding time for girls and women was even tougher.

Suddenly, however, by the mid-1990s, communities everywhere were under pressure to open more ice to women players, and that ice began to appear (not without a heck of a fight in some places, however).

Look at some numbers of hockey registrations. In Ontario, spring 1997 found more than 15,000 women players registered (this after practically a standing start just 20 years previously). Next in line was Minnesota and the Dakotas, with over 5,000 each, followed by Massachusetts, British Columbia, New England, Quebec, and New York.

Why the sudden interest? A lot, obviously, has to be credited to the hard work of women's hockey organizers, determined to make the sport available to both sexes. A lot goes to the fighters like Justine Blainey and Barbara Broidy.

Most, though, might be for a purer reason—the sport itself. And the sudden emergence on the world stage of serious women's hockey. Serious international women's hockey. And serious women's players.

Like Manon and Erin.

Quote, Unquote

"I thought you had to be dead to have a trophy named after you."

—Abby Hoffman, at the introduction of the silverware that would thereafter be awarded the Canadian women's hockey champions, 1992.

A Flash of Lightning

Manon. All hockey fans know the name. Most know the details of what the young woman from Quebec did in 1992 to put women's hockey on the front pages of sports sections across the world.

Manon Rheaume had grown up in Quebec playing hockey with the boys, including her brother, who would go on to an NHL career. Facing tough shots had just been something she had done, once she found herself in the nets.

She had been the first woman to play in a Major Junior A game—17 minutes as an injury replacement after getting called up from the Tier II farm club of the Trois-Rivières Draveurs. Then it had been a switch to women's hockey, playing goal for Canada in the world championships of 1992.

It was then she was invited by general manager and team president Phil Esposito to the fall 1992 training camp of the NHL's Tampa Bay Lightning. Everyone said it was a publicity stunt pulled by a man who knew how to get the media's attention.

Aw, I Knew That!

Q. What two players scored for St. Louis in Manon Rheaume's one period of NHL exhibition hockey in 1992 for Tampa Bay?

A. Jeff Brown and Brendan Shanahan.

Except Rheaume didn't take it like a publicity stunt, showing up for camp in superb shape and impressing Lightning coach Terry Crisp to the point he put her in goal for the first period of an exhibition game against the St. Louis Blues. Nine shots and two goals, plus some strong stops, led to a contract to play in the International League with Atlanta and, later, Nashville and Knoxville of the East Coast Hockey League.

She didn't play a lot (though she made a ton of money in endorsements, including over $500,000 one year), but the point had been made—if there was a position in hockey that a woman could compete with men, it was in goal.

And Rheaume wasn't the only one.

Erin Whitten, from Glens Falls, New York, by way of the University of New Hampshire, signed with the Toledo Storm minor pro club, where she was used as a practice player and the team's third goaltender. Kelly Dyer, out of Northeastern University, played in Florida's Sunshine Hockey League with Jacksonville and West Palm Beach. For West Palm, she started a game in 1994 and went 8–1 in 9 contests the following year.

All were not ready for the NHL, but they were close enough that many realized it would only be a matter of time before a woman came along who could handle it.

I Remember ...

In 1976, women's professional hockey had its own visionary in a former bullfighter named Charles Lewis. In that year, he tried to organize a pro league for women, riding on the popularity of the men's game. He set up headquarters in Tarzania, California, and went about putting his dream together. Unlike that of the NHL in 1917, or the WHA in 1972, Lewis' vision never came to life.

Stars of the Era

➤ Marian Hilliard was the best player on an excellent University of Toronto Varsity Blues club of the mid-1920s. She was known for her speed and playmaking. Hilliard was a charter member of the school's Sports Hall of Fame, inducted in 1987.

➤ Bobbie Rosenfeld was a tremendous multi-sport athlete who won a gold medal in the 1928 Summer Olympics in Antwerp on Canada's 400-meter relay team. She was a terror on the ice, often scoring at will and using her athleticism to dominate play. Rosenfeld went on to a long career as a sportswriter.

➤ Manon Rheaume was the first, and so far only, woman to tend goal in a National Hockey League game, an exhibition contest against St. Louis for Tampa Bay in 1992. She was a regular member of the Canadian women's national team in the 1990s and became a household name in Canada through her achievements and endorsements.

➤ Erin Whitten also played goal professionally after starring at the University of New Hampshire. She would go on to play for the United States women's team.

➤ Kelly Dyer made inroads in men's pro hockey in the Sunshine Hockey League, which later became the Southern League. Also a goal-tender, she would play on the U.S. women's team.

Aw, I Knew That!

Q. In what year was the first European Women's Hockey Championship held?

A. 1989, in West Germany.

The Least You Need to Know

➤ Women were playing hockey before the turn of the twentieth century.

➤ Hockey for women, especially in Canada, grew quickly through the 1920s and 1930s.

➤ The aftermath of World War II saw the women's game practically disappear before it was reborn in the 1960s.

➤ A number of court cases established girls' rights to play on boys' teams in certain cases.

➤ Women's hockey experienced incredible growth in the 1980s and 1990s.

➤ Manon Rheaume became the first woman to play in an NHL game, tending goal for Tampa Bay in a 1992 exhibition tilt.

Two Powers on a World Stage (1987–2001)

With women's hockey growing strong again in the 1980s, it seemed only natural that players in Canada and the United States would want to test themselves against the rest of the world. Unfortunately, there wasn't much of a "rest of the world" to test themselves against. Only Finland could ice a team that was anywhere near competitive with the North Americans. Still, an official world championship was finally organized for 1990. While waiting for the rest to catch up, the Canadians and Americans went at it tooth and short nails, with Canada coming out on top each time—except for one special moment when it counted most. In this chapter, we'll look at those tournaments and the rivalry between the two great women's hockey nations.

First Steps

Hazel McCallion, the flash from the Gaspé, had been a star player in her youth. Many years after her competitive career ended (but not the pickup hockey), McCallion was Her Worship, the long-time mayor of Mississauga, a suburb of Toronto. In 1987 she saw a dream she had shared with many other people come to fruition—an unofficial world championship.

Organized by Fran Rider and the Ontario Women's Hockey Association, seven teams went to the Toronto area to battle for the McCallion Cup—Canada, the United States, Sweden, Switzerland, Holland, Japan, and a second host entry representing Ontario (they were the Mississauga Warriors club team).

It was such an event that, as Brian McFarlane writes, even *Sports Illustrated* and *The New York Times* showed up.

The only country conspicuous by its absence was the Soviet Union, which didn't have women's hockey.

Though Canada and Ontario played for the title, with Canada winning, it was a game between the United States and the host nation that had everyone breathless—it ended 2–1 for Canada.

Flamingoes on Ice

The most significant development in women's hockey to that point occurred in March 1990, when the first world championships sanctioned by the International Ice Hockey Federation opened in Ottawa, Ontario.

As hosts, the Canadians were out in force, waving their pink and white flags, looking resplendent in their pink and white uniforms, fans' faces painted white with pink maple leafs …

Uh, just a minute …

Yep, someone, somewhere, thought it would be cute if the Canadian girls skated out in traditional Canadian international uniforms—same ones the men wore. Only they were pink!

Some thought it was great. Others, like sportswriter Jane O'Hara, were aghast. Pink?

The city of Ottawa went pink-crazy—everything was pink. And Canada, led by Angela James, France St. Louis, Geraldine Heaney, Dawn McGuire, Judy Diduck, and a whole roster of new national heroes, finished in the pink. So to speak.

Quote, Unquote

"They could have offered me a million and I still wouldn't do that."

—Manon Rheaume turns down an offer of $75,000 from *Playboy* magazine to pose nude.

Aw, I Knew That!

Q. Who was the most valuable player at the first women's world championship in 1990?

A. Cathy Phillips, the Canadian goaltender.

Eight teams showed up—Canada, the United States, Finland, Switzerland, Norway, West Germany, Japan, and Sweden.

Really, but for the United States and its fine goalie Kelly Dyer, and the plucky Finns, who surprised Canada by losing just 5–4, it was no contest as the hosts went on to win.

For the United States, Cindy Curley led all tournament scorers with 21 points, and a young forward named Cammie Granato chipped in 9 goals. She would be heard from many times in the coming decade.

Interesting note: Bodychecking was legal in Europe but not in North America, and the Euros thought they might gain some kind of advantage by insisting that hitting be allowed at the worlds. What they forgot, of course, was that the Canadian and American girls had grown up battling with their brothers and other boys in driveways and on rinks all over.

About 30 seconds into the first game, when a Canadian forward hammered a European opponent behind the net, the visitors realized that they had made a tactical error. After this tournament, no more bodychecking.

Except accidentally, of course.

Canada Again, and Again, and Again ...

Between world tournaments, the United States and Canada began to build a serious rivalry by playing exhibitions and, eventually, the Three Nations Cup, which would also add Finland, the only other team that could generally keep up, into the mix.

These games increased not just in intensity but in quality as ever-growing women's leagues, hockey schools, special programs, and the effects of NCAA college women's hockey contributed to stronger athletes.

In 1992, the second women's worlds went in Tampere, Finland, with two new countries—China and Denmark—along for the ride. It wasn't that surprising to see the Danes, but the Chinese, that was another story altogether, Chinese men never having been much involved in hockey, after all.

Quote, Unquote

"They are the wussiest uniforms you've ever seen. Real women don't wear pink."

—Jane O'Hara, *Ottawa Sun*, on the Canadian uniforms in the 1990 worlds.

Aw, I Knew That!

Q. Name the former captain of the Canadian women's team who also played for the country's national lacrosse team.

A. France St. Louis.

271

Canada won its three preliminary games by a combined score of 24–1, while the Americans won theirs by a total of 26–4. The final was no contest, however. Despite the efforts of Granato, who scored eight times during the tournament and was named the best forward, Canada's overall power and excellent defense that included Geraldine Heaney and goalie Manon Rheaume were too much.

Down went the U.S. women, 8–0, in the final.

Riika

If the Finns were ever going to make a mark in women's world hockey within a reasonable time, the program would need two things—strong organization and a legitimate leader.

By 1994, as Elizabeth Etue and Megan Williams write, they had both.

Finnish women had started playing hockey only in 1970, and 20 years later there were still only about 500 players in the country. The first women's worlds, however, inspired the same kind of growth in the Scandinavian country as it did in North America—in four years, the number more than tripled.

And the Finns were serious, organizing dry-land training and fitness camps, getting the national team together as often as possible, and committing to building a solid club.

Perfect timing then, in 1994, with the worlds in Lake Placid, New York, for Riika Nieminen to take the stage. Nieminen was an excellent athlete, having excelled in bandy (which accounted for her magnificent skating) and baseball, as well as hockey.

And despite her smallish frame, she was also tough and highly competitive.

Canada overwhelmed its opposition in Group A, but the United States, easy winners over Switzerland and Germany in its preliminary grouping, struggled to beat the Finns, 2–1.

I Remember ...

Stars in men's sports have had to put up with (and occasionally take advantage of) women fans hanging around the back door for years. But for women, it's a little more worrisome. Riika Nieminen of Finland found herself being followed from event to event during the early 1990s by a smitten male fan, who wrote her letters, left her phone messages, and even, according to writers Elizabeth Etue and Megan Williams, indirectly threatened a male friend of Nieminen at a hockey gathering.

It was a great moment for women's hockey—more competitive teams meant more respect and a greater chance to grow. But with Canada beating the Americans 6–3 to win gold again, there still remained one changing of the guard left before the game could say it had been truly opened up to more than just the red and white.

Close, But ...

By 1997, the Americans were hoping to finally solve the riddle of the Canadians.

The tournament was held in Ontario and featured eight teams, including the Russians, who claimed not to have a hockey program for women in 1990. They showed up for the first time and finished sixth of eight.

Canada again flew through the preliminaries, but ran into a revved-up Finnish club in the semi-finals, which came close to the upset, going down 2–1. That set up the final with the United States.

For the first time, the American women had a real chance to win the worlds, battling Canada to a 3–3 tie through regulation time. But in overtime, Nancy Drolet scored her third goal of the game to give Canada its fourth world gold medal.

Rather than get down, however, Team USA came to the realization that they had finally caught up. And next year was an Olympic year.

Quote, Unquote

"She's been begging me to slow down. She can't find time to train."

—Kent Hughes, agent for Cammie Granato, on the overwhelming number of endorsement and appearance opportunities for the U.S. star after Nagano.

Quote, Unquote

"Who *is* this clown?"

—Karyn Bye, Team USA, on her first thoughts from meeting coach Ben Smith for the first time in 1996. She learned who he was in a hurry.

An Olympic Dream

Women's hockey representatives had wanted hockey included in the 1994 Winter Olympics at Lillehammer, Norway, but they were turned back by, among other things, complaints from organizers that it would add a million dollars to the cost of staging the events.

Dissuaded, but not discouraged, women's groups tried again for 1998, and this time they were successful. The difference? First, the IOC was under a lot of pressure to increase the involvement of women in the Winter Games, and hockey would immediately put about 130 more females into the mix. Second, the IOC had seen how well-attended the first three world championships had been and wanted to jump on that bandwagon.

Not everyone was thrilled that women hockey players were going to Nagano. The main complaint was that the sport wasn't mature enough, what with only three teams capable of being truly competitive. And to be fair, women's hockey didn't have to go through nearly the scrutiny that many other sports had to in order to become official—especially in terms of the number of countries involved, the spread of those countries around the world, and the number of quality teams that could be iced.

But arguments aside, hockey women would get their chance. And the fans would have the opportunity to see something truly dramatic—one program reach the pinnacle and another succumb to intense pressure at exactly the wrong moment.

Ben Smith

One of the factors observers had been looking for with women's hockey to show its maturity was the eventual emergence of women coaches to lead the top teams.

The Canadians decided it was time to make a woman the head of the national program for Nagano (see later in this chapter), while down south, a man—a very experienced man—was put in place to guide the U.S. effort at Nagano.

While there is no reason to believe that a woman can't coach a hockey team as well as a man, if not better, the relative youth of the top-level women's game meant that female coaches still had not quite had enough time to catch up in experience to men's coaches at the highest levels.

As Cammy Clark writes, Ben Smith was a highly experienced, 50-year-old men's head coach with the strong Northeastern University program in 1996 (and a former assistant with the men's Olympic team in 1988), when he happened to glance at a flyer from USA Hockey advertising for a new head coach to run the women's team. Fascinated, Smith went for it, and, Clark says, it changed the course of the Olympic tournament.

I Remember ...

Ben Smith, the coach of the U.S. gold medal team in 1998, let very little of his personal life or his emotions out to his players while preparing them for the tournament. During the Olympics, on Valentine's Day, Smith came to practice with a bag of chocolate hearts that he handed out to the players. "Before this experience is over," he said to his surprised team, "I want you to know what you have meant to me. You players are the best people I have ever coached. I have enjoyed every single moment I have worked with you. I have come to care about you and my affection for you is unconditional. It will last forever."

Smith set a number of goals, but the most important, in his mind, was to change the constant feeling among the American women that they were second best—that the Canadians would always find a way to beat them, no matter what. It was ridiculous, of course, but quite normal for athletes. Team USA was right on Canada's doorstep in more ways than just geography, and it wasn't going to take much to change the pecking order.

What Smith, and none of the women on the national team could have known, of course, was that the Canadians would find a way to beat themselves.

Officer Miller

Shannon Miller was a police officer in Calgary, Alberta, who knew her hockey, knew how to teach the game, and was convinced she knew how to make her team winners.

What she didn't have was much experience as head coach in extremely emotional contests, especially not those she was going to find at the Olympic Games.

Miller had done well as an assistant coach with Team Canada in the 1992 and 1994 worlds, and the next year was named as the first female head coach of the nationals.

She was described, writes Etue and Williams, as "intense and intimidating" by players.

As someone who spoke her mind, Miller sometimes found herself in difficulties. Such as that which came up when long-time player Angela James was cut from the national team before the Olympics.

Miller had warned James, twice, to work on her defense (which was not only her right as coach, but her job), and James had not, according to Miller, satisfied the coach. So she was cut. James, angry, told the press that "she hoped it wasn't the case that a personal relationship between management and a player" was a factor.

By that, James was pointing at a possible lesbian love affair between Miller and one of her players, which obviously would be a terrible breach of the coach-player relationship. It went on in the press and the backrooms for two weeks before the Canadian Hockey Association exonerated Miller. But the damage had been done.

Aw, I Knew That!

Q. Only two players from Team USA's entry at the first women's worlds in 1990 were still with the club when it won the gold medal at the Nagano Olympics in 1998. Who were they?

A. Cammie Granato and Lisa Brown-Miller (she was Lisa Brown in 1990).

Quote, Unquote

"Hayley might already be better than any player we've ever seen in this game."

—Canadian coach Les Lawton, in 1994, after seeing future star Hayley Wickenheiser in Calgary. She was 15.

Miller was also under pressure for agreeing (very reluctantly, it should be pointed out) to a long series of exhibition games between her team and the Americans—13 of them that ended 7–6 for Canada. And then there was a huge 3–0 loss to Team USA at the Three Nations Cup in total just before Christmas 1997.

Clearly, the Canadians were going into Nagano carrying a huge load. And it would get worse.

Tension, Terror, and Triumph

For Canada, it came down to this: They had to win the gold at Nagano. Had to. Anything less (meaning second to the Americans) would be seen as a terrible failure.

For the United States, the goal was gold. But if there wasn't a gold and the game had been close it would be disappointing, again, but not completely disastrous.

Aw, I Knew That!

Q. In the 1998 Olympics at Nagano, which team, the United States or Canada, had the leading scorer in the tournament?

A. Neither. It was Riika Nieminen of Finland, with 7 goals and 12 points.

Under the strategy laid out by Smith, the Americans had been ever more physical with the Canadians, jumping on them at every opportunity, pressuring their defense. Leaning on them right out to the very boundaries of what the "no-contact" rules would allow.

And it worked. In the preliminary round, the teams met after they had finalized berths in the gold medal game, so it was technically meaningless. But it became competitively huge as Team USA came roaring back from a 4–1 deficit with six-straight goals in the third period for a 7–4 victory.

It was the first time the Americans had beaten the Canadians in a game at a major championship—worlds or this first Olympics—and the repercussions turned out to be tremendous.

Smith had his team both relaxed and convinced they could win the gold.

Miller, seemingly overwhelmed by stresses the women's game had never seen (media coverage was tremendous, especially back home in Canada), had her team tense, uptight, waiting for something bad to happen. Tension had turned into terror, and it showed on the ice.

Gold medal game. Manon Rheaume in one cage. Sarah Tueting for the Americans in the other. Though both goalies played well, Team USA jumped ahead 2–0 and held that lead right toward the end of the third period when Danielle Goyette, who as Clark points out had become one of the Olympics' leading scorers despite the recent death of her father, put one by Tueting at 15:59.

And that was it. The Canadians pressed, the U.S. defense shut it down, and an empty-net marker with eight seconds left ended the threat. Team USA had the gold medal.

Joy and celebration in the American camp. ("God, they're so beautiful. They're absolutely beautiful," said Granato when she saw the medals. "And they're ours, they're all ours.")

Stunned silence, confusion, agony, in the Canadian camp.

The press back home in Canada railed on Miller from one end of the country to the other (think about it—a women's hockey coach getting roasted in the media—the game really had taken a huge jump!), and the loss would cost her the job.

Canada would gain some measure of revenge by winning the 2000 and 2001 world championships, the former in overtime. But the Olympic gold was gone.

At least, gone until 2002, when the women would meet again in Salt Lake City, Utah, to put their game at the forefront of hockey attention and Canada would have a chance to gain Olympic honor back from Team USA.

Unless the Finns come and pull the upset, of course.

Great Games

February 2000

Canada and the United States went to overtime in the gold medal game at the world championships in Kitchener, Ontario, despite the fact the Americans had led the game 2–0 well into the second period, looking to end Canada's domination of the tournament going back to 1990 (they had never lost a game). In overtime, Danielle Goyette netted the winning goal to give Canada the victory. It was the second-straight sudden death loss for the United States in the gold medal game.

Canada 3, United States 2

Stars of the Era

➤ Cammie Granato first played for Team USA at the inaugural official world championship for women in 1990, and was still with the club as its captain in 2001. An excellent forward, she scored nine times as a rookie at the worlds, making the tournament all-star team in 1992 and 1997. At the Olympics she had four goals and eight points in six games.

➤ Angela James was the first superstar of women's international hockey. She led the 1990 worlds with 11 goals for Canada and made the all-star team in 1992. She found herself in the midst of controversy after being a late cut from the Olympic team.

➤ Riika Nieminen is the best non–North American player to come out of the 1990s. The Finnish star was better than everyone at the 1998 Olympics, leading the tournament with 7 goals and 12 points in 6 games. Three times she made the world championship all-star team.

➤ Cassie Campbell, an all-star defender with the Canadian team, became a media celebrity because she combined toughness and skill with beauty. In 1997 at the worlds, Campbell was named to the all-star team after collecting two goals and six assists.

➤ Geraldine Heaney, a defender, was another of the early stars for Canada, earning best defenseman honors at the 1992 worlds and making the all-star team.

The Least You Need to Know

➤ The first unofficial world championships was held in 1987 in Canada.

➤ Team Canada won the first official world tournament in 1990 and every world title since then up to and including 2000.

➤ Team USA closed the gap over the decade of the 1990s and won the first women's Olympic gold at Nagano in 1998, in a mild upset.

➤ Women's hockey struggled in the decade with competitiveness as only three teams—Canada, the United States, and Finland—could ice strong teams.

➤ Media coverage for the women's Olympic tournament was intense, especially in Canada, where the loss of the gold became a near national disaster.

The Minority Opinion

Willie O'Ree was the first black to play in the National Hockey League, making his debut in 1958. It would be more than a dozen years before another black appeared in the NHL, but since then more and more black Canadians and Americans have made an impact on the league—one became a superstar and may be among the top three goaltenders ever to play. But there was a minority influence in hockey long before O'Ree came along—stretching back to before the turn of the twentieth century. The best black player of the twentieth century may be one who never had the chance to make the National Hockey League, precisely because of his color. In this chapter, we'll look at those issues. Native players, continuing a tradition in hockey earned from their ancestors who helped invent the game, have always had a presence in pro hockey.

As (Native) Canadian as a Puck and a Stick

As we learned in Chapter 1, "Whose Game Is This, Anyway?" Native Canadians were involved in the creation of hockey through the contribution of shinny, which was melded with ice hurley to create Canada's game.

Down east, the Mi'kmaq played the game along with the white and black residents (see later this chapter), and indeed, manufactured the world's most famous sticks—Micmac—until the 1920s.

All through the twentieth century, Native players have made an impact on the game at all levels, including the NHL.

Despite the influence of Canadian Native Peoples on the game, the first regular Native performer in the league was American—Clarence "Taffy" Abel, who was the grandson of the chief of the Cherokee Nation. Abel, born in Sault Ste. Marie, Michigan, was a star in his home state and with the St. Paul Athletic Club before starting an eight-year career in the NHL that took him to 333 games with the New York Rangers and Chicago Blackhawks.

Tracking the Native Influence

Tracking the Native influence on the NHL is much more difficult than that of black players because many athletes have had joint parentage and many others don't list their ancestral backgrounds.

There have been some terrific players with direct ancestry, however.

➤ George Armstrong, from Skead, Ontario, was known as "The Chief" while captain of the Toronto Maple Leafs from 1957–1968. One of the most highly respected players of his time, Armstrong began his career in 1949 and played 1,187 games in the blue and white. Scored 296 goals and 713 regular season points in his career and was elected to the Hockey Hall of Fame in 1975.

➤ Stan Jonathan, of Ohsweken, Ontario, was picked 86th overall in the 1975 amateur draft by the Boston Bruins and went on to become one of coach Don Cherry's favorite players because of his toughness and ability with the puck. Had two seasons of 20 or better. Played eight years in the NHL before injuries shortened his career.

➤ Henry Boucha, from Warroad, Minnesota, was an Ojibwa who starred in hockey, football, and baseball. A graduate of the excellent hockey program at Warroad High School, he played at the

Aw, I Knew That!

Q. George Armstrong was one of three players in OHA/OHL history to win the outstanding player award twice. Name the other two.

A. Andre Lacroix (Peterborough) and Alyn McCauley (Ottawa).

worlds and Olympics for the United States before signing with the NHL. Considered a budding star, he suffered a bad eye injury on January 4, 1975, that cut short his career. Boucha played a few more seasons before retiring.

➤ Jim Neilson, from Big River, Saskatchewan, played 17 seasons in the NHL, mostly with the New York Rangers starting in 1962. He was a huge defenseman for his time, at 6'2", 205 pounds. Saw action in 1,023 games, scoring 69 times for 368 total points. Was twice an all-star.

➤ Ted Nolan, from Sault Ste. Marie, Ontario, played three seasons in the NHL with Detroit and Pittsburgh. Went on to coach the Buffalo Sabres and was coach of the year in the league in 1997.

Today's NHL features a number of Native players, including Chris Simon, Gino Odjick, Sandy McCarthy, and Craig Berube.

Early Black History

As William Humber points out, between the end of the American Civil War and 1911, the black population in Canada, the world's hockey hotbed, had dropped from 60,000 to about 16,000. Despite the small numbers, there were still small pockets of hockey interest in black communities and individual players of talent to come out of other areas, including Hipple Galloway of Dunnville and Charley Lightfoot of Stratford.

Down east, the Colored Hockey League was created in 1900, featuring the Africville Seasides, Dartmouth Jubilees, Halifax Eurekas, Truro Victorias, and Amherst Royals.

The games often drew large crowds, though as Humber points out, the mostly white fans would often expect "occasional self-mockery or clowning." They'd boo if they didn't get it.

That league lasted into the 1920s.

Bud Kelly was likely the best black player of the pre-1920s era. Part of Frank Selke Sr.'s 118th Battalion team during World War I (which played in London, Ontario), the story goes that the NHL's Toronto St. Pats were interested in the forward, but he played badly in a game that the club's scouts came to see, and so missed his chance at breaking the color barrier.

He certainly made a lot of money playing hockey, however—small-town teams made a lot of payments under the table to keep their best stars.

Quote, Unquote

"He was the best Negro player I ever saw."

—Frank Selke Sr., on Bud Kelly.

In the 1920s, George Barnes played intermediate hockey in Ontario, and he had the misfortune to "get involved in an incident" with Wid Green of Cayuga in 1929. Green suffered a severed muscle in the groin and died later in hospital.

There is no record of any disciplinary action against Barnes.

What blacks in hockey needed was someone to come along who could take the next step. That player appeared in the 1930s.

Three Flies in a Pail of Milk

In his autobiography, *A Fly in a Pail of Milk,* Herb Carnegie tells of the day his dreams of playing in the NHL came crashing down around him.

As a member of the Young Rangers Junior A club in Toronto in the late 1930s, Carnegie practiced often at Maple Leaf Gardens.

"One day," Carnegie wrote, "I was enjoying the practice when Ed (coach Wildey) called me over to the boards and pointed to a shadowy figure sitting part way up in the blue seats. 'See that man sitting in the blues? That's Conn Smythe, owner of the Toronto Maple Leafs. He says he'd take you tomorrow if he could turn Carnegie white.'"

That story was repeated often over the years, one version having Smythe saying, "I'd give anyone $10,000 if he could turn Herb Carnegie white."

Whatever the version, and Smythe never admitted to saying anything about Carnegie, young Herb knew right then he was going to be shut out of his NHL dream.

I Remember ...

In 1969, Herb Carnegie returned to Le Colisee in Quebec City for an oldtimer's game between the former Aces and the legends of the Montreal Canadiens. The Habs were introduced first and received a thundering ovation. When the Aces were introduced, and Carnegie's turn came up, the 15,000 fans in attendance greeted him with a prolonged ovation that, he wrote, "left me motionless and spellbound. Perspiration seeped down my spine." In Quebec, where race seemed to matter less than anywhere else in Canada, the fans welcomed him back with love and respect. Carnegie and his wife, Audrey, considering it just another game beforehand, had not even accompanied her husband. The next day, in the local daily *Le Soleil,* the headline read "Ovation Pour Carnegie!" An ovation for Carnegie.

Unwilling to give up hockey, Carnegie, and his younger brother Ossie, played anywhere they could make a buck, including Northern Ontario and in Quebec. Joined by Manny McIntyre of Fredericton, New Brunswick, the trio became the first (and only) all-black line in pro hockey, playing together in both Northern Ontario and Quebec.

In the 1950s, Carnegie got as close to the NHL as possible as part of the superb Quebec Aces in the Quebec Senior League, where he was a teammate of Jean Beliveau.

Though he had a tryout with the New York Rangers (it was thought the club was capitalizing on Jackie Robinson's debut with the cross-town baseball Brooklyn Dodgers), he never made the big club.

Beliveau would write that "It is my belief that Herbie was excluded from the NHL because of his color. He certainly had the talent."

Carnegie gave up hockey in 1954 and concentrated on a life in the financial world (in which he was hugely successful) and on his other sporting passion, golf. So good was he on the tees and greens that he won the Canadian senior amateur title and is considered one of the best senior amateur golfers ever in Canada.

One Eye on the Prize

In an interview conducted in early 2000, Willie O'Ree admitted something he had kept secret most of his life. In his final years of junior hockey he had taken a hit to the eye and suffered greatly reduced vision permanently.

O'Ree was born in Fredericton, New Brunswick, played junior hockey down east, in Quebec and Ontario, had a season with the Quebec Aces, and then, in 1957–1958 made his NHL debut—breaking the color barrier—with the Boston Bruins. He appeared in only two games that season but was back up again in 1960–1961 for 43 games, during which he scored 4 times and had 14 points.

O'Ree was known for his speedy skating and stickhandling, but had trouble at the big-league level finishing his scoring chances. What no one knew of course, was that O'Ree was accomplishing everything with one and a half eyes.

Quote, Unquote

"They won't let any black boys play in the National Hockey League."

—Advice from father of Herb Carnegie in the 1930s.

Aw, I Knew That!

Q. In 1961, Willie O'Ree was traded by the Boston Bruins to another NHL team. Name the team.

A. Montreal Canadiens. He would never play a game for them.

After the NHL, he went on to a long career in the Western Hockey League, first with the Los Angeles Blades and then the San Diego Gulls. He also played 50 games in the American Hockey League with New Haven in 1972–1973. His career did not end until 1979, in the Pacific Coast League, a season he played after a two-year retirement.

Always of two minds about his experiences, O'Ree once said he never had to go through what Jackie Robinson had to in baseball, but he also said, "Somebody was always saying something about my color. I felt it was my duty to stand up for myself."

It would be 13 seasons before another black player would make the NHL.

Mike and Bill

Mike Marson was a hard-working left winger with some scoring touch who compiled 94 points with the Sudbury Wolves junior club in 1973–1974. Taken in the second round of the amateur draft by the expansion Washington Capitals, he would play a full season with the club as a rookie with no time in the minors, scoring 16 times and assisting on 12 in 76 games.

Aw, I Knew That!

Q. This black player appeared in 145 games for the Los Angeles Sharks of the World Hockey Association. Name him.

A. Alton White.

With the size of Washington's black population, management thought having a couple of black players might help with ticket sales, and while that didn't really work out, it did give a shot to another black athlete, Bill Riley. Out of the British Columbia senior league, Riley played one game in 1974–1975 and then joined the Capitals, mostly full-time, the following year, giving the team two black players when no one else had any. Over 5 NHL seasons and 139 games, Riley had 31 goals and 30 assists.

Marson, up and down between the minor and the big clubs for 6 seasons, ending with Los Angeles in 1980, had 24 goals and 24 assists.

Though the barriers were now definitely down, hockey still was waiting for a legitimate full-time star.

Reality Sucks

Tony McKegney would say later, when his marvelous career was over, that he had never experienced overt racism until he was drafted in the summer of 1978 by the Birmingham Bulls of the World Hockey Association.

A huge star with the Kingston Canadians in junior A (52, 65, 66, and 55 goals over 4 years), McKegney decided to go where the money was, signing with John Bassett Jr.'s Bulls for 1978. As soon as the announcement was made in Alabama, however, the Bulls began getting irate phone calls from some fans threatening to cancel season tickets. Bassett, in a move he would forever feel shame over, caved in and released McKegney.

"I'd never run into anything like that in my life," said the left winger.

Birmingham's stupid loss was Buffalo's gain, however.

McKegney would play 912 games over 17 seasons with the Sabres, Quebec, Minnesota, New York, St. Louis, Detroit, Quebec again, and Chicago (he was one of those players not quite good enough to be untouchable but plenty good enough to bring lots back in a trade). During that time he potted an excellent 320 goals and 639 points, adding another 47 points in the playoffs. He had three seasons over 30 goals and notched 40 in 1987–1988 with St. Louis.

Oh, some of the players that teams got for McKegney? How about Real Cloutier, Adam Creighton (taken with a first-round draft choice), Adam Oates, Paul MacLean, Robert Picard, Greg C. Adams, and Jacques Cloutier.

Tony McKegney was the first legitimate black star.

And Then, Along Came Grant

Grant Fuhr. Goaltender. Spruce Grove, Alberta. Adopted son of white parents. Hockey-crazy from birth. Aggressive. Talented. Among the top five goalies of all time. Black.

Yes, Grant Fuhr was hockey's first black superstar. While the Edmonton Oilers were down at the other end setting all sorts of scoring records during their glory years, Fuhr was the guy at the other end stopping the inevitable odd-man rushes coming back toward the Oilers' goal.

He was money in the bank, especially in the play-offs. Joining the Oilers in 1981 as a rookie right out of junior, Fuhr helped lead Edmonton to five Stanley Cups. He was six times an all-star. Was top goaltender twice. After suffering with injuries in his final Edmonton season, he was traded to Toronto and then played with Buffalo, Los Angeles, St. Louis, and Calgary, finally announcing his retirement (sort of, you never knew with Grant), in the spring of 2000.

Quote, Unquote

"Sometimes, I would wonder why I was trying to be a pro player when there were none to look up to. I'm proud of the fact that I was the first black to establish myself in the NHL."

—Tony McKegney, who played 13 NHL seasons, scoring 320 times.

Aw, I Knew That!

Q. This goaltender scored with the Detroit Juniors in 1993 and with Manitoba of the IHL in 1996. Name him.

A. Fred Brathwaite.

Fuhr is considered a lock for the Hall of Fame (eligible 2003). He would be the first black player so inducted.

A Growing Concern

As the National Hockey League turned to the new century, the number of black players in the loop was growing all the time.

A new influx of emigration to Canada had swelled the size of the black community in that country, which meant more young blacks playing the game. As well, hockey programs for blacks, such as that started by Herb Carnegie (Future Aces, a combined education and athletics affair), had also made an impression. In the United States, more and more young blacks turned to hockey from traditional sports such as basketball, football, and baseball.

Aw, I Knew That!

Q. Edmonton's backup goalie for the deciding game of the 1990 Stanley Cup final was the second black backstop to dress for the team. Who was he?

A. Eldon "Pokey" Reddick.

The result was more than a dozen names on rosters for 1999–2000: players such as Anson Carter in Boston, Edmonton's Mike Grier (the first American-born African American in the league), Donald Brashear of Vancouver, Jarome Iginla, and goaltender Fred Brath-waite in Calgary, and many more had made active rosters.

And more were in the minors.

The trail laid by Carnegie, O'Ree, Marson, Riley, McKegney, and Fuhr was finally leading to the payoff for black hockey players.

Quote, Unquote

"That's what was strange to me; that it was someone with his background and his race."

—Mike Grier, a black star on the Edmonton Oilers, of Chris Simon's alleged on-ice racial slur against him. Simon is Ojibway.

Stars of the Era

➤ George Armstrong scored 296 regular season goals and added 26 in the playoffs during his 21-year Hall of Fame career. The long-time captain of the Toronto Maple Leafs, he scored the famous empty-netter in the 1967 finals that sewed up the last Stanley Cup victory of the century for his club.

➤ Jim Neilson played for three NHL clubs but 12 of his 16 seasons were for the New York Rangers. A big defenseman, he was an incredible plus-43 (goals on for, goals on against) for the 1968–1969 Blueshirts.

➤ Herb Carnegie should have been the first black player in the NHL, but an unofficial color bar prevented it from happening. An excellent scorer, he played on the first and only all-black line in pro history, alongside his brother Ossie and Manny McIntyre.

➤ Tony McKegney was the first black star in the NHL, scoring 639 points in 912 games. He played on seven different clubs, including twice with Quebec.

➤ Grant Fuhr finished his twentieth NHL season as a goaltender in 2000. Six times an all-star and twice the league's top goalie, it was Fuhr who manned the battlements for the Edmonton Oilers when their hot scorers were often caught up the other end looking for goals. One of the best goaltenders of all time.

The Least You Need to Know

➤ Native players were involved in the NHL almost from its conception.

➤ Blacks were playing hockey at the turn of the twentieth century.

➤ Herb Carnegie was prevented from playing in the NHL by an unwritten color code.

➤ Willie O'Ree was the first black in the NHL.

➤ Tony McKegney and Grant Fuhr were black NHL stars of the later twentieth century.

Chapter 26

Sources: Juniors, Collegians, and High Schoolers

To support a century of professional and international hockey teams in North America, there had to be a source: a well-spring of young talent. For most of the twentieth century, the junior leagues in Canada provided almost all of those players. Most every legendary performer in the National Hockey League traced his roots back to a junior club. That began to change in the final two decades—more and more players appearing who had skipped Major Junior for a scholarship to an American college. And another avenue (along with all those players from Europe of course) opened with the discovery of the talent playing in American high school leagues. In this chapter, we'll look at the North American sources for NHLers and other pros.

To Honor the Dead

Junior hockey (mostly 17- to 20-year-olds with a few one-year overagers and a handful of 15- and 16-year-olds) traces its roots to Ontario in 1890, when the Ontario Hockey Association came together and officially sanctioned the age group, split into A and B levels depending on quality of play, size of town, etc. Seeing its success, other provinces jumped on board as well, especially Quebec, Manitoba, Saskatchewan, and Alberta.

Eventually, it made sense for the top junior clubs from each province to play each other and determine a Dominion hockey champion.

When World War I began in August 1914, it put a serious dent in junior hockey because so many of its players signed up to fight in France. But it would also provide the impetus for creating one of the most famous trophies in hockey.

When the Canadian Amateur Hockey Association decided to get everyone together on a national championship starting in 1919, Captain James T. Sutherland proposed a Memorial Cup Trophy, to honor the dead, that the OHA immediately donated to the CAHA for its Canadian winner.

Three men were specifically honored by the trophy: Captain Alan Davidson and Captain George T. Richardson, both former Kingston Frontenacs who were killed in the trenches, and John Ross Robertson, a terrific organizer, player, referee, and coach who died in 1918.

University of Toronto Schools (a high school club) won the first championship over the Regina Patricias in 1919, followed by the Toronto Canoe Club Paddlers in 1920, before the trophy went west to the Winnipeg Falcons in 1921.

Aw, I Knew That!

Q. Name the only player to win a Memorial Cup championship, Allan Cup (senior) championship, Olympic gold medal, and Stanley Cup in his career.

A. Dunc Munro, UTS juniors, Toronto Granites Seniors, Canada, and the Montreal Maroons.

If You Play It, They Will Come

In the 1920s and the 1930s, crowds flocked to junior hockey across Canada (in the United States, local club teams would begat a stint with a college team as the main way of developing as a player), brought in by town-to-town rivalries and, at the Memorial Cup level, the East-West format wherein Eastern and Western Canadian representatives would meet in a best-of-seven series played most often in Toronto.

And in a nice touch, over the first 10 Memorial Cups the two sections of the country split the wins evenly. What made fans particularly excited was the prospect of their town, and they were often very small, getting some national publicity and prestige by winning the cup.

Check out some of the winners in the pre-war era: Fort William (north shore of Lake Superior), Owen Sound, Newmarket, Elmwood, St. Boniface, and Oshawa. These were towns that normally didn't register in the national consciousness.

With a few exceptions, such as Americans like Taffy Abel, these junior leagues were pumping all the talent on a yearly basis into the NHL. And those clubs noticed. In the most significant development for junior hockey, the NHL teams began to buy up or financially support certain junior franchises in order to have a place to develop athletes they had found themselves and signed as young as 13.

Montreal, for example, had numerous clubs inside Quebec, in Peterborough, Ontario, and Regina, Saskatchewan. Toronto had working agreements with St. Michael's College and the Toronto Marlboroughs, along with dozens of clubs across the land. Of course, those two NHL clubs had a huge advantage over the four American ones because kids naturally wanted to play for the team they supported.

But that didn't stop the American teams from forming junior systems across Canada.

During World War II, junior teams were hit hard again as players signed up for service (one among the casualties, Red Tilson, died in battle and had a trophy named in his honor for most valuable player in the OHA junior A).

Great Games

April 1990

The Oshawa Generals and Kitchener Rangers had already played a seven-game series to decide the Ontario champion two weeks before when they met in the final of the Memorial Cup at Hamilton in front of 17,083 fans. The game went into double overtime before defenseman Bill Armstrong of the Generals scored on Mike Torchia of the Rangers at 2:05 of the second extra frame. It was the second double-overtime game between the two teams at the tournament.

Oshawa 4, Kitchener 3

More Modern Times

After the second war, junior hockey continued to flourish. By then, C and even D levels had been added to allow even smaller communities to be involved. And with district and regional playdowns, it was technically possible for a tiny town to still challenge for the Memorial Cup. Writer Brian McFarlane's Inkerton Rockets (near Ottawa) were one of those teams, making it to the 1951 quarterfinals before exiting thanks to the overwhelming Quebec Citadelles and their star, Jean Beliveau.

The second half of the century would see a number of important developments and changes for junior hockey:

I Remember …

In the mid-1950s, Turk Broda, the former goaltending great, was coaching the junior Toronto Marlboroughs and future NHLer Carl Brewer, one of the more eccentric players in the game. One night Brewer was called for a delayed penalty, but it took forever for the Marlies to touch the puck and draw a whistle. Meanwhile, Brewer had come to the bench and promptly hid under it. "Where's Brewer?" asked the referee. "What are you talking about, Brewer isn't even dressed," was Broda's reply, twinkle in his eye. The ref couldn't find him, but just when he was about to forget the penalty, Brewer started laughing, giving it away. A perfect example of Brewer's idea of a practical joke.

➤ After the war, the Memorial Cup tournament began to move out of its permanent home in Toronto and travel around the country.

➤ In 1969, the NHL, with six new teams to look after and many more on the way, went to a universal draft (taking in juniors, collegians, high schoolers, Europeans, and anyone else a team would care to draft). That meant the final end of sponsored junior clubs by the pro organizations.

Quote, Unquote

"Scotty's been in the Memorial Cup three years in a row. That's a mark no one else has had."

—Sam Pollock, manager of the Montreal Canadiens, on his young Peterborough coach Scotty Bowman, 1959. He knew how to identify talent.

➤ In 1970, the OHA, Western Canada Hockey League, and Quebec Amateur Hockey Association voted to separate the top level of Junior A into Major Junior A, leaving everyone else to battle for a new crown—the Centennial Cup (now the Royal Bank Cup). There would be no more Inkertons.

➤ In 1972, the East-West format was dropped in favour of a round-robin that would see four clubs making the Memorial Cup tournament—the winners of the three leagues plus the team from the host city. A town in each league would host while the leagues themselves rotated the hosting duties.

➤ In the 1980s, the Major Junior A clubs separated from their provincial organizations and formed the Canadian Hockey League, a separate entity that took over running the Memorial Cup.

➤ Also in the 1980s, Major A hockey began to expand to the United States, first in the west with clubs such as Spokane, Portland, and Seattle, and then in the east with Detroit, Portsmouth, and Erie.

➤ In the 1990s, the Quebec League began to expand east itself, moving into New Brunswick and Nova Scotia.

➤ In the late 1980s, Major A clubs began to pay much more attention to the educational needs of its players, who before that had usually been forced to drop out of school in order to concentrate on hockey. Scheduling was set up so road trips during the week were shorter, practices were scheduled for after-school hours, and some clubs even hired tutors or education assistants to help the student athletes with their work.

Speaking of student athletes, because the NCAA American college rules denied scholarships to those who played Major Junior A (they felt the small weekly "allowance" made Major Juniors "pros," and we'll avoid a discussion here about college football and basketball athletes with their new cars and expensive jewelry), the Provincial or Tier II Junior A and Junior B loops became more important later in the century. Brett Hull, out of British Columbia, was one example of a player who went through that system, heading to an American college after high school.

Aw, I Knew That!

Q. Name the member of base-ball's Hall of Fame who owned half of the 1991 Memorial Cup champion Spokane Chiefs?

A. George Brett.

Quote, Unquote

"That's all right. That's okay. You'll all be working for us one day!"

—Popular cheer at Harvard University when their team falls behind.

Fun and Games

The most unique and enjoyable part of college hockey in the United States, says writer Kevin Allen, is not the players, or the missing center red line, or even the NCAA tournament, called the Frozen Four (a play on basketball's Final Four). It's the wild fans, whose enthusiasm, choreographed cheers, and wild antics make the college game so different from hockey played elsewhere.

As we learned in Part 1, "A Little History, Repeated," college hockey has been played in the United States since before 1900 (the first recorded game was February 3, 1896, Yale tied Johns Hopkins—but it was going on long before that), and heroes, especially the famous Hobey Baker, were regularly made there.

Those Darn (Old) Canadians

The college game itself didn't really take off across the country until after World War II, when the NCAA established the national championship at Colorado Springs. Eddie Jeremiah's Dartmouth team was the power in the 1940s (46 wins in a row at one point), but Michigan jumped them in the first NCAA's in 1948 and would go on to win 7 times up to 1964.

What had the eastern clubs upset for years was the way western teams like Michigan, Colorado College, and the University of Denver would recruit far older Canadian players (some well into their 30s) as a way of guaranteeing victory. While it was technically okay, it was hardly within the spirit of college sports—these were supposed to be kids in the first five years out of high school, still finding their legs and growing into their bodies.

Not all western coaches did this—Allen writes that John Mariucci was so angry about all the old Canadians he refused to play Denver again after 1958 and kept the promise except when forced to do so at the NCAA championship.

Eventually, the rules were altered and the older Canadian influence disappeared. But many college coaches still looked north, often almost exclusively, for players.

Aw, I Knew That!

Q. The first American-born collegian to jump directly from school to the NHL did it in 1928. Who was he?

A. Myles Lane, Dartmouth College, 1928. He signed with the New York Rangers.

Quote, Unquote

"There were games when the only American on the ice was the referee."

—Bob Ridder of USA Hockey, on the number of Canadians in western college lineups in the 1950s.

An Irish Family Feud

While there have always been many strong college teams across the United States, even today there is nowhere that the college game is played as intensely as within the Boston family rivalry between Boston University, Boston College (which has competed almost entirely with Americans), Northeastern University, and Harvard. The four hold an annual tournament called the Bean Pot (begun in 1952), named for the silver bean pot trophy given to the winner. Out of that tournament has come some of the most intense rivalries on the ice, and one especially hot rivalry off the ice that involved two coaches named Kelley—Jack, at BU, and Snooks, at BC. When Jack retired from BU in 1972, he was given the gift of a beautiful chair, inscribed with "Boston College," by the BC school officials. It's said that Jack, after losing to BC, broke that gift chair into a bunch of little pieces.

Ken, of Cornell

When goaltender Ken Dryden took the National Hockey League by storm in 1971, many people would look at his background and wonder, "Cornell? He's out of Cornell? What kind of a hockey background is that?"

A very strong one, as a matter of fact. Dryden chose not to play Junior A hockey in Canada, accepting a scholarship to Cornell instead. Coached by Ned Harkness, who was always desperately trying to stay one step ahead of Boston University's strong clubs, Cornell won the NCAA's in 1967 and 1970 (BU would take it in 1971 and 1972).

They were obviously more than just Dryden, but fans could be forgiven for wondering that when you consider the goalie played 83 games in 3 seasons and lost exactly 4 times. He was undefeated (26–0–1) in 1966–1967, in leading the Big Red to the national crown.

But Cornell would prove it was more than that in the year after Dryden graduated when Cornell put together an undefeated season in front of a 5'5", 125-pound tyke named Brian Cropper.

Badger Bob

The most famous coach, next to Herb Brooks, to come out of the NCAA and make a name for himself in the NHL, was Bob Johnson, known as Badger Bob for his long career at the University of Wisconsin Badgers.

Aw, I Knew That!

Q. This coach was the first to go from an NCAA team to the NHL. Who was he and what happened?

A. Ned Harkness, out of Cornell, coached the Detroit Red Wings for all of 38 games in 1970–1971.

Quote, Unquote

"Uncle Sam has the cheek to develop a first-class hockey player ... who wasn't born in Montreal."

—Unknown Montreal journalist, 1910, on American college star Hobey Baker.

Johnson, whose most famous quote, "It's a great day for hockey," continues to outlive him, took the Badgers to three NCAA titles (1973, 1977, and 1981). He did everything to promote the game in the state of Wisconsin and later, as a coach in the National Hockey League.

He was named head coach of the Calgary Flames in 1982 and stayed with the club for five years—only once, in his rookie season with a rebuilding club, finishing with a less-than-.500 record. Johnson eventually left Calgary unable to solve the Alberta rivals in Edmonton (not that anybody else could, either), and resurfaced with the Pittsburgh Penguins in 1990–1991. Badger Bob took that club to the Stanley Cup and seemed set to do it again the following year before he took gravely ill, dying on November 26, 1991.

Opening the Talent Doors

With more Canadian players choosing to skip Major Junior A and get an education before going pro, and with ever more American athletes available who could match the Canadians' skills, the NCAA gradually became an important source of players for the NHL.

Aw, I Knew That!

Q. Bill Stewart of the Chicago Blackhawks was the first American-born coach to lead his team to a Stanley Cup. The second American was a former college coaching legend. Who was he?

A. Bob Johnson, 1991, Pittsburgh.

The victory by the United States at the Lake Placid Olympics in 1980 went a long way to helping that a long, of course, but there was too much talent in U.S. colleges in the final two decades of the century for the NHL to ignore. Red Berenson (who shares the NHL record with six goals in one regular season game) was the first of the post-war college players signed by the big league, out of Michigan in 1962.

After that it was a mere trickle for a while, but from 1980 onward the trickle became a dribble and then a nicely running stream. Check this out: Minnesota-Duluth produced Brett Hull; Lake Superior State gave us Doug Weight; Cornell offered Ken Dryden and Joe Nieuwendyk; Boston University gave Keith Tkachuk; and Vermont gave John LeClair.

And there were many others.

I Remember ...

To look at Bob Johnson behind an NHL bench you would never imagine that he was an excellent athlete. In fact, he played in baseball's minor leagues, but soon realized that his calling was as a coach—a hockey coach. Despite his pro sports background, Johnson never lost the old college spirit. In 1966 he was hired by Wisconsin as its first hockey coach and immediately went to work on school spirit. As did his wife, Martha. She became famous at Dade County Coliseum for the cowbell she would ring at one end of the rink that kept the regularly sold-out crowd of 8,662 on its toes. So much a hockey family were they that the Johnsons' son, Mark, made it to the NHL (as a player)—before his father did.

High Schools

In Canada, high school hockey is mostly a second-tier competition because most good players have gone to Junior A, or, in later years, to Provincial A, in order to qualify for a U.S. scholarship. There are exceptions of course—Notre Dame College in Wilcox, Saskatchewan, has a superb high school hockey program, as do Upper Canada College and St. Michael's College School in Toronto (private schools all).

High school hockey in the United States, however, is a very different matter. Though junior hockey leagues are growing in America, there are a half-dozen Major A teams based out of American cities, and a number of United States–born athletes have gone north to compete in Major A—high school hockey is where it's at for most teenaged players.

The hot spots for the high school game are New England and the northern midwest, including Minnesota, Wisconsin, the Dakotas, and Michigan. The Minnesota state championship tournament, for example, which runs an entire week, draws wild sell-out crowds to all its games in Minneapolis-St. Paul.

Bob Carpenter of St. John's Prep School (Danvers, Massachusetts) was the first American high schooler taken in the first round (1981 by Washington, third overall), and Brian Lawton of Mount St. Charles High School (Rhode Island) was the first high schooler chosen first overall in the NHL draft, going to the Minnesota North Stars in 1983, straight from graduation.

Phil Housley of South St. Paul High School (St. Paul, Minnesota) went in the first round in 1982, as did Tom Barrasso of Acton-Boxboro High School (Acton, Massachusetts), who went in the first round in the same 1983 draft as Lawton.

The race to take high schoolers in the first round tailed off in the 1990s, partly because of the continued growth of the college game (kids wanting to get an education first), and partly because of the number of Americans heading to Major A.

Great Games

March 1995

The University of Michigan and the University of Maine skated out for the national championship game that year about as closely matched as you could imagine—as the game would prove. Tied 3–3 after regulation, goaltender Blair Allison for Maine and Marty Turco for Michigan began an exhibition of talent under pressure that would go on through two overtimes and into a third before Dan Shermerhorn scored for Maine 28 seconds into the sixth period for the win. Between them, Allison and Turco combined for 99 saves.

Michigan 4, Maine 3

The CIAU

College, or university, hockey in Canada also goes back well before 1900, and it was there in the early days that many future pros cut their teeth. As junior hockey grew, however, the influence of Canadian universities on the game lessened. Without scholarship programs, the best young players would either choose junior or take the U.S. college route, leaving the Canadian college game as a home for Major A players who didn't get drafted, those who didn't go south, or those few who could afford to pay their way through school and keep playing hockey.

Nonetheless, a number of top NHL coaches have come out of Canadian university play, including Mike Keenan and Tom Watt, both from the University of Toronto; Doug MacLean from the University of Prince Edward Island and University of New Brunswick; and Pierre Page, Dave King, Harry Neale, Gary Green, Jean Perron, Clare Drake, and Doug Carpenter.

CIAU players who have made the jump in recent years include Al MacAdam, Steve Rucchin, Cory Cross, and Stu "The Grim Reaper" Grimson.

Canadian University teams play a final four–type tournament for the University Cup each spring.

The Least You Need to Know

➤ Junior hockey in Canada provided almost all the players for the pro ranks throughout most of the twentieth century.

➤ College hockey in the United States took off after World War II and now also provides a number of players for the pros each year.

➤ High school hockey in parts of the United States features play almost on a level with Major A in Canada.

➤ Canadian universities have sent a number of top coaches into the pro ranks.

Part 7

The Rules

Every game has to have rules, especially one that involves the speed and physical play of hockey. As you've seen throughout this book, the rules have slowly developed from a time when seven players were on the ice for each side, each goal was two posts frozen in the ice behind which stood a man with a cowbell, ready to ring it if the wooden puck went through, there were no lines painted on the surface, and the fans stood frozen to the snow banks. The standard rule book for the game in North America is the one published yearly since 1917 by the National Hockey League. Other leagues, including college, high school, women's, and youngster's organizations, have made changes to those guidelines to fit what they are trying to achieve. Whatever an individual rule book says, the idea is the same: Keep the mayhem to a minimum and ensure a fast, elegant, and enjoyable brand of the fastest game on ice.

Setting the Table

If you grab a copy of the 2000–2001 National Hockey League rule book, you'll find a rink diagram (shown later in this chapter), a detailed look at the goal crease, an explanation of how to build a proper goal, and 148 pages explaining what you can and can't do during a game, divided into 6 sections and 93 specific categories. Those 93 sermons from the mount run the gamut from Rule 1: Rink ("The game of 'Ice Hockey' shall be played on an ice surface known as the 'RINK'") to Rule 93: Video Goal Judge. It would take you hours to work your way through it and weeks to sort out what the book actually said.

In this chapter, we're going to take you through the rule book on a tour that doesn't require a lawyer or Andy Van Hellemond, the NHL's officials director, along as interpreter. These are the NHL rules, by the way. The international rules do differ in some instances, and we'll try to flag those as they go by.

Ice Hockey vs. Hockey

It must be understood from the beginning that if you are going to be a serious fan of the game, you must never, ever, call it "ice hockey." Only people who have no idea what's going on call it "ice hockey." The game is "hockey." Just "hockey." You may turn up your nose at anyone who calls it "ice hockey," as though they have just crawled out from under a puck.

You have our permission.

What Is Hockey?

Take two teams of six players, put them on skates, give them lots of padded equipment, and hand each of them a wooden stick. Tell one from each group to go stand between those pipes down there at each end, instruct each team to use the stick to shoot the doughnut-sized piece of chilled vulcanized rubber (one inch thick and three in diameter) you're currently holding through the other team's pipes, then toss the rubber thing out in the middle of them and get out of the way.

That's hockey. The rest is detail.

The Rink Its Own Self

According to Section One of the NHL rule book, a rink is 200 feet long and 85 feet wide. An international rink is 100 feet wide, which alters the game immensely (see Chapter 12, "A Federation for the Worlds"). It's only been in recent years, however, that all the rinks in the National Hockey League have fit the league's guidelines. The old Boston Garden, Chicago Stadium, the Auditorium in Buffalo, and a number of other buildings had playing surfaces that were shorter, not as wide, or a little wider than the book said they should be. Some had "square corners" from which the puck would bounce crazily. Others had shorter spaces between the bluelines than they were supposed to, which changed the way the home team built their club.

All those rinks are gone now, replaced by cookie-cutter expanses. We miss the old days.

Anyway, as you can tell by the following figure, there are two blue lines that divide the rink into a pair of defensive zones with a neutral zone in between. And there's a big red line down the middle that further divides the neutral zone. (We'll get to what the lines are for when we discuss offside in the next chapter.)

Aw, I Knew That!

Q. What country can rightly lay claim to the invention of the ice-cleaning machine?

A. The United States. The modern machine was invented by Frank Zamboni of Paramount, California, and patented in 1949.

At each end of the rink there are small red goal lines that cut from the boards right across the front of the goal. In front of the goal is the crease, a different-colored area that is eight feet wide, six feet out, and has a little quarter-circle thing at the top. Only the goalie is allowed in the crease unless an opposition player is pushed in by a defender. The crease is a compromise between the old semi-circle in international play and the old rectangle that the NHL used forever. Now, it's a rectangle with a circular top.

At the midpoint of the goal line and falling behind it, red in color, and held up by two 46-inch-high posts set 72 inches apart and joined at the top by a crossbar, is the net. The net is the whole point of the exercise. Put that little black rubber puck thing into that net.

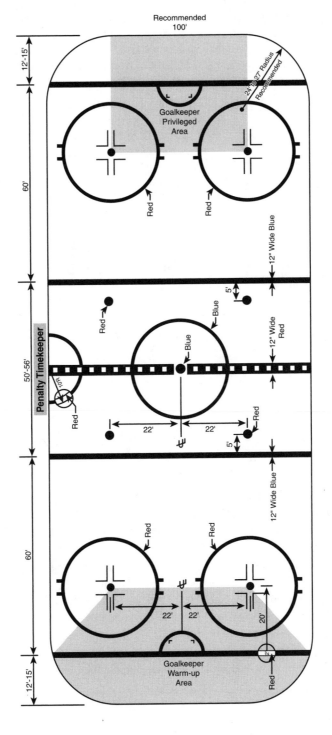

NHL rink.

There are nine red dots spread around the surface of the rink, where face-offs occur. Over by the door to the penalty box there's a little half-circle, which players are supposed to stay out of when the referee is yakking with the guy in the penalty box who writes down details of the bad thing somebody just did.

Quote, Unquote

"If Conacher had put his big mitts around Chadwick's neck, it might have been curtains."

—A bystander on an incident from the late 1940s in which Chicago coach Charlie Conacher grabbed referee Bill Chadwick by the shirt with murder in his eyes.

On one side of the rink are the two player benches. Each has two doors, one for entrance and one for exit, though when players are changing on the fly they often don't use the doors, preferring instead to jump over the boards. This is a real skill, involving both the avoidance of falling flat on your face and looking like a goof, and of not slitting the throat of the guy next to you with those razor-sharp skate blades.

The benches are 24 feet long. At least that's how long the rule book says they should be. You can easily tell if a specific rink has a bench that's not quite that long by checking for the backup goaltender. If he's standing behind the bench or perched on a stool, you know the bench isn't the right length.

Check out your home team's bench.

I Remember ...

The placement of both player benches on the same side of the rink became the rule about 20 years ago because of constant complaints about the setup in the old Montreal Forum. The Canadiens' bench and the penalty box were right next to each other. The opposition's bench was on the other side of the rink. That meant when a Habs' player finished serving his penalty, he could simply step out of the box and right into the Montreal bench—a huge advantage that coaches learned to use, especially if the play was just moving up the ice when the penalty ended. You could pop the guy out of the penalty box into one end of your bench and pop another right out into the rush at the other end of the bench, saving yourself about 25 feet and a lot of time. The opposition, meanwhile, had to wait until the penalized player skated all the way across the ice to their bench if they wanted to replace that guy right away. It took a long time, but the NHL finally put a stop to that.

One other thing: You see all those advertisements painted on the boards? They weren't allowed until the mid-1980s, when Marcel Aubut, president of the Quebec Nordiques, decided he could make a lot more money if he followed the lead of European teams and sold ads on his boards. When the other owners saw the bottom line, out went the no-ads rule.

Not with That Number You Don't

On to Section Two of the rule book. There are six players on the ice for each team: a goaltender, left and right defensemen (or defenders, in women's hockey), a center, and left and right wings. (Or if you wish, a forward line has a Democrat in the middle surrounded by a Liberal and a Republican.) If one or both clubs takes a penalty you'll have less than six players, but a team can never have less than four. Oh, and if one club, trailing by a goal or two, decides to pull the goaltender for an extra attacker with around a minute to go in a game, there will be six skaters and no goalie. Or if that club has a penalty, it might be five skaters and no goalie on the ice.

Confusing, isn't it?

A team has to be dressed in matching uniforms—helmets, sweaters, pants, socks—and the number on the back of the sweater (at least 10 inches high, please) must be between 1 and 98. It used to be between 1 and 99, but when Wayne Gretzky retired, his 99 retired with him. In the old days, no player who wasn't a goalie would be caught dead with a number higher than 29, but some teams had retired so many low numerals that sticking to that became difficult. And then Gretzky picked 99, Mario Lemieux 66, Jaromir Jagr 68, and so on. Having a big number became cool.

I Remember ...

In the 1978–1979 season, the National Hockey League decreed that all teams must sew player names on the back of the shoulders, above the numbers. Many clubs had been doing it for years, however Harold Ballard, the controversial owner of the Toronto Maple Leafs, decided he wasn't going to go along with what league president John Ziegler said, citing possible cuts in program sales if he went with sweater names. Ziegler pushed. Ballard pushed back. Finally, Ballard said he was relenting. In a game at New York, the Leafs skated out in their dark blue road uniforms featuring their names on the back—in dark blue lettering on a dark blue background. The president didn't think that was very funny and threatened a fine. Ballard gave in. But he'd had his joke with Ziegler.

Each team has a captain, identifiable by the big "C" on the left front shoulder. The captain is usually someone everyone respects, but sometimes it's the guy who makes the most money. There are also two alternate captains (look for the "A"). Only the captain and the alternates can yak at the referee on the ice—officially, at least.

You can dress 18 skaters and 2 goaltenders. But count the players in the pregame warm-up and you'll often get more than 20. That's because some poor sucker or two came in, stretched, got dressed, put all that tape around the top of his skates and around his socks to keep the pads from flopping around, got himself in the mental frame of mind to go out and Be a Player, and then was told his services weren't going to be required because the other guy they thought might be too injured to play also took the warm-up and was fine.

Up to the press box, big fella.

It's All Bobby Hull's Fault

Part Three of the rule book deals with equipment, and subject number one is the stick.

For decades, the hockey stick had a very straight blade, perfect for shooting both on the forehand and the backhand. Then along came Bobby Hull, the Golden Jet, in 1957–1958. The Chicago Black Hawk liked to put a curve in his blade—a big curve. That would turn his 100-plus mile an hour slapshots into 100-plus mile an hour knuckleballs that made life miserable for goaltenders and probably hastened the acceptance of the goalie mask.

It was ultimately determined that the curve on his stick, and suddenly a lot of other players', was too much, so rules were brought in that limited it.

Rule 19 contains five subsections dealing with length of shaft and blade, curve of stick, width of blade, and more of the same for goalies.

By the way, if you think somebody is using an illegal stick, you can ask the referee to check it. If you're right, they get a two-minute penalty. If you're wrong, you get a two-minute penalty for delay of game. It's this rule that has led to equipment managers hiding the stick blades from prying eyes before a game.

Goaltending equipment rules have been changed significantly over the years as well, especially recently. All goalies have been known to push the outside of the rule envelope—anything to get an edge on that fella out there who wants to whip that little rubber thing at your head as fast as he can.

Goalies tried making the leg pads wider and wider. The NHL stopped that. They tried making the catching glove ever wider by adding wing flaps. The NHL stopped *that*. And one of the best dodges was started by Garth Snow, then in Philadelphia, who came up with the idea of wearing a specially altered sweater, four sizes too big, with little wing things sewn on so when he raised his arm he looked like the Angel Gabriel. Well, an orange and black Gabriel. Shingles, as the wings came to be called, were pushing it too far.

So the NHL called all the goalies together in the late 1990s, talked it out, and new rules were brought in, leaving goaltenders to come up with something else that might work.

This is why Rule 21 has 33 sections and subsections and 4 detailed drawings.

There are some issues that have caused controversy in recent years that the NHL rule book doesn't cover—yet.

In older days, players wore protective gloves that came up over the full wrist and up a fair portion of the forearm. As equipment has become lighter, most players have switched to these little stubby gloves they say give more freedom of movement when stickhandling. They barely cover the wrist at all. Wrist injuries have gone up as a result.

One of the best arguments against these teeny gloves is that Wayne Gretzky, who wore teeny shoulder pads and shin pads and a helmet that for a long while wasn't within league standards, refused to wear them. The greatest offensive force in NHL history wore old-fashioned gloves and never suffered a single wrist or hand injury. Didn't stop him from scoring, either.

Another controversy without a rule involves face shields or visors. Eye injuries are up in the NHL, but players still insist that they should have the choice of whether to protect their eyes with a plastic shield or not. Conservatives say the shields encourage players to play with their sticks up higher, and anyway, only a wimp would wear a visor. They used to say that about helmets as well, but the rules now require that everyone has to wear one.

Let's skip Section Four: Penalties for now (see Chapter 28, "The Meat and Potatoes") and head on to …

Quote, Unquote

"There's nothing but ice water running through his veins."

—Frank "King" Clancy, Hall of Fame player and referee, on ref Mickey Ion's coolness under fire. Ion was elected to the Hall in 1961.

No, They Are Not Escaped Convicts

Out on the ice you'll notice four striped figures skating around to a chorus of boos just before the players take the pond. These are the game officials, just like any other sport has.

Two of those striped figures are referees (look for the orange Day-Glo armbands). The other two are linesmen.

It was only two years ago that the NHL decided to experiment with two referees instead of one, and despite some complaints, it looks like they're going to stick with two refs. There's less chance of nasty boys trying something behind the ref's back if there are two backs to try it behind.

Anyway, one of the refs drops the puck on the face-off to start the game and each period. That's the

Aw, I Knew That!

Q. Which referee is credited with inventing the system for indicating penalties with specific hand motions?

A. Bill Chadwick, who refereed from 1951–1955.

only time they'll touch the puck all night. Refs are there to whistle play to a stop, call infractions, and stand back and watch fights to see who gets more penalty minutes.

The linesmen have an easy-to-describe, difficult-to-accomplish job. They handle all the face-offs except those the referees get. Linesmen call the offside and icings. They break up fights, often getting a stray punch in the head for their efforts. There are 13 reasons in the book why a linesman would blow his whistle to stop the play (it's sort of like the 11 ways to score from third base with less than 2 out). Refs are generally paid more than linesmen. We can't for the life of us figure out why.

Around the outsides of the rink there are "minor officials" who hold a plethora of jobs. At each end of the ice are the goal judges, usually protected by Plexiglas from fans who in the past were known to hurl objects at them for "bad" calls. Goal judges decide if a puck has entered the goal (it has to be all the way over the line or the plane of the posts and crossbar) and then turn on a red light to indicate a goal. However, a goal judge can be overruled by the referee. And with the invention of the goal camera and the replay official way up in the press box, the goal judge can also be overruled by electronics.

Why are there still goal judges? We're not sure.

Aw, I Knew That!

Q. What famous referee began his athletic career as an outstanding pro football player, scoring three touchdowns in the 1938 Grey Cup championship of the Canadian Football League?

A. Roy Alvin Storey. You can call him "Red."

Over in the penalty box is the penalty timekeeper, who keeps the game sheet up to date with penalty offenders, looks after the penalty box attendants who themselves open and close the gates for players, and, on rare occasions, finds himself in the middle of potential scraps when players attempt to get at each other by climbing over the scorers and clock operators.

Also near the penalty timekeeper is the official scorer, who runs around before the game to get the lineups from each team and keeps track of the goals and assists and when goalies might be changed—those sorts of things.

Next to the official scorer is the game timekeeper, who actually runs the clock.

Upstairs in the press box sit the statisticians. The NHL is now totally computerized and can keep track of everything from playing time to who won face-offs, to who took what shots from where, and so on.

Aw, I Knew That!

Q. What famous jockey was such a hockey fan that he used to ride afternoons at California tracks and work nights as a penalty box attendant at Los Angeles Kings games, opening the gate to let the players in and out?

A. Sandy Hawley, member of the Thoroughbred Horse Racing Hall of Fame.

The Least You Need to Know

➤ Never call it "ice hockey." It's just "hockey."

➤ Hockey features your five skaters and a goalie against their five skaters and a goalie.

➤ Most North American rinks are 200 by 85 feet. International rinks are 200 by 100 feet.

➤ There are two referees and two linesmen in the NHL. Most other leagues have one referee and two linesmen.

➤ In simple terms, the refs call the penalties and the linesmen call the offsides and icings.

Chapter 28

The Meat and Potatoes

In This Chapter

➤ What really goes on out there

➤ Minors and majors

➤ How you get the gate

➤ Fisticuffs

➤ Caught on the lines

Once you have the basics down for your hockey game, you can toss the players out on the ice and let them have fun—for about 30 seconds, when it becomes obvious that you need some pretty specific rules for governing things before anarchy breaks out. Football, basketball, baseball, and any number of other games would require such rules if any of them featured players traveling at better than 30 miles an hour on a sharpened steel blade, each wearing a suit of armor and carrying a big stick.

In this chapter, we'll have a look at the real meat and potatoes of hockey's rules.

No Mayhem Allowed (Honest)

Leading off Section Six: Playing Rules in the NHL rule book (we'll get to Sections Four and Five in a minute) are the attempts to keep mayhem to a minimum. You can't abuse the officials; you can't attempt to maim an opponent with your stick, skates, or body (you can't throw your helmet at them, either); you can't, unless you are a goalie, play with a broken stick, because that pointy end might seriously wound someone. That's why you'll see a player drop a broken stick like it's a nightmare prom date—

more than a few seconds with that weapon in your hand and you get two minutes in the box. The goaltender has to replace a broken stick at the first whistle.

I Remember ...

According to broadcaster and writer Dick Irvin, a few years back young referee Richard Trottier was working a game on Long Island involving the New York Islanders and their legendary coach Al Arbour. Upset at Trottier, Arbour yelled out, "You're the worst referee I've ever seen. You're the worst," every time the official skated by. At some point, linesman Ray Scapinello came by and reminded Arbour that the coach had always thought Ron Wicks was "the worst referee" he'd ever seen. Arbour thought about that a moment, and the next time Trottier came by he yelled out, "You're the *second* worst referee I've ever seen. The *second* worst."

Don't Try This at Home

Players are sent to the penalty box for being bad. How long they stay is determined by what they did. Penalties are divided into 2-minute minors, 4-minute double-minors, 5-minute majors, 10-minute misconducts, and game misconducts or match penalties. A game misconduct simply means you miss the rest of that game. A match penalty means you miss the game and get a trip to the commissioner's office for a little face-to-face.

Now let's get to the real bad boy and bad girl stuff and the penalties you'll get if you try these moves.

➤ **Boarding** (two-minute minor, double minor, or five-minute match penalty, which is where they kick you out of the game and your team has to kill a five minute disadvantage). You are allowed to check someone into the boards (players learn young how to take a check properly *if* they see the person coming). You aren't, however, allowed to attempt to put the opposing player into the third row of the seats. It's a judgment call by the referees. Judgment calls are where refs truly earn their money.

➤ **Butt Ending** (double-minor or match penalty). Other than kicking a fellow player, taking the butt end of your stick and deliberately burying it in the gut or other soft part of your opponent is considered the lowest form of debauchery by fellow players.

➤ **Charging** (minor, double-minor, or match). This is another judgment call. If the ref thinks you took too many strides to get to the man you just crunched with a body check, it's charging. The number of strides used to be generally accepted as three, but it's now more of a "was there an intent to maim?" approach to the call.

➤ **Checking from Behind** (major penalty of five minutes and a game misconduct). Another judgment call. If you sneak up behind someone and hit them in the back, whether into the boards or not, you can get tossed from the game.

➤ **Clipping** (minor or major plus game misconduct). This is one you almost never see, partly because the play goes so quickly it's hard to do. Clipping in hockey is the same as football—taking someone out below the knees.

➤ **Cross-Checking** (minor, double-minor, major, or match penalty). Another judgment call. This is when you hold your stick with your hands spread wide apart and whack somebody. If you watch defenders work in front of the net when there's a forward trying to block out the goalie's vision, you'll see lots of cross-checking going on. You can get away with it in that instance if you don't do it too hard. Even with advances in equipment, cross-checking hurts. That's why it takes a lot of courage to stand in front of the net.

➤ **Delay of Game** (minor). If you delay the game by shooting the puck into the stands (they're especially hard on goalies for this) it's two minutes. You can also get called for delay if you knock the net off its moorings on purpose, if you take too much time going to the penalty box, or if the coach gets mad at a ref and takes his or her sweet time getting the players back on the ice for a face-off. Calling for a stick measurement (see Chapter 27, "Setting the Table") and being wrong is considered Delay of Game.

➤ **Deliberate Injury of Opponents** (match penalty). Intent to injure gets you an automatic game misconduct and a little trip to the Commissioner's office, which usually means suspension for a number of games.

➤ **Elbowing** (minor, double-minor, major, or match). Pretty straightforward: Hit another player with your elbow and you get the gate. Another judgment call for how serious it was.

➤ **Falling on the Puck** (minor or penalty shot). If you fall on a puck and hold it for a face-off (three or four seconds) with no one threatening your health and physical well-being, you can get sent to the box. Same for a goalie. However, if a skater falls on the puck in the crease and holds it for a face-off, that's a penalty shot. Penalty shots are very cool. They put the puck at center, everyone else

Aw, I Knew That!

Q. Who was the last official from the "Original Six" era (pre–1967 expansion) to retire?

A. Linesman John D'Amico.

goes to the bench, the whistle blows, and you get to skate in on the goalie for one chance to score. Penalty shots are the most exciting plays in hockey. In international hockey especially, they use the penalty shot style of play to settle games if one period of overtime doesn't solve anything.

➤ **Gross Misconduct** (match penalty, suspension, and fine). This is the nasty stuff: shoving a referee or linesman, spitting on another player or official, trying to kick someone, or hitting someone over the head with your stick—that sort of thing.

➤ **Handling the Puck** (minor). This can be complicated, but basically you can't pick the puck up with your hand unless you wear the big bulky pads and are paid to be a goalie. You also can't throw the puck down the ice (but you can bat it forward with your hand unless it goes to another player on your team or if you do it in the defensive zone).

➤ **Head-Butting** (double-minor, major, or game misconduct). You almost never see this.

➤ **High-Sticking** (minor, double-minor, major, or match). You can't bring your stick above your shoulders while hitting somebody. You also can't bring your stick above your shoulder and hit someone with it.

➤ **Holding** (minor). You can't hold someone with your hand, nor can you put two arms around your opponent. This is why you sometimes see a defender with one arm around a player and the other up in the air to remind the ref that he isn't holding.

➤ **Holding an Opponent's Stick** (minor). This is a relatively new rule. You can only put your hands on your own stick, not the other player's.

➤ **Hooking** (minor, double-minor, or major and game misconduct). Again, it's a judgment call, but you can't pull somebody down using the crook of your stick. If you pull them down with a hook and they go into the boards, that's when you get the big one.

➤ **Interference** (minor). Boy, this is probably the most argumentative rule in the book, for which there are nine subsections and six "Notes" describing possible interpretations. Basically, you aren't allowed to interfere with someone's progress or knock them over when they don't have the puck. You can if they have just that instant passed the puck or if the puck is pretty close to them going by. In recent years, coaches of less-talented teams have come up with the neutral zone trap and the left-wing lock, which is basically an illegal interference disguised as good defense. It's a little like setting a pick in basketball, only with both guys moving *very* quickly. If you master this one, you can throw away this section of the book because you've probably grasped all the other rules as well.

➤ **Interference by/with Spectators** (match penalty or they kick the fan out, or both). You, as a spectator, can't lean over the boards and grab a player. Players can't come over the boards and grab you. This is almost never seen these days, although it happened fairly often (players going into the stands) back in the early years of hockey.

➤ **Kicking a Player** (match). This is the lowest form of physical expression. Even your own teammates will hate you for doing this.

➤ **Kicking the Puck.** You can kick the puck all you like (it's hard to do), but you can't kick it, or use your skate to guide it, into the net.

➤ **Physical Abuse of Officials** (pack up baby, you're in for a long vacation). Like most leagues, the NHL takes a very dim view of shoving or hitting an official. Descriptions of this fill four pages in the rule book.

➤ **Slashing** (minor, double-minor, major, or match). Another nasty that happens way too often. This is obviously using your stick to slash out at another player. Slashing often leads to fighting, which we'll deal with in a minute.

➤ **Throwing the Stick** (misconduct, penalty shot). If you throw your stick at another player, it's a misconduct—10 minutes in the bin. If you hit him with it you'll probably get the whole game. If anybody on the bench throws a stick, or if a player has a breakaway (a clean chance on the net) and a trailing player tosses his stick at him, it's a penalty shot. If you throw your stick at an opponent breaking in on an empty net (pulled goalie) it's an automatic goal.

➤ **Tripping** (minor, double-minor, major, match). If you use your stick or your leg to trip somebody, it's the gate for you. If the tripee goes face-first into the boards, the goal, or the goaltender, that's a more serious matter. There's also the nefarious slew-footing, a new penalty for using your leg or foot to take a player's feet out from under him. Slew-footing has caused some nasty injuries in recent times, until the NHL decided in 2000 to crack down.

Okay, that's the basic stuff. Now let's deal with hockey's little albatross. It's politically incorrect, left over from the dark ages, favorite of the ultra-conservatives, little problem—fighting.

Quote, Unquote

"In my book, he still holds the record for complaining and bitching."

—Former referee Bruce Hood, writing in his book on former Chicago, Boston, and New York Rangers superstar Phil Esposito.

Quote, Unquote

"Wake up, you old fart! ... Pardon me, I said I just farted."

—Linesman Ray Scapinello recounts what a player said one time in Montreal as the ref skated by—and what he said when the ref looked back.

There's Nothing Like a Good Hockey Brawl

Before we launch too far into this, a point must be made: Compared to the early days of hockey when serious violence was part of the game, or to the 1970s when fighting was so commonplace it hardly caused any rumpus in the media at all, modern hockey has almost no fisticuffs. (And it should be pointed out that there are those who believe there are actually more fights today, just no bench-clearing brawls to make them look worse. It's all in the way you count the stats.) Where you often used to get two or three fights a game, there's hardly two or three fights across the whole league on a night when all the teams are playing.

Having said that, it seems to us that fighting's time has come to an end. We say that knowing lots of people still disagree.

The argument goes like this: Fighting is a safety valve that allows players involved in the world's fastest, toughest game on ice—players who are armed with a stick they don't always look after properly—to blow off steam. There's nothing wrong, the argument goes, with two guys dropping their gloves and pounding the snot out of each other as long as it's an even match. Great stuff. They no longer allow it in college hockey, high school hockey, women's hockey, international hockey, or house league hockey.

It's very complicated, involving subtexts of visors, an increase in stick work, being a man, standing up for your team, protecting the star players, and on and on.

We'll leave the argument itself alone, but let's try to explain the rules regarding fighting.

➤ If two players drop their gloves at the same time and pound each other out, they both get five minutes for fighting. If they do it to each other a second time during the game, they are usually asked to leave.

Aw, I Knew That!

Q. What linesman was called The Ironman?

A. Neil Armstrong. He worked 16 years, 1,733 regular season games, 208 in playoff games, and 10 all-star games and never missed an assignment for illness or injury.

➤ If one player goads another into a fight, that's known as Being the Instigator. That means an extra two minutes. Conservatives hate the Instigator rule because it has eliminated the goon—a designated fella who was there to look after a superstar. If somebody took a poke at Wayne Gretzky, say, Dave Semenko would go over and pound him out. But this doesn't happen any more, which the conservatives say makes the superstars easy targets. It's interesting to note that both Gretzky and Mario Lemieux, the modern game's biggest stars, are against fighting.

➤ If two players duke it out and a third jumps into the fray, that's Third Man In, which is an automatic early shower. This rule came in during the 1970s to stop teams from intimidating other teams simply because they had more goons.

➤ If one player throws a punch at another, that's Roughing—two or four minutes. If one player throws a punch and the other throws a punch back and it ends right there, both get Roughing. If there's a lot of pushing and shoving after the whistle and the ref figures it's gone on too long, that's also Roughing.

➤ If anybody leaves the bench to get involved in the fight (precipitating a bench-clearing brawl), that player gets an automatic 10-game suspension, as does that player's coach. You never, ever, see the benches clear anymore. In the 1970s, you saw it all the time.

➤ If two guys from one team hit another guy from the other team over the head with a chair, that's the World Wrestling Federation.

I Remember ...

Don Cherry told the great writer George Plimpton this story one year. Seems Eddie Shore, the Hall of Fame defenseman then owning and coaching the Springfield Indians of the American Hockey League, got so mad at referee Frank Udvari (who had the guts to stand up to Shore) one night, that he pulled his entire team off the ice and refused to send anybody on. Unfortunately, he forgot to call in goalie Don Simmons, who was busily keeping the ice nice and clean in front of his net. Udvari warned Shore he'd drop the puck if the coach didn't send his players out. Shore refused. Udvari dropped the puck, and five skaters from the other club took off with it for the Indians' net. This is when Simmons chose to look up and probably almost swallowed his tongue. Somehow, four shots missed and Simmons jumped on the puck after stopping the fifth. It was about the only five-man breakaway in recorded history.

We can sum all this up with the following anecdote:

A player comes over the opposing blueline and puts a nifty move on the defenseman, zipping right by him. The defender trips him up with his stick (two minutes). The other guy gets mad, gets up, and slashes the defender with his own stick (two minutes). They stare at each other for a second, and before the linesmen can get there to break it up, one guy drops his gloves and goes at the other (Instigator—two minutes). The aggrieved party (the original defender) drops his own gloves, and they duke it out (five minutes each). Upset, another offensive player jumps into the fight (Third Man In—game misconduct). Meanwhile, the other players pair off and start dancing around, without really fighting. One pairing gets a little too aggressive, refuses to stop when the ref says so, and they both get Roughing (two minutes). On the way to the penalty box, one of those two calls the ref something particularly unprintable (generally unprintable happens all the time), and gets a misconduct (10 minutes).

That's a total of 40 minutes in penalties and 4 guys in the box. (Game misconducts are counted as 10.)

Ah, the good old hockey game.

You Take One of Mine and Two of Theirs ...

Section Four in the NHL rule book deals with all the different penalties (in minutes) you can get, as described earlier in this chapter. It also handles who plays with what number of players short. Follow along:

➤ If one team takes a minor, they play four skaters against five. They are Killing a Penalty. The other team is on a Power Play. This latter term can be very embarrassing for the attacking team if their Power Play stinks—which brings up the oft-heard hockey joke, "Gee, too bad they couldn't just decline it."

➤ If both teams take a minor at the same time, the teams still play five skaters against five. (Remember, the goalie is not considered a "skater" even though those tending the twine tent are often the best skaters on the team.)

➤ If one team takes a minor and during the Power Play the attacking team takes one, they play even strength until the first penalty is over. Then the second team is on the Power Play, sometimes for just a few seconds.

➤ Major penalties do not mean you have to play a man short unless the five minutes were for some nefarious infraction such as serious slashing, boarding, etc. When two players duke it out, they both get five, but neither plays with a body short.

Oh, one other thing about penalties, and this is important: If a ref sees an infraction but the aggrieved team still has the puck, he will wait until the team that committed the sin has touched the puck before blowing the whistle. This is known as the Delayed Penalty. If you see the arm go up indicating a call is coming, check back down the ice. You'll see the aggrieved team's goalie racing for the bench so they can put an extra skater out there, since you can't get scored on if the other team can't touch the puck without the whistle blowing.

Note: There have been very rare occasions where the offensive team has passed the puck back to the blue line (also called the point) and it has skipped over the defenseman's stick and rolled right down into the open net. That counts as a goal. Very humiliating.

Looking back on this, it sure can be confusing. But it doesn't take that many games to figure it all out. Then the only confusion is how the penalty timekeeper can keep all of this straight without blowing a blood vessel in the brain.

Why Do They Keep Blowing the Darn Whistle?

It's time to deal with the line violations—offside and icing. Please refer back to the figure of the ice surface.

Okay, as simple as possible:

➤ If you are racing down on the opposition blueline with the puck and one of your own team goes over the blueline before the puck does, that's offside.

➤ If you pass the puck over the defending blueline after one of your teammates crosses it, that's offside.

➤ If you pass the puck to a teammate across the defending blueline after he himself crosses the line, that's offside.

➤ If you pass the puck across any two lines to a teammate (look back at the figure), that's offside.

That wasn't too bad, was it?

Aw, I Knew That!

Q. What coach started the "waving the towel" trend by fans in the NHL by waving a white towel in mock surrender at the officials one year at the end of a playoff game?

A. Roger Neilson. He was with Vancouver at the time. When the Canucks got home for the next contest, most of the crowd had towels they were waving at the officials.

Now, if you cause an offside, the puck is faced off just outside the opposing blueline, on one of those two red dots. If the linesman thinks you did it on purpose, say to get a change of players because you were tired, the puck comes all the way down into your own zone and is faced off in one of the two circles in front of your goalie.

And if the play is offside but the opposing team immediately gets the puck and makes an honest attempt to move it back out of its own zone, that's a Delayed Offside—the linesman raises his arm but the whistle isn't blown. The play keeps going that way.

Since we're on a roll here, let's explain icing.

If you shoot the puck from anywhere on your own side of center, all the way down past the other team's red end line, and their player gets to the puck first, that's icing. The linesmen get to show off a little by swooping down, scooping up the puck, and racing full speed down the ice for a face-off in the offending team's zone.

Pretty simple, except this rule is also very controversial. In many college leagues, and in all international play, as soon as the puck crosses that end line, the whistle goes. In the NHL and many junior leagues, they have what's called Touch Up Icing. That's when the defending team is required to touch the puck to get the icing call. This, in turn, often causes all-out races for the puck, because if an offensive player gets there first, there is no icing, and that can be a big advantage.

The problem is, when they are racing at 30 to 35 miles an hour after the puck, with the defender usually in front with his back to the attacker, you can get pretty nasty collisions that result in injuries, almost always to the defender, on the end boards. There is a movement to get the NHL to change this rule to the instant whistle.

Aw, I Knew That!

Q. According to hockey broadcaster, researcher, and writer Brian McFarlane, what's the unofficial record for number of "icings" in a game?

A. 87. The New York Americans apparently iced the puck 87 times in a game with the Boston Bruins in the 1930s to keep the Bruins from scoring. This was before the act resulted in a whistle. Angry, Bruins' manager Art Ross made sure his players "iced" the puck exactly 87 times in the return match at New York. Shortly thereafter, the league brought in the current rule to stop such shenanigans.

On the Face-Off

Last, let's take a look at the face-off. Two players face each other over a red dot. The linesman (almost always) makes sure they are lined up fairly, and then drops the puck so it hits the ice flat, with no bounce. The players clash sticks and try to knock the disk backward to a teammate, or forward, where they and a teammate can take off in hot pursuit.

You'd think this would be an easy thing. There are 13 subsections to Rule 54. Rules on where each player can stand. Where teammates can stand. How close the teammates can be to the two who are facing off. Who has to put the stick down on the ice first (both). How you can get yourself tossed out of the face-off and replaced with someone else (don't antagonize the linesman while you're jockeying about).

Face-offs are arguably the most important part of a hockey game, especially in the late going. Face-offs are fascinating—or infuriating, if your player gets tossed out of the circle.

The Least You Need to Know

➤ If you get mad and use your stick against another player in some way, you'll probably be asked to leave the game for either a few minutes or for the rest of the game.

➤ Penalties are divided into 2-minute minors, 4-minute double-minors, 5-minute majors, 10-minute misconducts, and game misconducts or match penalties.

➤ Fighting is still a part of hockey, although many want to see it banned.

➤ Icing and offside are the standard line violations in hockey.

➤ Face-offs are the most important single moments in hockey games.

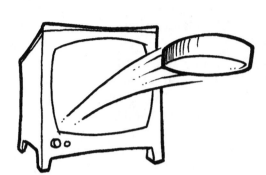

I Can't Watch Hockey on TV Because I Can't Follow the Puck!

Some tips on watching hockey on television by someone who should know: Mark.

➤ **Don't try to follow the puck.** At the beginning, most people will just watch the puck, thinking that to follow the puck is to follow where the action is going. But that's not normally where the player who will score the goal is. You have to learn to watch *away* from the puck—like watching away from the ball in basketball. Very few goals are scored by the guy with the puck; they are scored by the guy *about to get* the puck.

➤ **Don't get upset when the puck comes too the near boards and disappears.** Because television shoots from one side of the ice, especially in the old days before the camera that's now mounted right on the glass, you were blind for one side of the ice surface. But you learn to know what's going on. Watch the bodies. Which way are they going? Is the body obviously moving the puck up the ice? It can be hard at first, but stop thinking *puck* all the time.

➤ **Don't get fooled by angles.** When I was young, I thought someone could score from anywhere. But players pass to the middle when shooting because they know that's where they are going to score from. Once in a while they can get one in from a bad angle, but not often. Look for the people in a good position. Don't be afraid to take your eye off the puck.

➤ **Try not to panic.** When the guy is carrying the puck down the near boards, just assume he's got it. Don't worry about it. You're going to see it in a couple seconds. It's going to come into view. It's like in baseball: You don't always see the ball when it's hit in the air—the camera doesn't follow it, the camera switches to the guy who is going to catch it, and you have to just assume it's going to happen.

➤ **When a puck is shot from the point (the blueline), look at the net and see if it arrives there.** The camera follows the shot. Watch games when a guy shoots from the blueline. It's the last time you see that guy in the frame. The camera is doing the same thing you want to do. When it switches to the wide shot so you can see the goalie, your eye gets confused. Let your eyes go to the net. If the puck doesn't arrive, it's in front of the goalie somewhere, and the cameras will find it for you.

➤ **Don't try to find the puck in the middle of a scramble.** When a goalie is diving around looking for the puck in a scramble in front of the net, my hope or fear (depending on whether I'm pulling for the offensive or defensive team) is that the puck is going in the net. You are anticipating that the puck is going to wind up there, so take a look there. That worry or anticipation is part of the excitement of hockey. It's the same if a guy is coming down the wing and lets go a hard shot—you don't watch the goalie (though you'll see him in your peripheral vision anyway), you watch the net to see if the puck goes in.

➤ **Learn to anticipate.** When you watch a two-on-one break, take a look at the player without the puck. When you see two guys battling for the puck behind the net, look at the front of the net to see who's there. When you watch a power play and the puck is going back and forth at the blueline (the point), take a look in front of the net to see if there is anyone screening the goalie.

➤ Learn these tips, and then pretend you know what you're doing.

It's a lot of fun to sit and watch a game with someone else and say "Now, don't watch the puck ..."

The Top Ten Players of All Time

1. Wayne Gretzky
2. Bobby Orr
3. Gordie Howe
4. Mario Lemieux
5. Maurice Richard
6. Patrick Roy
7. Terry Sawchuk
8. Bobby Hull
9. Viacheslav Fetisov
10. Eddie Shore

The Top Ten Teams of All Time

1. Team Canada 1976 (Canada Cup)
2. Montreal Canadiens, 1976–1977 (only eight losses all season, just one loss at home, Stanley Cup)
3. Edmonton Oilers, 1985–1986 (119 points, 446 goals for, Stanley Cup)
4. Montreal Canadiens, 1957–1958 (96 points, three players in top 10 scorers, Stanley Cup)
5. Detroit Red Wings, 1951–1952 (100 points, undefeated in the playoffs, Stanley Cup)
6. Soviet Union, 1954 world championships (first Soviet world title winners)
7. United States, 1980 Olympic champions
8. Soviet Union, 1979 Challenge Cup (beat the NHL two games to one)
9. Toronto Maple Leafs, 1941–1942 (won four straight in final after going down three games to none; Stanley Cup)
10. Czech Republic, 1998 Olympics champions

The Top Ten Moments of All Time

1. Paul Henderson's series-winning goal for Canada in game eight at the 1972 Summit Series against the Soviets.
2. Czechs defeat the Soviets twice at the 1969 world championships, just months after the Soviet invasion of Czechoslovakia.
3. Mike Eruzione's goal at the 1980 Winter Olympics for the United States beats the Soviet Union.
4. Bobby Hull signs with the Winnipeg Jets of the World Hockey Association, 1972.
5. Wayne Gretzky scores 92 times, a record, for Edmonton in the 1981–1982 season.
6. The NHL is formed in 1917.
7. Gordie Howe plays for Hartford of the NHL in the 1980 playoffs at age 52.
8. Bobby Orr scores the Stanley Cup–winning goal for Boston against St. Louis in 1970.
9. Mario Lemieux scores the winner against the Soviets in the 1987 Canada Cup final.
10. Maurice Richard scores 50 goals in 50 games for Montreal in the 1944–1945 season.

The Ten Most Influential People in Hockey History

1. **Anatole Tarasov.** He forever changed the face and pace of the game. He changed strategy and off-ice training. He took his country's players to incredible heights. The Soviet coach changed the NHL's perception of itself.

2. **Frank and Lester Patrick.** They developed rules, created leagues, built the first artificial ice surface in Canada, and influenced changes in the game that have been handed down for generations. And all before they even came to the NHL. Almost every modification they introduced has been kept or developed.

3. **Alan Eagleson.** Starting in the 1960s as an agent, in the 1970s and 1980s as an international hockey negotiator, the emergence of the Eagle left the business of hockey forever changed. His conviction on fraud charges in the 1990s only served to alert us to his incredible influence.

4. **Bobby Orr.** Revolutionized the game of hockey as played from the defense position. Changed the pace of the game forever. From his NHL birth in 1966, hockey was never the same.

5. **Wayne Gretzky.** Makes the list for both his on-ice achievements and, almost as importantly, those off the ice. Allowed the NHL to build a firm base in the United States. Playing in Los Angeles directly influenced the birth of two more franchises. Once-in-a-lifetime personality.

6. **Lord Stanley of Preston.** For recognizing the growing sport of hockey, promoting its growth and supplying a trophy that has and will influence every hockey player's dreams.

7. **Foster Hewitt.** His voice was hockey to English Canadians for over 50 years. Sold the excitement of the game from sea to sea with his *Hockey Night in Canada* radio and television broadcasts.

8. **Scotty Bowman.** In his sixth decade of coaching in the NHL. From 1968–2001, over 300 different coaches or managers have been on the job. None have been more successful (eight Stanley Cups as a coach). Changed the game from behind the bench while changing with the times himself.

9. **Frank Selke Sr.** The Father of Montreal's great 1950s dynasty, he developed the farm system in Montreal that helped build the greatest organization in pro sports history. Laid the blueprint for other managers to follow.

10. **Paul Henderson.** His three game-winning goals in the 1972 Summit Series vs. the Soviets made him a legend and an icon forever. Never before or since has one single goal prompted such intense and emotional discussion.

Bibliography

Allen, Kevin. *USA Hockey: A Celebration of a Great Tradition.* (Triumph, 1997)

Avery, Joanna, and Julie Stevens. *Too Many Men on the Ice: Women's Hockey in North America.* (Polestar Book Publishers, 1997)

Banks, Kerry. *Pavel Bure: The Riddle of the Russian Rocket.* (Greystone Books, 1999)

Batten, Jack. *The Leafs: An Anecdotal History of the Toronto Maple Leafs.* (Key Porter Books, 1994)

Benedict, Michael, and Darcy Jenish. *Canada on Ice: Fifty Years of Great Hockey.* (Penguin, 1999)

Carnegie, Herb. *A Fly in a Pail of Milk: The Herb Carnegie Story.* (Mosaic Press, 1997)

Cohen, Tom. *Roger Crozier, Daredevil Goalie.* (Thomas Nelson & Sons, 1967)

Coleman, Jim. *Hockey Is Our Game: Canada in the World of International Hockey.* (Key Porter Books, 1987)

Diamond, Dan, ed. *Hockey Hall of Fame: The Official Registry of the Game's Honour Roll.* (Doubleday Canada, 1996)

Diamond, Dan, et al. *Total Hockey: The Official Encyclopedia of the National Hockey League.* (Total Sports, 1998)

Dryden, Ken. *The Game.* (Macmillan Canada, 1983)

Etue, Elizabeth, and Megan K. Williams. *On The Edge: Women Making Hockey History.* (Second Story Press, 1996)

Fischler, Stan. *Coaches.* (McGraw-Hill Ryerson, 1994)

———. *Golden Ice: The Greatest Teams in Hockey History.* (McGraw-Hill Ryerson, 1990)

———. *Hockey's 100.* (Stoddart, 1984)

———. *Hockey Stars Speak: In Depth Interviews with the NHL's Biggest Stars.* (Warwick Publishing, 1996)

———. *The Rivalry: Canadiens vs. Leafs.* (McGraw-Hill Ryerson, 1991)

Fischler, Stan, and Shirley Fischler. *All-Time Book of Hockey Lists.* (McGraw-Hill Ryerson, 1993)

———. *Fischler's Hockey Encyclopedia.* (Fitzhenry & Whiteside Ltd., 1975)

———. *Red Line: The Soviets In The NHL.* (Prentice Hall, 1990)

Greenspan, Bud. *Frozen in Time: The Greatest Moments at the Winter Olympics.* (General Publishing, 1997)

Greig, Murray. *Big Bucks and Blue Pucks*. (Macmillan Canada, 1997)

Gzowski, Peter. *The Game of Our Lives*. (PaperJacks, 1983)

Hood, Bruce. *Calling the Shots: Memoirs of an NHL Referee*. (Stoddart, 1988)

Houston, William. *Pride & Glory: 100 Years of the Stanley Cup*. (McGraw-Hill Ryerson, 1992)

Howe, Gordie. *Gordie Howe: My Hockey Memories*. (Firefly Books, 1999)

Hunt, Jim. *Bobby Hull*. (Ryerson, 1966)

Hunter, Douglas. *Champions: The Illustrated History of Hockey's Greatest Dynasties*. (Penguin Studio, 1997)

———. *The Glory Barons: The Saga of the Edmonton Oilers*. (Viking, 1999)

———. *Scotty Bowman: A Life in Hockey*. (Penguin Books, 1998)

IIHF Guide. 1976 edition. (ISCO Publishing Co., 1976)

IIHF Guide. *Official Yearbook 1999/2000*. (Horst Eckert Copress Sport, 1999)

Irvin, Dick. *Behind the Bench: Coaches Talk About Life in the NHL*. (McClelland & Stewart Inc., 1993)

———. *The Habs* (McClelland & Stewart, 1991)

Jarman, Colin, ed. *Guinness Dictionary of Sports Quotations*. (Colin Jarman &Guinness Publishing Ltd., 1999)

Kelly, Malcolm G. *The Complete Idiot's Guide to Canadian Sports History and Trivia* (Prentice Hall Canada, 1999)

Kendall, Brian. *100 Great Moments in Hockey*. (Viking, 1994)

Lapp, Richard, and Alex MacAulay. *The Memorial Cup: Canada's National Junior Hockey Championship*. (Harbour Publishing, 1997)

Liebman, Glenn. *Hockey Shorts*. (Contemporary Books, A Tribune Company, 1996)

MacInnis, Craig, ed. *Remembering Bobby Orr*. (Stoddart, 1999)

Macskimming, Roy. *Gordie, A Hockey Legend: An Unauthorized Biography of Gordie Howe*. (Greystone Books, 1994)

Mahovlich, Ted. *The Big M: The Frank Mahovlich Story*. (HarperCollins, 1999)

Martin, Lawrence. *The Red Machine: The Soviet Quest to Dominate Canada's Game*. (Doubleday Canada, 1990)

McDonell, Chris. *For the Love of Hockey: Hockey Stars' Personal Stories*. (Firefly Books, 1997)

———. *Hockey's Greatest Stars: Legends and Young Lions*. (Firefly Books, 1999)

McFarlane, Brian. *It Happened in Hockey*. (Stoddart, 1991)

———. *More It Happened in Hockey*. (Stoddart, 1993)

———. *One Hundred Years of Hockey* (Deneau Publishers, 1989)

———. *Proud Past, Bright Future: One Hundred Years of Canadian Women's Hockey*. (Stoddart, 1994)

———. *Stanley Cup Fever*. (Pagurian Press, 1978)

———. *Still More It Happened in Hockey*. (Stoddart, 1994)

———. *The Blackhawks: Brian McFarlane's Original Six*. (Stoddart, 2000)

———. *The Ultimate Hockey Quiz Book*. (Key Porter Books, 1999)

McKinley, Michael. *Etched in Ice: A Tribute to Hockey's Defining Moments.* (Greystone, 1998)

Michel, Doug, as told to Bob Mellor. *Left Wing and a Prayer: Birth Pains of a World Hockey Franchise.* (Excalibur Sports, no date)

Morrison, Scott. *The Days Canada Stood Still: Canada vs. USSR 1972.* (McGraw-Hill Ryerson, 1989)

Mulvoy, Mark. *Great Moments in Sports.* (Rutledge Press, 1981)

O'Brien, Andy. *Fire-Wagon Hockey: The Story of the Montreal Canadiens.* (Ryerson, 1970)

Our Hockey. (Fizkultra (I) Sport Publishing, 1972)

Plimpton, George. *Open Net: The Professional Amateur in the World of Big-Time Hockey.* (Penguin, 1985)

Podnieks, Andrew. *Canada's Olympic Hockey Teams: The Complete History, 1920–1998.* (Doubleday Canada, 1997)

Rheaume, Manon, with Chantal Gilbert. *Manon: All Alone in Front of the Net.* (HarperCollins, 1993)

Spencer, Teena, with Will Ferguson, and Bruce Spencer. *The Girlfriend's Guide to Hockey* (Key Porter Books, 1999)

Sports Illustrated. Winter Olympics Issue. (1988)

Stewart, Barbara. *She Shoots, She Scores. A Complete Guide to Women's Hockey.* (Doubleday, 1993)

Strachan, Al, ed. *One Hundred Years of Hockey: The Chronicle of a Century on Ice.* (Key Porter Bools, 1999)

Tretiak, Vladislav. *The Hockey I Love.* (Lawrence Hill & Co./Fitzhenry & Whiteside Publishing, 1977)

———. *Tretiak: The Legend.* (Plains Publishing, 1987).

Tureo, Mary. *Crashing the Net.* (HarperCollins, 1999)

Vipond, Jim. *Gordie Howe: Number 9.* (Ryerson, 1970)

Weir, Glen, with Jeff Chapman and Travis Weir. *Ultimate Hockey.* (Stoddart, 1999)

Web Sites

www.iihf.com   The official Web site of the International Ice Hockey Federation

www.nhl.com   The official Web site of the National Hockey League

www.cs.utoronto.ca/~andria   Andria Hunter's women's hockey Web site

www.hockeydb.com   Hockey statistic database

Personal Interviews

Craig Campbell	Paul Patskou	Alyn McCauley
Ken Dryden	Paul Stewart	Harry Neale
Ron Harrison	Terry Crisp	Sid Smith
Rick Ley	John Garrett	Alpo Suhonen
Scott Morrison	Dick Irvin	Alan Adams

Index